C000065824

Kill the Queen!

THE EIGHT ASSASSINATION ATTEMPTS ON QUEEN VICTORIA

Barrie Charles

AMBERLEY

Front cover illustration reproduced by kind permission of the London and Metropolitan Archives.

First published 2012

Amberley Publishing
The Hill, Stroud
Gloucestershire, GL5 4EP

www.amberleybooks.com

Copyright © Barrie Charles, 2012

The right of Barrie Charles to be identified as the Author
of this work has been asserted in accordance with the
Copyrights, Designs and Patents Act 1988.

All rights reserved. No part of this book may be reprinted
or reproduced or utilised in any form or by any electronic,
mechanical or other means, now known or hereafter invented,
including photocopying and recording, or in any information
storage or retrieval system, without the permission in writing
from the Publishers.

British Library Cataloguing in Publication Data.
A catalogue record for this book is available from the British Library.

ISBN 978 1 4456 0457 2

Typesetting and Origination by Amberley Publishing.
Printed in Great Britain.

Contents

Author's Note & Acknowledgements

These are, essentially, the true stories of the people who plotted, attacked, and tried to assassinate Queen Victoria. Once I had completed the research for this book, I realised that many of the currently published accounts on the subject, even some well-regarded histories of Queen Victoria, contain numerous errors. I believe that what follows is a considerably more accurate account of the people and the events.

However, the source information is largely based on contemporary reporting in newspapers and the information held in public records and government files, which, of course, are not always error-free. Where possible I have tried to consult multiple sources, but this was not always feasible. I may have inadvertently introduced my own mistakes too, for which I apologise. I have also tried to divine the thoughts and motives of the assailants, something which, by its nature, must at times be speculative, but I hope it breathes some life into the narrative.

My gratitude goes to the patience of the many staff in the libraries and archives that I consulted during the research for this book, both in England and Australia, particularly the employees of the British Library and the National Archives. I have also made extensive use of secondary sources for background information and certain details, for which I acknowledge all the authors, as detailed in the 'Sources' appendix. This is particularly true for Chapter 8, much of which is based on the extensive researches of Christy Campbell, as detailed in his book *Fenian Fire: The British Government Plot to Assassinate Queen Victoria*.

I am also grateful for specific help from Adrienne Phillips in Chapter 2; Audrey Holland in Chapter 4; Valentine Bolam in Chapter 5; and Mark Stevens in Chapter 7. I also wish to thank for their assistance George and Gail Tait in New South Wales and Des Aldridge in Victoria, along with my patient proofreaders, Jackie Tuson, Maggie Charles, and David Charles.

But above all, I would like to thank Stephen Wade, who, during his excellent course on Crime Writing, gave me the idea for this book.

Barrie Charles

1

The Pot-Boy, 1840

The two guns bulging from his trouser pockets, Edward Oxford left the house with a feeling of purpose and determination. They might think of him as a thin youth of no consequence, but he would show them. It was six weeks since he had been sacked from his job at the Hog-in-the-Pound public house because, they said, of his laughter. 'Maniacal', the customers called it. They described him as a mere 'pot-boy' and accused him of being haughty, but why should he deign to talk to those ignorant drunks?

He crossed the street and made his way towards Westminster Bridge. This was not the first time that he had been shown the door, and he was tired of being treated as a nobody. He was a senior member of a secret society called 'Young England', and soon people throughout the land would know of him. His plans were laid; he knew what to do.

He began taking action only three days after losing his job, using £2 from his previous quarter's wages to buy two pistols from a shop on the Blackfriars Road. He also bought bags for the pistols and a powder flask for 2s. For the following month, he assiduously practised using the guns at shooting galleries in Leicester Square, Westminster Road, and the Strand. Then, last Wednesday, he visited a shop at 10 Bridge Road, Lambeth, where an old school friend, John Gray, sold him half a hundred copper firing caps. He was running short of money and could only afford a quarter-pound of gunpowder, but the shop only dealt in half-pound amounts. They did not stock bullets either, so Gray recommended him to a gunsmith in Borough.

Edward crossed Westminster Bridge. The tide was out and the foul-smelling Thames was a mere trickle through the slimy brown mud. Picking his way between the heaps of horse dung, he crossed the roadway by the remains of the Palace of Westminster, destroyed in the disastrous fire of 1834. The din of the workmen starting on the rebuilding added to the clatter of the iron-shod wheels of the carriages on the cobblestones, the noise of the crowds and livestock, and the clamour of the costermongers, but Edward ignored them all as he escaped into the relative calm of Birdcage Walk.

His mother was away in Birmingham and, over the last week, he had continued practising, firing from the back window of his lodgings. But that morning, Wednesday 10 June, he decided the fateful day had come. He dressed smartly in his gambroon trousers[1], light silk waistcoat, and brown frock coat, which he had saved for best from a funeral two years earlier. He waited until three o'clock before setting off on his 2-mile walk.

The previous Easter, when he was out by Hyde Park Corner with two fellows from the Hog-in-the-Pound, his plan had begun to form. He had seen the crowds of people waiting to catch a glimpse of the Queen on her daily outings and learnt of her routine. He knew how to set about his task from reading the adventures in books such as *The Black Prince*, *Jack Shepherd*, and *The Pilot*.

In St James's Park, the birdcages no longer lined the thoroughfare, but he could still see the Ornithological Society on Duck Island. Afternoon strollers were about beside the placid waters of the lake. The licensed milk-sellers were at work with their cows and pails. For them and the others around, it was just an ordinary day.

Outside Buckingham Palace, the people hoping to catch a glimpse of Her Majesty paid no heed to Edward. He passed the Marble Arch entrance at the end of The Mall, acting like any other visitor, and continued for another hundred yards along Constitution Hill. The avenue led from the garden gate of the palace towards the triumphal arch at Hyde Park Corner, and was lined with trees, which afforded protection.

Edward selected a good spot about a third of the way along the road, his back to the iron railings of Green Park. Although several people were about, it was less crowded than near to the palace, and none would suspect his intentions. He prepared for a long wait, his arms crossed, the two pistols concealed beneath his brown coat. It was just after 4 p.m.

Two hours later there was the sound of cheering from the palace. A few more moments elapsed before the Queen and Prince Albert emerged from the garden gate in an open carriage pulled by four horses, with postillions[2] and two outriders. The royal couple, with Victoria on the left and Albert on the right, raised their hands to wave to their subjects.

It was a low carriage and the sovereign was clearly in view as the party proceeded down Constitution Hill heading for Hyde Park. In a short while they had nearly covered the ground to where Edward stood. He walked forward, nodding his head as if to affirm the rightness of what he was about to do. As the carriage came alongside, he quickly pulled a pistol from his coat. At a distance of only six paces, he fired.

Several of the onlookers heard the loud report, and some women screamed, but the Queen was not hit and she appeared unaware that her life was in danger. Edward pulled out his other pistol with his left hand and balanced it on his right arm. Then the Queen at last saw him pointing the gun at her. She ducked instinctively, while Albert pulled her down. Edward fired again.

* * *

Victoria was not a universally popular monarch. She was only twenty-one and her inexperience in government, her sex, plus some unfortunate incidents, had set some parts of the populace against her. When she was born in 1819, she was only fifth in line to succeed, but from the outset it was recognised that one day she could become Queen. Her father was the Duke of Kent and brother of George IV, but he died from complications following a cold when she was not yet one. His equerry, the ambitious Captain John Conroy, immediately sought to become indispensable to the Duchess, and they tightly constrained and controlled Victoria's upbringing. She was never left alone, even at night; her education was by carefully selected tutors; she only came into contact with a narrow circle of permitted visitors and had few in the way of friends.

Through childhood, Victoria's position in the order of succession fluctuated, but by the time that George IV died in 1830 and was succeeded by his brother William IV, she was next in line. It was only around that time, when she was eleven, that she realised what she could become. Although Queen Adelaide could yet have a child, Victoria was then trained as a future Queen, while the 'Conroyals', as the Captain and Duchess were sometimes slanderously referred to, schemed to advance their position as possible regents.

When King William IV died in the early hours of 20 June 1837, Princess Victoria's life fundamentally changed. Despite her protected upbringing, she had developed strength of character beyond her years. Her eighteenth birthday, the age at which she could become Queen, had just passed, and she determined that her accession to the throne would also mean an escape from the gilded prison which had enclosed her life. Although Victoria was technically still a minor, the Conroyals' control vanished.

Her training had at least prepared her for how she should behave. When the Privy Council met later that morning to introduce her to her government, she rejected all offers of support. She walked alone into the Red Saloon at Kensington Palace, a diminutive figure as small as a child, not beautiful but prepossessing, with fair hair, prominent blue eyes, a tiny chin, and a clear complexion. According to the Duke of Wellington, her regal bearing and voice meant that 'she not merely filled her chair, she filled the room'. Many in the country feared that this slight young woman would be susceptible to the prejudiced and malign influences of her courtiers and politicians, but she proved to have sterner qualities. She quickly decided to make her main residence at Buckingham House in London, which had been bought by George III, rebuilt by George IV, and refurbished by William IV, but not finished. When told that the new palace would not be ready for Her Majesty's occupation, she simply gave a date and ordered that it should be completed by then. It was.

But Victoria was inexperienced and she relied heavily on her first Whig prime minister, Lord Melbourne, who was kindly and calm in his advice. If Victoria had a failing, it was that she became too emotionally and intellectually dependent on certain trusted men in her life. Melbourne was the first, and she became very close to him, despite the fact that the Whigs were bent on reducing some of the privileges of the aristocracy. At one point there was even idle speculation that they might marry, even though he was forty years older. In May 1839, Melbourne resigned after the Whigs had nearly lost an important parliamentary division, and Victoria was devastated. She wrote in her diary, 'That happy peaceful life destroyed, that dearest kind Lord Melbourne no more my minister [...] I sobbed and cried much.' The dismayed Victoria was expected to ask Sir Robert Peel of the Tories to form a government. But, in what became known as the 'Bedchamber Crisis', Peel asked that some ladies of the Queen's household, who were related to Whig ministers, be replaced by Tory ladies, and Victoria stubbornly refused. Peel declined to form a government and, much to the Queen's pleasure, Melbourne soldiered on.

This failure was not welcomed by the populace, where Chartism was rampant. The Chartists, the country's first working-class political movement, rose to prominence in the mid-1830s, fuelled by the appalling conditions in the factories and towns, and campaigned strongly for universal adult male suffrage and a secret ballot. In 1839, they presented a petition with over a million signatures to the government, which was rejected out of hand by Parliament. In November, the men of the Welsh valleys marched in protest over the terrible conditions in the mines, and twenty were killed by musket fire in the so-called 'Newport Rising'. In the politically aware sections of London society, revolution was feared.

Victoria's popularity declined further over the Lady Flora Hastings affair. In February 1839, the Queen noticed that the unmarried lady-in-waiting had a bulge in her figure and assumed that she must be with child. Victoria's knowledge of the reproductive process was at best sketchy, but she did know that a man was involved, and she recollected that

Lady Flora had spent a night on a carriage journey with the hated Captain Conroy. She accused her of being pregnant but, after a humiliating medical examination, Lady Flora was pronounced a virgin. In fact she was afflicted with cancer of the liver, which caused her death a few months later in July, and the Queen was blamed for making her last months even more painful.

Another blunder from the point of view of political diplomacy occurred soon after this affair. Victoria had been struck by the handsomeness of her cousin Albert, the Prince of Saxe-Coburg Gotha, and during his second visit in October 1839 they became very close. She wrote in her diary that he was excessively handsome, with beautiful blue eyes, broad shoulders, and a fine figure. The young Queen had fallen in love, but the origins of her beau were a problem. On the one hand the country was delighted that their young Queen might wed, but after five Hanoverian Kings and their German brides, they were seriously disappointed by his nationality. Parliament was also less than keen to have to provide a purse for another penniless German prince at a time when the Chartist numbers were being swelled by the poor and unemployed. Victoria would not allow politics to overrule her heart, and their engagement was announced on 3 November 1839. However, she did bend a little with the mood and agreed that Albert would only be the Queen's Consort, with no power of his own. In many ways, that too suited her well.

The wedding took place at noon on 10 February 1840, in the Chapel Royal at St James's Palace. Victoria entered in a rich white satin dress trimmed with orange blossom and wearing a royal diamond necklace and a sapphire brooch, a present from Albert. Her eyes showed the signs of tears, but her face was full of happiness. Although Albert was a little short for the ruling classes at 5 feet 7 inches, beside Victoria he looked statuesque and handsome, trim in the borrowed uniform of a British field marshal and decorated with the Ribbon of the Garter. The ceremony completed, both young people looked deeply happy, each just twenty years old and profoundly in love.

Victoria ignored procedural correctness and was determined that only her friends would be at the ceremony, and of the 300 wedding guests only five were Tories, who had been most vociferous in criticising the Queen's choice of consort and casting doubt on his Protestantism. Afterwards, Victoria kissed her aunt, the Dowager Queen Adelaide, but only shook the hand of her mother. The royal couple returned to Buckingham Palace, where they changed before attending a simple wedding breakfast for around forty people, and soon after departed for Windsor. That evening she wrote in her diary:

MY DEAREST DEAREST DEAR Albert sat on a footstool by my side, and his excessive love & affection gave me feelings of heavenly love & happiness I never could have *hoped* to have felt before! He clasped me in his arms, & we kissed each other again & again! His beauty, his sweetness & gentleness – really how can I ever be thankful enough to have such a *Husband*! [...] to be called by names of tenderness, I have never yet heard used to me before – was bliss beyond belief! Oh! This was the happiest day of my life!

Victoria became pregnant almost immediately. Despite her condition, she continued the process of government, reading the contents of the red dispatch boxes that regularly arrived at the palace, although increasingly Albert helped with selecting the papers. On 1 June he gave his first speech in English, as honorary president of the Anti-Slavery Society, to great applause. But ten days later, they experienced a more hostile encounter.

It was as they drove along Constitution Hill on an outing in the early evening summer light that Edward Oxford struck. Albert wrote what happened next in a letter to his grandmother the following day:

> We hardly proceeded a hundred yards from the Palace, when I noticed, on the footpath on my side, a mean-looking man holding something towards us; and before I could distinguish what it was, a shot was fired, which almost stunned us both, it was so loud, and fired barely six paces from us. Victoria had just turned to the left to look at a horse, and could not therefore understand why her ears were ringing, as from its being so very near, she could hardly distinguish that it proceeded from a shot having been fired. The horses started and the carriage stopped. I seized Victoria's hands, and asked if the fright had shaken her, but she laughed at the thing.
>
> I then looked at the man, who was still standing in the same place, his arms crossed, and a pistol in each hand. His attitude was so affected and theatrical that it quite amused me. Suddenly he again pointed his pistol and fired a second time. This time Victoria also saw the shot, and stooped quickly drawn down by me. The ball must have passed just above her head, to judge from where it was found sticking in an opposite wall [...] I called for the postillions to drive on.

Underneath, Victoria was shocked, but she knew how she should behave, and her iron will came to the fore. To show the public that they had not lost confidence, they continued with their outing through Hyde Park. When they returned they found cheering crowds massed around the palace, on horseback, in carriages, and on foot. For the next few days, everywhere they went they were applauded, and at the theatres and elsewhere, crowds would spontaneously burst into renditions of 'God Save the Queen'. The attempted assassination provided a very welcome boost to Victoria's popularity.

* * *

The would-be assassin, Edward Oxford, was a slightly made youth of eighteen; around average height at 5 feet 6 inches and good looking, with small but expressive dark eyes, auburn hair, and a fair complexion. He was born on 9 April 1822 in Birmingham, the third of seven children. His mother, Hannah, came from a respectable Midlands family, but his paternal antecedents were more murky. Some who knew the antics of his father and grandfather thought that they were the cause of his reckless and scandalous behaviour.

His grandfather, John Oxford, was a seaman of foreign extraction. Described as a small 'man of colour', but not a black man, he suffered from bouts of madness and fits of drunken anger. He was born in the village of Much Hadham in Hertfordshire in 1769, but the family moved to London, where he met his future wife, Sophia Kent. They married a couple of months later in St Marylebone, London, on 5 February 1795.

Edward's grandmother told him the story of the disaster that occurred three years later, after his grandfather returned from a voyage to the East Indies. On Edward's father's first birthday,

John Oxford arrived at his father-in-law's house, near Petworth in Sussex, where his wife was staying. He had high notions of himself and felt that his in-laws were not showing him sufficient respect. After a bout of drinking, he became violent. He shattered the windows, threw two clocks down and broke them, and smashed everything in the house. Help was summoned, and three men, together with his brother-in-law, tied him up with cords. He was taken on horseback into town, and the magistrate sentenced him to a fortnight in the Petworth bridewell.[3]

He was released to return to London, where he went to sea again. In 1801, he joined the crew of the new 32-gun, fifth-rate frigate, HMS *Medusa*, which was to be his ship for the rest of his naval career. Fortunately, he wasn't on her very first voyage, when she was commandeered by the navy's rising star, Vice-Admiral Nelson, to sail from Deal to Boulogne to take part in the blockade, when many of the hands were killed or wounded in an ill-planned sortie. But he was on board during the battle of Cape Santa Maria on 5 October 1804. HMS *Medusa*, under the command of Captain Gore (later Rear-Admiral Sir John Gore), was one of four British frigates that intercepted four Spanish frigates heading for Cadiz laden with treasure from the New World. Spain was not at war with Britain, so their commander, Rear-Admiral José de Bustamante y Guerra, thought he had nothing to fear from the approaching British squadron. The *Medusa* lined up on the weather-beam of the *Fama*, and each of the other three boats paired with a Spanish counterpart, while a boat was sent to the flagship demanding that they shorten sail and surrender. Their admiral refused.

The Spanish fired first, but a terrible response from the experienced British gunners wreaked havoc. Nine minutes after the first shot, the *Nuestra Señora de Las Mercedes* blew up. Within half an hour both the *Medea* and the *Santa Clara* had surrendered. The last boat, the *Fama*, struck her colours, but after the *Medusa* ceased fire, she re-hoisted them and made off. HMS *Medusa* and HMS *Lively* gave chase, but it took three hours before they overhauled the ship and she surrendered. The Spanish toll was 258 killed and eighty wounded, while the British lost just two dead and seven wounded. The ships were taken to Gibraltar and then Plymouth in what was described as an act of piracy by the Spanish. Spain declared war on Britain in support of Napoleon, something the government had thought would happen soon anyway. A year later Nelson defeated the combined Spanish and French fleet at Trafalgar.

The captured cargo raised nearly £1 million for the government, but the courts decided that there was no prize money since the two countries were not at war. However, *ex gratia* payments were made and may well have led to some considerable sums being passed to John Oxford. He was uninjured, although a later accident on the *Medusa* led to a permanent contusion[4] to his right foot.

His eccentric and violent outbursts continued during spells of shore leave, and were still occurring many years later in 1821. At the time, the family were living near the dockyard in Deptford, and his wife Sophia had to call for help. The beadle[5] and two or three other men had to restrain John and put him in a straight-waistcoat, and he was kept tied up for about ten days. A couple of months after he had recovered from this ordeal, he went to sea again. Finally, in 1826, he was admitted to the Royal Hospital for Seamen at Greenwich, where he was put under the care of Sir Richard Dobson for a 'complaint in the head'. According to his daughter, Sophia, who used to visit him in the hospital, he would stand guard at the gate with his halberd[6] over his shoulder, and say he was St Paul, put there because the Pope of Rome had escaped. He died a few years later, in 1831.

So, if John Oxford was an Englishman born and bred, where had his 'colour' originated? In fact it was inherited from his father, Edward's great-grandfather, another George Oxford, who was Afro-Caribbean. He came from the slave plantations of Antigua, where he was a servant to the part-owner, Stephen Lavington. When the latter died on a visit to South Carolina in 1758, his wife Jane decided to return to England. She settled in her brother-in-law's house at Moor Place, a large Elizabethan house in Much Hadham, Hertfordshire. She brought with her the black servant George Oxford, an unusual sight in London, never mind the deep countryside. But George did not remain a servant much longer, for in 1763, he left her employ and married Mary Ann Ross in Much Hadham parish church. He subsequently became a respected village shopkeeper and baker.

It is not clear when George Oxford gained his freedom, but he must have been favoured. A good, clear signature on the marriage register indicates that he was literate (as was Mary Ann Ross), and somebody must have provided the money to start his business. Over the next eight years, George and Mary Oxford gave birth to four children in Much Hadham, including Edward's grandfather, after which they moved away, probably to London. There, George must have passed on his learning to his son, because John Oxford was also literate.

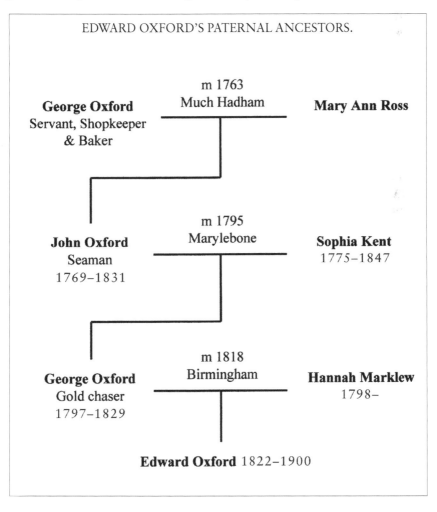

EDWARD OXFORD'S PATERNAL ANCESTORS.

George Oxford
Servant, Shopkeeper
& Baker

m 1763
Much Hadham

Mary Ann Ross

John Oxford
Seaman
1769–1831

m 1795
Marylebone

Sophia Kent
1775–1847

George Oxford
Gold chaser
1797–1829

m 1818
Birmingham

Hannah Marklew
1798–

Edward Oxford 1822–1900

Edward's father, George Oxford, inherited some of his grandfather's colour (he was described as a 'mulatto' by the *Leicester Chronicle*). He was apprenticed as a jeweller, and later earned a very good living as a gold-chaser, decorating gold items such as snuff boxes or fob watches with engraved, inlayed, or high relief embellishments. He was a skilful worker, one of the first and perhaps the best in Birmingham, and could make £10–20 a week, a very great sum.

Hannah Marklew was the daughter of the landlord of the Anchor and Hope in Birmingham, and George Oxford, who frequented the pub, was desperate to marry her. He threatened to cut his own throat with a razor on several occasions, should she refuse. Finally, he appeared with a double-barrelled pistol, which he said he would fire into his own face unless she consented. She eventually agreed, but they kept the plan secret from her parents. Her father disliked him, and sometimes refused to serve him in the pub, but he would just send out for drink to other establishments, and show his importance by paying the score of other customers. The day before she was due to marry a letter arrived in response to an enquiry of his previous master as to his character. It was not good, and Hannah told George that she had changed her mind.

George flew into a rage and showed her the marriage licence, which he had obtained without the consent of her parents, even though she was only twenty years old. He also pulled out a big roll of banknotes, which he flung onto the fire, where it was burnt to ash. She relented, and the next day, 28 April 1818, they were married. They continued to keep their wedding secret, but then, during a quarrel with Hannah's mother, George told her, and Hannah's parents were horrified.

He lived a life of eccentricity and extravagance, driving around the town with a frivolous appearance and outrageous manners, and was referred to by some as the 'tawny beau'. At home, he continued to act strangely and was given to violent outbursts. On several occasions he led his horse around the parlour, and after the birth of his first child, Susan, he struck a file into the breast of his wife so that milk flowed out. While she was pregnant for a second time, he would make the actions and noises of a baboon, and the little boy was born an idiot with a simian face and could only grunt and stick his tongue out like his father. He died when he was less than two and a half, soon after Edward was born.

One day not long after that, when they were out walking, Edward's father left them abruptly, returned and locked up the house, and told the neighbours he was going to America. In fact, he went to Dublin for four months, where he squandered a great deal of money, before returning. There were many other incidents of violence or neglect, and on several occasions he took poison or overdosed on laudanum, which he may well have become addicted to.

He was later implicated with a gang of coiners[7] and moved to London, where he lived wretchedly and had to make a living selling pies. George Oxford died on 10 June 1829, exactly eleven years before his son became so notorious. During their marriage, Hannah gave birth to seven children, but only Edward and Susan survived. At the time of her husband's death, Hannah was with him in London, but then she returned to Birmingham for a while, before finding a position as housekeeper with Mr William Prescott, a banker, in London.

Edward's early life was spent in Birmingham. He lived with his maternal grandfather and was somewhat protected from the antics of his father, although his shocking behaviour and the frequent absences of his mother must have affected the young boy. Perhaps partly because of his broken home, Edward became disturbed and bottled up his anger. He burst into tears for no reason, even when there was nobody near, and often flew into a rage with no provocation. He also sometimes wilfully destroyed things with no apparent cause. In Birmingham, he was sent to school at Mr Walter's until he was about ten, when he went to join his mother in London and attended, for a few months, Mr Robinson's in Lambeth. He found the work easy, and his reports said that he was an intelligent and able pupil, but he could not settle. The teachers complained of his inattentiveness and bad behaviour, and he was often caned. Soon he was moved to another school in Camberwell, but that didn't last, and several other establishments followed elsewhere.

Edward had a fascination with guns and gunpowder. He would play at letting off cannons, and once, soon after he had come to London, the cannon exploded and his eyebrows and eyelashes were burnt off, leaving his face a mess. His tears and rages continued, and sometimes after these fits he laughed hysterically. For a time, the family lived on Westminster Bridge Road, where Hannah kept a pastry cook's shop, but she had to lock her son in the cellar several times to stop him upsetting the customers. Finally, she was forced to give up the pastry shop, and later ran a small coffee house on Borough Road, but Edward made such a disturbance when the gentlemen were reading their newspapers that the business failed and the goods were taken in restitution.

Edward's first job, after the coffee house folded in 1836, was working for his aunt, Mrs Clarinda Powell, at the King's Head in Hounslow where she was the landlady. He took to the job, which gave him a little independence, and was a good worker, but rather put the patrons off by his occasional bursts of maniacal laughter. One evening, he went around turning off all the gaslights, leaving the packed pub in complete darkness. Meanwhile, his mother took over the Red Rover public house in Market Street, Southwark Bridge Road, which was another failure, and in December 1836 she sought refuge from Borough Gaol in the Insolvent Debtors Act, when her debts were listed as £390 and her assets between £3 and £4.

On several occasions Edward's anger turned to violence. One day in Hounslow, he was out with a boy of about the same age who was amusing himself with a bow and arrow. Edward held up his hand and invited the boy to fire at it. He missed, so Edward said, 'Now let me fire at your hand.' The youth, ashamed to refuse, agreed and stood a considerable distance away. Edward took aim, released the bow, and hit the poor boy's hand violently in the centre.

On another occasion, in July 1838, Edward got into a fight with the harness boys at a local stable, which led to his first brush with the law. The foreman of the yard, John Yates, was called, and he told Edward to leave. 'Not for you or any such old bugger,' Edward retorted. The foreman seized him by the collar and ejected him, and Edward went into the King's Head, crying. He told his aunt, who emerged and abused Yates. Edward then came out with a large screwdriver, telling Yates that he would 'knock his bloody brains out'. He struck the foreman on the head, drawing blood. At the magistrate's court, he was found guilty of assault and fined £1 with 10s 6d costs.

Soon after that incident, the King's Head closed, and Edward moved to the Shepherd and Flock run by Mr Minton in High Street, Marylebone, but after eighteen months he was dismissed for attacking a fellow barman, William Hazelwood, with a knife. All this time, Edward felt that he was destined for greater things, not a life of such menial employment. During the winter of 1839/40, he asked his mother to fund him to the tune of £50 to become a midshipman, and when she said it was a foolish idea, he pointed out how proud she would be when he was Admiral Edward Oxford.

He spent a few months at the Hat and Feathers, managed by Mr Parr on Wilderness Row in St Luke's, and then he was recommended to the Hog-in-the-Pound by his uncle, Charles Marklew, who was landlord of the Ship Tavern in the City. He started work at the Hog in January 1840 for an annual salary of £20. He only lasted four months.

After he was dismissed, he went to live with his mother and sister at No. 6 West Place, West Square, Lambeth, where she had two rooms in a lodging house managed by the elderly Mrs Sarah Packman. Edward occupied the front room. He had some of the normal interests of any eighteen-year-old youth, and was probably interested in the two young milliner daughters of his landlady. He certainly wrote a letter to one young woman who had taken his fancy, Emily Chittenden, a nursery maid at his previous employment. Appended to the address on the envelope were the following lines:

> Fly postman, with this letter-bound
> To a public-house, the Hog-in-the-Pound.
> To Miss Chittenden there convey,
> With speedility obey.
> Remember, my blade,
> The postage is paid.

On 6 June, the Saturday before the outrage on Constitution Hill, he went to see another young lady of his acquaintance, Mary Ann Foreman, who had been a barmaid at the Shepherd and Flock. He asked her to come and see him in the Hog-in-the-Pound, even though he no longer worked there.

Whether these romantic desires had any influence on his decision to seek notoriety is unknown. But certainly his unemployment gave him the time to prepare for the deed, and the absence of his mother in Birmingham removed any restraining influence. On Wednesday 10 June, he carried out his plan.

* * *

A crowd had gathered around Edward by the time that Constable Charles Brown reached the scene. They began to chant, 'Kill him! Kill him!' Edward remained calm, and when Brown grabbed him by the collar, he said, 'You have no occasion to use violence. I am the person. I will go quietly.' One of the bystanders said, 'Perhaps there are more of them'; to which Edward replied, 'I have friends'. The mob let the police lead the assailant away, confident in the knowledge that soon there would be another public hanging for them to witness at Newgate.

Two police constables from 'A' division took him to Westminster station house in Gardener's Lane. At the police station, Edward was asked for basic details by the inspector, but there was no formal interview. The room where he was held was visited by a succession of people, wanting to see the man, and discussing amongst themselves the situation. Apart from Mr Gregorie, the magistrate for Queen Square police court, there was the Honourable Augustus Murray, the Controller of the Royal Household; the Marquis of Normanby, Mr Fox Maule, Under Secretary at the Home Office; Mr McCann, surgeon of Parliament Street; Earl Cadogan; the Earl of Uxbridge; and many other noblemen and gentlemen.

Edward's lodgings were searched and a box uncovered that contained details of a secret society called 'Young England', a sword and scabbard, two pistol bags, a black crêpe[8] cap with two red bows, a powder-flask containing about 3 oz of gunpowder, a dozen percussion caps, a bullet mould, and five bullets.

Edward managed to sleep quite soundly in his cell in the police house and ate a substantial breakfast the following morning, before being taken to the Home Office to be interviewed. In the afternoon, he went before the Privy Council, who were sitting as the 'Board of Green Cloth', a court with jurisdiction over the verge (about 12 miles) of the Royal Household.[9] Edward was committed to Newgate Prison, charged with high treason.

YOUNG ENGLAND
Rules and Regulations

1. That every member shall be provided with a brace of pistols, a sword, a rifle, and a dagger; the two latter to be kept at the committee-room.
2. That every member must, on entering, take the oath of allegiance to be true to the cause he has joined.
3. That every member must, on entering the house, give a signal to the sentry.
4. That every officer shall have a factitious [*sic*] name; his right name and address to be kept with the secretary.
5. That every member shall, when he is ordered to meet, be armed with a brace of pistols (loaded) and a sword to repel any attack; and also be provided with a black crape cap, to cover his face with his marks of distinction outside.
6. That whenever any member wishes to introduce any new member, he must give satisfactory accounts of him to their superiors, and from thence to the council.
7. Any member who can procure a hundred men shall be promoted to the rank of captain.
8. Any member holding communications with any country agents must instantly forward the intelligence to the secretary.
9. That whenever any member is ordered down the country or abroad, he must take various disguises with him (as the labourer, the mechanic, and the gentleman), all of which he can obtain at the committee-room.
10. That any member wishing to absent himself for more than one month must obtain leave from the commander-in-chief.
11. That no member will be allowed to speak during any debate, nor allowed to ask more than two questions. All the printed rules to be kept at the committee-room.

A. W. SMITH, Secretary.

LIST OF PRINCIPAL MEMBERS				
Factitious Names				
President	*Council*	*Generals*	*Captains*	*Lieutenants*
Gowrie	Justinian	Fredeni	Oxonian	Hercules
	Ernest	Othoe	Louis	Mars
	Alowan	Augustus	Mildon	Neptune
	Augustia	Anthony	Amadeus	Albert
	Coloman			
	Ethelred			
	Kenneth			
	Ferdinand			
	Godfrey			
	Nicholas			
	Hanibal			
	Gregory			
Marks of Distinction				
A black bow	A large white cockade	Three red bows	Two red bows	One red bow

First letter addressed to Mr Oxford, at Mr Minton's, High Street, Marylebone.

YOUNG ENGLAND, *May 16, 1839.*

SIR, – Our commander-in-chief was very glad to find that you answered his questions in such a straightforward manner; you will be wanted to attend on the 21st of this month, as we expect one of the country agents in town on business of importance. Be sure and attend.

A. W. SMITH, *Secretary.*

P.S. – You must not take any notice to the boy, nor ask him any questions.

Second letter addressed to Mr Oxford, at Mr Farr's, Hat and Feathers, Goswell Street.

YOUNG ENGLAND, *Nov. 14, 1839.*

SIR, – I am very glad to hear that you improve so much in your speeches. Your speech the last time you were here was beautiful. There was another one introduced last night by Lieutenant Mars, a fine, tall, gentlemanly-looking fellow, and it is said that he is a military officer, but his name has not yet transpired. Soon after he was introduced we were alarmed by a violent knocking at the door; in an instant our faces were covered, we cocked our pistols, and with drawn swords stood waiting to receive the enemy. While one stood over the fire with the papers, another stood with lighted torch to fire the house. We then sent the old woman to open the door, and it proved to be some little boys who knocked at the door and ran away.

You must attend on Wednesday next.

A. W. SMITH, *Secretary.*

Third letter addressed to Mr Oxford, at Mr Robinson's, Hog-in-the-Pound, Oxford Street.

YOUNG ENGLAND, *April 3, 1840*

SIR, – You are requested to attend to-night, as there is an extraordinary meeting to be holden, in consequence of having received some communications of an important nature from Hanover. You must attend, and if your master will not give you leave, you must come in defiance of him.

A. W. SMITH, *Secretary*.

Edward's mother arranged for a solicitor to represent him, but on being asked, Edward said that he would defend himself, and the authorities refused access. Later he changed his mind and was represented by Mr Pelham, solicitor, and counsels Mr Bodkin and Mr Sydney Taylor. They proposed the defence of lunacy, and Edward must have gone along with it, as on 18 June he wrote a letter from Newgate Gaol to his solicitor asking him to write to the Home Secretary requesting some childish books to read, such as *My Little Tom Thumb* and *Jack and the Beanstalk*, and to ask him 'as a prisoner of war whether I may not be allowed on a parole of honour?' and 'on what grounds, ask him, does he detain one of Her Majesty's subjects?' On the other hand, the Home Secretary received a report from another prisoner that Edward Oxford appeared perfectly sane.

In the press, intense speculation abounded as to whether Edward was in league with others, perhaps the Chartists or the Germans. A letter from the Irish campaigner Daniel O'Connell, the MP for Dublin, claimed it could not possibly be the act of a poor 'pot-boy', but rather a plot by the Orange faction in the Tory party that sought to assassinate the 'first sovereign that ever showed impartial justice to the people of Ireland' and wreak murderous destruction on the Catholics.

The Home Secretary also received numerous letters from concerned citizens worried about the future safety of the Queen. A William Gougenheim, translator of languages, was concerned at the sight of four or five large water carts parked near the palace, which made him think of 'the machine infernale of the Rue Saint Nicaisse in Paris; it was a watering cart full of gun powder and Bonaparte had a very narrow escape'.[10] Others were inspired by the Young England documents that had been reported in the newspapers. A letter for Edward was intercepted that came from a certain George Campbell, saying that he and John were safe in Dublin and to 'say nothing tell nothing' and 'to not fear death'.

The trial was initially set for Monday 23 June, but after representations from the defence on the need to bring witnesses to the city, was delayed until 9 July. The judges selected for the hearing were Lord Denham, Mr Baron Alderson, and Mr Justice Patteson, while the Attorney General led the prosecution and Mr Taylor the defence. Edward's defence lawyers went to considerable effort to prepare and present their case, not paying heed to the inability of Edward's family to pay. After the trial, his solicitor wrote to the Home Secretary asking whether the Crown would cover the expense, which amounted to nearly £600.

Edward was tried under the Treason Act of 1351, enacted by Edward III, with various modifications under later sovereigns.[11] These defined high treason as waging war on the sovereign, being adherent to his enemies, planning the death of the sovereign, slaying the Lord Chancellor, or having sex with the sovereign's eldest unmarried daughter or the wife of his eldest son. The law required that the trial be heard before three judges, but in many other ways the proceedings were conducted in a similar manner to a murder trial. Edward Oxford was indicted:

> That he, being a subject of our Lady the Queen, on the tenth of June, as a false traitor, maliciously and traitorously did compass, imagine, and intend to bring and put our said Lady the Queen to death; and to fulfil and bring to effect his treason and treasonable compassing, he, as such false traitor, maliciously and traitorously did shoot off and discharge a certain pistol, loaded with gun-powder and a bullet.

The prosecution brought forward numerous witnesses to testify to the defendant's purchase and practice with the weapons, and the act itself. The defence responded with an equal volume of testimony, which focused on signs of insanity in the defendant, his father and grandfather[12], given by his mother and other relations, teachers, and employers. His mother also confirmed that all the Young England papers were in Edward's handwriting. Expert evidence from leading medical men of the time supported the defence: Dr Thomas Hodgkin[13] (an eminent pathologist) diagnosed a 'lesion of will' that meant he could not control his impulses; Dr William Dingle Chowne (the manager of Charing Cross Hospital) agreed that he could not control his will; Dr James Fernandez Clarke (an acclaimed medical author) thought he was a hysterical imbecile; and Dr John Connolly (the reformist head of the Hanwell Lunatic Asylum) believed he suffered from a disease of the brain that could be inferred from the shape of his head. The latter also reported that, on asking the prisoner why he shot at the Queen, Edward replied, 'Oh, I may as well shoot at her as anybody else.' Mr Taylor also threw doubt on whether the pistols had in fact been loaded with ball or not. Edward himself had only muddied the waters by saying, 'If your head had come in contact with the balls, you would have found there was ball in the pistol.'

Edward thought the proceedings fascinating, as the high and mighty of the land discussed every aspect of his life to date over the course of two days. He often smiled and looked around the courtroom, later cross-questioning his attorney on who exactly the lords and ladies in attendance were. When the discussion became more tedious, he would occasionally chew on the bunch of rue strewn on the dock bench.[14]

At the end of the trial, the jury retired and returned after three-quarters of an hour with a special verdict, 'We find the prisoner, Edward Oxford, guilty of discharging the contents of two pistols, but whether or not they were loaded with ball has not been satisfactorily proved to us, he being of unsound state of mind at the time.'

There followed some legal wrangling between the Attorney General and Mr Taylor, where the latter contended that if the jury found it unproven that the defendant had sought to endanger the life of the Queen, then he must be acquitted of the charge. The Attorney General questioned how any jury could let such a dangerous man go free. Lord Denham instructed the jury to decide on the matter of whether the pistols were loaded. They retired for another hour, and on their return did not directly answer the question, but found the prisoner guilty of the charge, he being at the time insane. Lord Denham corrected the wording, and declared the verdict to be, 'not guilty on the ground of insanity', and instructed that the prisoner be confined in strict custody during Her Majesty's pleasure.

Edward showed no emotion at the verdict.

* * *

On 18 July, Edward Oxford was taken from Newgate Gaol to Bethlem Hospital[15] in Southwark, literally just a stone's throw from where he used to live in West Square, and secured in the criminally insane wing. The place had an awful reputation for its treatment and restraint of violent inmates, and, as late as 1814, it was still possible to pay a penny (free on Tuesdays) to visit and peer at the antics of the insane. During that year, there were 96,000 such visits. In 1815, the institution moved to new premises in St George's Fields, Southwark.[16] When Edward was admitted, the hospital had around 400 inmates, of whom about half were classed as incurable, and eighty-five were criminally insane. By then the regime had become much more humane. The hospital was kept scrupulously clean, whitewashed once a year, swept daily, and the sleeping rooms built on a slope to a drain for the purpose of regular scouring.

Edward soon grew used to the routine. Inmates were locked up between 8 p.m. and 8 a.m., with wake-up at 6 a.m. (7 a.m. in winter) and normal bedtime at 8 p.m. For safety, food was served on wooden trenchers with implements made of bone. Breakfast was at 8 a.m., dinner at 1 p.m., and tea at 5 p.m. It looked unappetising, but the alternative of force-feeding with a stomach pump was much worse. Clothes were removed at night-time. During the day, patients were kept busy, and recreation facilities were laid on. But some aggressive patients were still kept in chains. Hydrotherapy with warm and cold baths was popular, and aperients were widely used as constipation was believed to be a frequent concomitant of insanity.

Conditions were worst where Edward lived, in the criminal wing, which consisted of two self-contained blocks (female and male) at the back of the hospital. They were built more like prisons, with their own exercise yards. The dismal arched corridors were feebly lit at either end by a single iron-barred window, and divided in the middle by gratings more suitable to fierce carnivores than afflicted humanity. The department was overcrowded, and the opportunities for employment were limited: playing fives, running in the exercise yard, knitting and reading. Edward, not a large or strong man, was locked in the same room as other, more violent, inmates for much of the time. When he could, he took advantage of what leisure facilities existed, and he started studying French. The long years passed slowly with little change.

Reform finally came twelve years later, with the arrival of the first resident physician as superintendent, Dr William Charles Hood, and George Henry Haydon as steward.[17] Dr Hood soon sized up Edward and told a later visitor that 'he was quite sane, and had always been so'. Haydon became Edward's mentor and saviour, a kindly blue-eyed giant the same age as Edward, who excelled in drawing and had spent five years in Melbourne selling sketches to the papers and working as a clerk and an architect. He was not at all like the average lunatic asylum manager, and was a liberal teetotaller who, unusually for the time, had been a defender of the culture and rights of the aboriginals. Back in England, his interests remained broad; he qualified as a barrister as well as working at Bethlem for thirty-seven years until he retired in 1889.

The better-behaved were moved to a normal ward, and Edward Oxford, as a model inmate, prospered. The hospital had a well-stocked library, and work was seen as therapy.

The men were employed in the garden, in brick-laying, and in the workshops, while the women helped with the cleaning and needlework. Incentives were given in the form of tobacco for the men and a daily allowance of bread, cheese, and small beer for those engaged in household work. Recreation was also encouraged for those who were well-behaved, with the men playing outside at ball, trap-ball, leap-frog, and cricket, and inside at cards and dominoes, while the women played the pianoforte and held evening dances. Visitors were allowed, but strictly controlled, and letters were censored.

With Haydon's encouragement, Edward put his time to good use, reading and drawing, learning to play the violin and, by 1854, he was said to have acquired a sound knowledge of French, German, and Italian, and a smattering of Spanish, Greek and Latin. He became an accomplished knitter of gloves, carpenter, painter and decorator for the hospital, and, according to one doctor, could play fives, chess, and draughts, better than any other inmate.

Following the death of Prince Albert in 1861, Edward wrote a poem, which began:

> Whilst yet erect, just like some fair young oak
> That scarcely deigns before the storm to bend,
> Death laid him low, as by the lightning's stroke,
> And England lost a true and steadfast friend.
>
> A husband dear, to one than whom this earth
> None better, and few equal e'er has seen;
> Whose many virtues, and whose priceless worth
> Adorn the Wife, the Mother, and the Queen.

In 1864, Bethlehem closed its criminal wing, and on 30 April, Edward was moved (one of the last) to the new Broadmoor Criminal Lunatic Asylum, which stood on a wild heath near the village of Crowthorne in Berkshire. To those who had been confined to Bethlem's prison blocks, the move to Broadmoor, with its terraces and views across the Berkshire Downs, must have seemed almost like release. Because of the terms of their incarceration, the place was nicknamed 'the Queen's great pleasure house'. Edward was rather unwell when he arrived, having suffered from constipation and oedema[18] in his lower legs for the previous six months. He then contracted urethritis, but gradually his health improved and he continued his industriousness, working as a housepainter and becoming proficient as a wood grainer.

Three years later, he was released on the condition that he emigrated to the colonies and never returned. Twelve officers from the Metropolitan Police, led by a Chief Inspector of the Detective Force, photographed Oxford and took notes on his appearance, and it was made clear that if he ever returned, he would be incarcerated for good. Thirty copies of his photograph were distributed to the Metropolitan districts. A warrant for his release was issued by the Secretary of State on 2 October, and the medical superintendent arranged the passage. He was accompanied to Plymouth in late November, and placed on board the *Suffolk*, a 200-foot-long, 976-ton steamship, which left on 3 December 1867, bound for Victoria, Australia.

Immediately after his release, Edward wrote to his old mentor, George Haydon, 'Last night for the first time for nearly twenty-eight years I slept, or rather went to bed, with the key of the bedroom door on *my* side. You may fancy my feelings if you like, but you won't be able to feel as I then felt.' He thanked Haydon, saying, 'I shall take with me a grateful remembrance of all the kindness I have received at your hands.' He recalled the help he had received in times of trouble and added, 'Had it not been for that, my sorrows, great as they have been, would have been intensified ten-fold.'

Edward knew emigration was the right thing:

In leaving England forever I do what is certainly the best, for a man who has once been in the grip of the law [...] It makes no matter what his offence, or whether he has paid the full pound of flesh ten-times over, the taint clings to him like a leprosy, & makes men worse than himself affect airs of superiority over him. All that, at a distance, & where he is unknown, is prevented. He can then find his own level, by putting on the bold front necessary [...] in the future no man shall say I am unworthy of the name of an Englishman.

Edward changed his name to make sure that he was unknown, and when he landed in Melbourne on 7 February 1868, he was called, appropriately enough, John Freeman. He gave his age as forty-three, two years younger than he actually was, and found employment as a housepainter. He gradually adapted to his new life. Melbourne was booming following the huge influx of immigrants with the gold rush, which had seen Victoria's population grow from 100,000 in 1851 to around 700,000 when Edward arrived.

Thirteen years later, on 16 March 1881, he married a widow twenty years his junior, Jane Bowen. Edward claimed to be only fifty-three, rather than his true fifty-eight. He gave his father's profession and the names of his parents correctly for the marriage register, although their surnames were magically transformed to Freeman. His new wife was English too, having been born Jane Tapping in Thame, Oxfordshire, in 1842. Her father was a baker and confectioner, but they had not remained in the town long, and she was much travelled and much married. She followed her aunt Sarah to Fremantle, Western Australia, where Jane married John McKinley in 1861. But her husband survived less than four years, and in 1865 she married James Bowen. He was an accountant for the British India Steamship Navigation Company, and had spent some time in Bombay. They lived in Western Australia for five years, and then came to Melbourne after James became ill, suffering from chronic rheumatism. He died a painful four years later in 1874, at the young age of thirty-six, leaving Jane with a six-year-old son, James William Bowen, and an older child from her earlier union.

Although she worked as a dressmaker, she must have been left tolerably well off, as she lived in Emerald Hill[19], a smart suburb developed during the 1860s. Edward moved to the area and rented a three-storey, twelve-room, brick-built property with his new wife, at 43 Howe Crescent, Albert Park, a classy address. They lived there for five years before moving to a slightly more modest, but equally impressive eight-room property, four doors down the road. John Freeman also moved up the ladder socially too, and got to know the Dean of Melbourne, becoming his nominee as Churchwarden and Honorary Secretary of the vestry at St James's church, the old Melbourne Cathedral. After a couple of years in Emerald

Hill, he ceased to describe himself in official documents as a 'painter', preferring instead, 'gentleman' or 'writer'.

On the occasion of the Queen's seventieth birthday in 1889, he was invited to attend the Governor General's levee[20], a high point of the Melbourne social calendar. It was a public holiday, the ships in the harbour dressed with flags, and the Victorian Ensign flying from public buildings. The public were treated to a procession of fire brigades through the city streets, a military review in Albert Park, and a series of football matches, including one against a Maori team recently returned from England. But John Freeman was the guest of His Excellency the Governor, and mingled with high-ranking politicians, military officers, foreign consuls, and representatives of all the accepted religious denominations.

As well as his social standing, his learning had also progressed, and in 1888 he published a book entitled *Lights and Shadows of Melbourne Life*, which is well written and evocative of the time. It celebrates the exuberant wealth and bustle of the city, whilst dwelling on the low life: the unemployed and destitute, the pubs, lodging houses, markets, and costermongers; a common approach of the time that made the reader feel proud and superior.

After twenty-one years of silence, he resumed his correspondence with Haydon, by sending him a copy of the book. He wrote, 'You are the only man in the world, besides myself, who could connect me with the book [...] Even my wife [...] is no wiser than the rest of the world.' George Haydon died in 1891, so afterwards there was nobody left who knew the truth, unless someone discovered the connection in Haydon's papers.

Edward also wrote some short stories about rural life at the end of the eighteenth century, which he sent to Haydon before his death to see if he could find a publisher. He may well have written them for local newspapers, as he now called himself a 'journalist' in official returns. He asked Haydon to offer the stories under his true identity, without revealing his current whereabouts, as this would make the articles more saleable. He hoped to earn sufficient income to provide for his wife should he die, as 'my career as a colonist has been an honourable and successful one in everything save in the acquisition of money'. But nothing came of this endeavour in the short time before Haydon died.

Certainly the name Edward Oxford was remembered, and his despicable deed remained in the public consciousness for a long time. Several connected with the case, who had fallen on hard times, appealed to the Crown many years later for a pension or gratuity based on their involvement. Both the sister and widow of Joshua Lowe, who had first seized Edward, wrote in 1879 claiming that Lowe had saved the sovereign's life, and his daughter tried it on in 1907, nearly seventy years after the event. A retired constable, Thomas Townsend, claimed he was the one who had arrested the villain, although he actually appears to be unconnected with the case.

In his letters to Haydon, John Freeman was of the opinion that, 'There are many old friends [...] in England who would be pleased to hear of me again; and I should like a certain illustrious lady to know that one who was a foolish boy half a century ago, is now a respectable, & respected, member of society.' More likely, if she had known, Victoria would still regret that he had not been made an example of.

John Freeman died on 23 April 1900, aged seventy-eight, his correct age now reflected on the official register. His wife arranged for him to be interred in the same grave as her previous husband, where her aunt Sarah was also buried. The funeral was the following day, and the cortège left his home at 39 Howe Crescent at 3 p.m. and made slow progress across town to Melbourne General Cemetery. After reaching the Church of England section of the graveyard, his body was interred following the usual burial service. Of all the mourners present, none were aware who he truly was.

It is clear that Edward Oxford was very clever, if not approaching genius, and like others renowned for more worthy achievements, an eccentric. His genetic inheritance and his upbringing in a broken household with a strange and violent father and grandfather produced a very disturbed boy. But his screaming, maniacal laughter, and belief that he was destined for great things might equally have been the antics of a bored child with too much imagination and no way to channel his abilities. After his incarceration, he always held that there were no balls in the pistols and he never meant to harm the Queen, only to make a name for himself. In another age, or with parents of a superior class, his life might have been very different.

But Edward Oxford was not the only person to attack the Queen; he was the first of many. What was different in Victorian times compared to the modern day? Why, when terrorism is supposedly rife, has Elizabeth II reigned relatively undisturbed for almost as long? The fact that Edward Oxford escaped execution and supposedly had an easy life in an asylum certainly was one factor, amongst others. Would things have been different for Victoria if the court had not been so merciful?

When Edward Oxford heard of the next attempt on the Queen's life, less than two years after his own, he said, 'If they had hanged me, there would have been nothing of the kind again.' But they didn't and there was. The authorities would try not to be so magnanimous a second time.

2

The Unemployed Carpenter, 1842

Victoria was upset by Edward Oxford's attack, but she knew she had to be stoical. Being the head of state meant she was bound sometimes to be the target of unfavourable attention. Besides other provocations, there was nothing she could do about the fact that some of her subjects found her unacceptable as sovereign because she was a woman. Only a few months after she had acceded to the throne, a man had approached her carriage and, shaking his fist, had shouted, 'You — usurper, I'll have you off the throne before this day week.' He claimed to be the son of George IV and had shown a card carrying the name King John II. But his real name was Captain Goode, formally of the 10th Foot, and he was declared insane.

Albert, concerned as ever, helped the Queen take her mind off the subject of unwelcome attacks with an amateur concert at the palace, where the royal couple sang a duet together from an opera by Luigi Ricci. They were both still young. But after Victoria's protected childhood, and Albert's upbringing in the courts of Germany, they were growing up fast. In August, Albert reached his majority, and Parliament designated him Regent in the event of Victoria's death while her forthcoming child was still a minor. The attempted assassination had not affected the pregnancy, and as her term approached, the doctor asked about her need for sedatives. She declined, saying, 'I can bear pain as well as other people.' Labour started three weeks early, and after twelve hours, a little girl was born, subsequently named Victoria, the Princess Royal. When Dr Locock, the chief physician in attendance, announced to the Queen, 'Oh Madam, it is a princess,' she reportedly replied, 'Never mind, the next will be a Prince.' Just for helping nature take its course, Victoria paid Locock the exorbitant fee of £1,000, equivalent to the yearly wage of around forty labourers.

The baby was called 'Pussy' by her parents, and Albert in particular grew close to the infant, developing a rapport with her greater than with his succeeding children. But Victoria suffered from postnatal depression, so the Prince began to organise the Queen's daily schedule, partly in an attempt to keep her occupied and lift her spirits. They had been rising late, but now they breakfasted at nine o'clock and then took a walk, before starting on the incoming and outgoing correspondence. Relaxing after the business, they would draw or etch together before lunch at two. Generally, she would receive her ministers in the afternoon before their drive in the park. Dinner was at eight, usually with guests, and before or after they would read to each other, with Victoria preferring fiction, and Albert more serious work. He then read the lesson for the day to her, as he had done every evening since their marriage.

Naturally, the baby was farmed out to a wet nurse, as was normal amongst the aristocracy, which probably accounts for the fact that Victoria quickly became pregnant again, just a few months into the New Year. The only effective and available contraception was abstinence, something unacceptable to the young couple. Artificial methods of birth control were frowned on by the Church, and even the Queen's doctors were confused about the rhythm method, assuming that humans were like animals, on heat around the time of the period, and that mid-month was safest.

Victoria felt very depressed after she realised that she had conceived again. The nine-month cycle of body changes began once more, and Albert had to try hard to lift her mood. One novelty occurred in June, when the Queen took advantage of the new Great Western Railway line and very much enjoyed a train ride from Slough, near Windsor, to Paddington. They travelled in a specially built ornate state carriage with a crown on the roof, and Victoria announced herself 'charmed', although Albert worried that the speed of 50 miles an hour was dangerously excessive.

Naturally, the affairs of state often demanded her attention, and she continued to value the recommendations of Lord Melbourne. But then, in August 1841, the Queen lost her favourite advisor when Sir Robert Peel won the general election with a large majority. The Prince encouraged Victoria to put the crown above party politics, and arranged a compromise over the 'bedchamber ladies' and other court appointments. At the Privy Council meeting to welcome her new government, the Queen, despite being seven months pregnant, was composed and fair.

Victoria's second child was born on 9 November 1841, after a difficult labour. 'My sufferings were really very severe,' she wrote, 'and I don't know what I should have done, but for the great comfort and support my beloved Albert was to me.' But her earlier prediction proved correct: it was a male heir. They named him Albert Edward, the Prince of Wales.

Albert's influence was growing, and during her lying-in period, Peel kept the Prince informed with daily dispatches. The country was embroiled in the Opium War, which had started in 1839 following the destruction by the Chinese authorities of stores of the illegal drug belonging to British merchants. British military might proved superior to that of the poorly organised Chinese and, in 1842, the Chinese sued for peace and signed the Treaty of Nanjing, which provided for compensation, leased Hong Kong to the British for 155 years, and opened up trade to British merchants.

A few weeks after the birth, the Queen resumed her duties. Discontent in the populace continued, unaffected by the change of government, and Chartism grew further in popularity. In May 1842, a deputation of 100,000 people presented a petition to the government that was reputedly 6 miles long and contained 3¼ million signatures.[1] Parliament rejected the request to expand the electorate to include the working and middle classes by 287 votes to 49. Despite the unrest the rejection would cause, the royal couple carried on their life unchanged, ignoring the fear of possible further attempts on the Queen's life.

They didn't have long to wait. On Sunday 29 May, the Queen and Albert attended divine service as usual at the Chapel Royal. It was on their return that the villain struck. They were in a closed carriage, but about halfway down The Mall, a man in a shabby hat ran towards the vehicle. He pulled out a small pistol, thrust it into the carriage window, and pulled the trigger. There was a click. The gun had failed to go off.

The villain escaped. Later, a wood engraver from Holborn, Mr Pearson, reported that he saw the would-be assassin draw a pistol from his breast and point it at the carriage, but it did not fire. The attacker then made off and Pearson, who had a serious speech impediment, did not raise the alarm, as he felt the man would be far away by the time he could make a policeman understand. He claimed he heard the man say, 'They may take me if they like, I don't care; I was a fool I did not shoot.' Another bystander who failed to take any action heard the man say, 'I wish it had been done.'

That evening, the royal couple debated with Sir Robert Peel what to do. The Queen did not want to succumb to fear and shut herself away, so Peel proposed deliberately trying to draw the assassin out the following day. Despite the danger, Victoria readily agreed. For his part, Peel promised to deploy a considerable police force in plainclothes along the route.

On Monday afternoon, Prince Albert left Buckingham Palace around 3 p.m. to attend the Stannary Court in Somerset House, giving judgement as Lord Warden of the Duchy of Cornwall. On his return, they set off together in an open barouche[2] and four. 'You may imagine,' wrote Albert later to his father, 'that our minds were not very easy. We looked behind every tree, and I cast my eyes round in search of the rascal's face.'

Victoria selflessly instructed that no ladies should accompany her in the carriage. Her equerry, Colonel Charles George James Arbuthnot, rode much closer than normal at her side, with Prince Albert's equerry, Colonel Wylde, close by on his side. However, the royal couple did not change their positions; Victoria continued to sit on the right and Albert on the left. This made it easy for the would-be assassin to position himself on the roadway.

Despite the royal couple's fears, nothing happened on the outward journey. They wondered if there would be any further attempt that day, and worried that they would have to take further outings in fear of their lives. But the plan worked. It was around 6.15 p.m. when the carriage drove down Constitution Hill towards the palace at its top speed of 12–13 miles per hour. Suddenly, a man strode forward not far from the point where Oxford had made his attempt. Just two or three yards away, he pulled out a pistol and fired at the Queen. This time the gun went off.

* * *

The gunman, John Francis, was a desperate and confused young man. But he knew what he was doing; he was following the path carved by Edward Oxford two years earlier. In many ways he was not unlike his role model in age and appearance. Nineteen years old and about 5 feet 6 inches tall, he was considered quite handsome by many, with his dark eyes, hair, and whiskers. Perhaps he was rather on the stout side, and his face was light olive in colour, which led some to say that he had 'a foreign cast of countenance', but he knew that he was now destined for fame, or at least notoriety.

Those who were acquainted with his parents would never have expected their son to carry out such a deed. John's father, also called John Francis, was a fifty-one-year-old Welsh craftsman from Aberystwyth, while his mother Elizabeth came from Somerset and was in her mid-forties. They had both moved to London more than twenty-five years earlier and married in 1817. Subsequently there were five children, two boys and three girls, with John Jnr born in November 1822, their second child and first son.

John Snr was a stage carpenter, and had worked at the Theatre Royal in Covent Garden for twenty-three years. He was particularly skilled at building the intricate mechanisms for pantomime tricks, and contributed to the success of the venue through many seasons, especially during the time of the renowned clown, Grimaldi. The theatre also featured innovative musical entertainments, opera, and ballet, and was the first in the world to use the intense power of limelight[3], replacing the traditional open-flame gaslights.

When he was old enough, John Francis became an apprentice to his father. Initially, the boy was probably pleased to follow in his father's footsteps, a sign of approaching manhood. They lived at the lower end of Tottenham Court Road, close to Oxford Street, which was a major thoroughfare. Over a thousand horse-drawn omnibuses and stage coaches, and more than four thousand hackney carriages, gentlemen's conveyances, wagons, and carts passed along the road every day. Crossing the busy street each day on their way to work, John and his father would walk the half a mile through the narrow and sometimes dangerous lanes of Holborn and Covent Garden, past the flower and vegetable market, which in the early morning was a powerfully odorous chaos of wagons, porters, vendors, and buyers.

But as he grew into adulthood, John became disillusioned with his occupation. He served out his apprenticeship, but he frequently got into quarrels and found the work hard for the pittance that he was paid. Once he had to find his own employment, he never lasted long in any job and was often out of work. Then, about a year before the attack on the Queen, he went completely off the rails and found another way to remedy his lack of funds. He had been unemployed for six weeks when late one afternoon he arranged to meet a friend at the Cambrian Stores, a public house near Leicester Square. He had known Charles Mendham for a couple of months, but while his friend waited, John visited his lodgings in Cannon Street and asked for him there. When he was told that his friend was out, he asked if he could wash his hands and went up the stairs. When Charles returned later, he found £32 4s missing from his portmanteau. The police came to arrest John that same day, but he only had 7s on him, and nothing was found at his home in Tottenham Court Road. He was discharged for lack of evidence.

Not long after this incident, in the Caledonian coffee house in Mortimer Street, just north of Oxford Street, he made friends with a fellow about his own age called William Elam. John was finding it increasingly hard to live at home, under the watchful eye of his parents day and night, and six months after the robbery, he had a final argument with his parents and left. He took a single room with William, close to the Caledonian in Great Titchfield Street, at a cost of 3s a week each for half a bed and board. All went well at first, and their landlord, Mr Forster, a tailor, found him good tempered and inoffensive, with regular habits, and always on time for his meals.

Despite his best efforts to find employment as a journeyman carpenter, he found it difficult to get work. In a competitive marketplace, it was essential to demonstrate the right attitude and provide good references, and John was challenged on both fronts. He gradually ran out of money and was reduced to spending hours at a time in the Caledonian sitting over a single cup of coffee. By Saturday 21 May 1842, his rent arrears amounted to £1 14s.

The following Monday, by way of a distraction, John went to watch the hanging of the notorious murderer Daniel Good. The atrocious killing, and Good's subsequent evasion from the police, had been widely reported in the newspapers, and avidly read by the public. As part of an investigation into the theft of a pair of trousers, Constable William Gardner was searching the stables of a gentleman in Putney, where Good worked as a coachman. In the last stable, illuminated by his lantern, he came across what he at first thought was a plucked goose. It turned out to be the naked torso of Jane Jones. She had been killed with an axe; her head and limbs hacked off. Before the policeman could raise the alarm, her lover, Daniel Good, had locked him in the stables and escaped. In an extensive manhunt, the murderer managed to evade police across London for two weeks.[4]

Good was tried, convicted, and sentenced to death. Crowds started to gather at Newgate to see the hanging the evening before the execution, seeking the best vantage points, while seats by the windows of the houses opposite were selling at up to £15 apiece. A huge mob watched Good meet his end at eight o'clock the following morning, and John Francis was one of those packed into the street. Afterwards, back at the coffee house, he joked that 'it was a damned *good* job that Good was executed, and that was much too *good* for the fellow'.

Despite his outward show of nonchalance, John was becoming desperate to find a way to gain a living and avoid having to return to his parents as a failure. He railed against the fate inflicted on the poor, and dreamed about becoming a success in business. Ignoring realities, he took steps to fulfil his fantasies. The same day as the hanging, he contracted to rent a shop and parlour at 63 Mortimer Street, just around the corner from Great Titchfield Street, for 24s a week. 'I am going to open a tobacconist,' he told the owner, despite his lack of knowledge of the trade and his complete lack of funds. John hired a painter to put 'Francis, Tobacconist' over the door, and arranged for cards to be printed announcing that he would open that Thursday. To acquire the stock, he told the supplier that he was inheriting several thousand pounds from his grandfather. A large quantity of snuff, tobacco, and cigars was delivered to the shop.

He duly opened the emporium on the Thursday, but when his supplier demanded payment for the goods, he said he did not yet have it, and instead would borrow £10 from his father to be paid on account. The next morning, he shut the shop temporarily and went back to his room. Once he had closed the door, he pulled out Elam's box and broke into it. He took £5 10s in gold and half sovereigns.

When Elam returned home around midday, he immediately discovered the theft. He spoke to the landlord, Mr Forster, who went straight round to the shop. He confronted John, saying, 'What have you been about? I suppose you know what I have come for.' John affected a lack of concern, and said, 'Oh, I suppose you want the money', and gave him the gold. Mr Forster said that he was not welcome back at his lodgings, and he would keep hold of Francis's box for the moment, in case it contained other stolen goods.

Later that afternoon, the supplier returned and demanded payment, and when none was forthcoming, took away the stock. John shut up the now empty shop. Unable to return to his lodgings, he took himself off to St Ann's coffee house in Oxford Street, where he rented a room. His fantasy had crumbled, but now he thought of another way to make his name and be provided for.

He went straight out and walked across town to Westminster, where he entered a pawnbroker at 19 Tothill Street. He asked the assistant whether he had any pistols, and negotiated the purchase of an old flintlock for 3s, with a trigger that only appeared when it was put on full cock. He scraped together his change and paid with three fourpenny pieces, a sixpence, and the rest in coppers, including several farthings. He then went to a shop around the corner in Upper Parliament Street, and bought a flint for a penny, and the shopkeeper also fitted a piece of leather to tighten the flint. Finally, at eight o'clock in the evening, he purchased a halfpennyworth of gunpowder, about half an ounce, from a shop in York Street.

Almost all his money was now gone, and on the Saturday he did little. On Sunday morning, he hid the pistol under his coat, and headed off in the direction of The Mall. Returning angrily later that afternoon after his abortive attempt, he spent another twenty-four hours with next to no money for food.

On his last day of freedom, John somehow found twopence to buy another ounce of gunpowder from a shop near Piccadilly Circus. Stubbornly determined, and convinced that this was the right solution to his troubles, he headed for Constitution Hill. He was dressed in the same clothes: a dark frock coat somewhat too large for him, a light waistcoat, black stock[5] with a pin in it, drab trousers, boots, and an old wide-brimmed hat. He met a friend, another young man, who witnesses later described as a low-looking fellow in a flannel jacket. They walked up and down in earnest conversation, and John was heard to say, 'Damn the Queen; why should she be such an expense to the nation? It is to support her in such a grand style that us poor persons have to work hard.'

His friend left and John took up position on the footpath next to the water pump, about halfway along Constitution Hill, with his back to the wall of Buckingham Palace gardens. It was only about ten yards from where Oxford had fired. John walked up and down as he waited, obscured from view as he passed behind the trees on that side of the road.

He was noticed by a constable, William Trounce, who thought he was acting somewhat suspiciously, because he seemed to be hiding from the policeman's gaze behind a tree. As the Queen's open carriage approached at a fast pace down Constitution Hill, Trounce was only a few feet away, but with his back to the man. John steadied himself with his left hand on the iron water pump and pulled out his pistol with his right. Trounce was saluting the Queen as he fired.

Colonel Arbuthnot wheeled his horse and shouted to the policeman, 'Secure him!' Trounce turned round, grasped John by the collar and grabbed the gun. Two bystanders, both army men, ran up to help the constable, one shouting, 'Seize the murderer!' The Queen's carriage rolled on – she had not been hit. Indeed, some bystanders thought the pistol had misfired, just a 'flash in the pan'. But others reported seeing plumes of smoke, hearing the report, and the barrel of the gun was warm when taken from the prisoner.

John was quickly hustled away to the porter's lodge at the palace. He was searched, and found to have only an empty pocket book, a twist of powder, two keys, a pair of gloves, and a single penny piece. Shocked by the fact that his plan had actually worked, with one of his eyes rolling in a disturbed fashion, he remained sullen and would not reply or answer questions. He was taken from the equerries' door in Pimlico by cab to the station house in Gardener's Lane, accompanied by Inspector Russell, the guardsman, and Constable Trounce. Later, a witness arrived to say that she recognised the attacker, and that his name was John Francis.

* * *

On hearing the news of the attempt on the Queen's life, both Houses of Parliament adjourned their business, and those in the Privy Council made their way to the Home Office. Less than two hours after the attack, John Francis was brought from Gardener's Lane station house, entering the Home Office through the rear door. At the front was a great press of onlookers, alerted to the events of the early evening. Inside were the assembled dignitaries, which included the Home Secretary, Sir Robert Peel, and the Duke of Wellington. Also present were the Attorney General, the Police Commissioner Colonel Rowan, and Mr Hall, the chief magistrate of Bow Street. John stood in awe as some of the witnesses were interviewed.

The meeting broke up at 10 p.m., and John was taken to Tothill Fields prison, where he suffered the indignity of being stripped naked and bathed before admittance. Somewhat recovered, he now decided to cooperate with the authorities and answered questions in a firm tone of voice, and became quite indignant when his father was referred to as a scene-shifter rather than a stage carpenter. He was asked if he had enough money to purchase food, and replied, in despairing tone, that he had not.

The following morning, he was taken back to the Home Office in a hackney cab, accompanied by the prison governor and two policemen. The Privy Council sat again in the Council Chamber on the second floor, and the growing crowds outside could glimpse their deliberations through the floor-length windows facing Horse Guards Parade. At 3.30 p.m., Sir Robert Peel left the meeting and walked to the palace, returning with the warrant for the prisoner's committal. By now, more than a thousand people were milling around the front entrance, as two Hackney carriages were brought to the Home Office. The first pulled up in Whitehall, but was just a decoy. As the crowds pressed in around the carriage, John was hustled out the back door and into the second.

At Newgate he was taken to a separate cell, where, after some food, he managed to sleep soundly. Two keepers were tasked with sitting up with him through the night and never leaving his presence. He was woken at six o'clock in the morning, like all the other inmates. He felt composed and caused no trouble to the authorities, and around midday he was allowed to take some exercise in the prison yard for about an hour and a half. John was not interviewed or spoken to, but he repeatedly told the turnkeys that the pistol was charged with nothing but powder. No ball was found in the vicinity of the attack, and when the police visited his lodgings and opened his box, they found only dirty linen, some scraps of poetry and other writings.

John Francis's father learned about the attack earlier that day whilst working in Deptford. Scarcely believing that this could possibly be his own son, of whom he had heard nothing for several months, he went immediately to the Home Office. There the fact was confirmed, but he was unable to see his son. Two days later he obtained a visiting order and went to Newgate on the Thursday. There was no show of emotion; he simply shook his son's hand and said, 'Well, John, how are you?' On the Saturday, his mother and sister were also allowed to visit.

The trial took place two weeks later, on Friday 17 June, at 10 a.m. The judges were Lord Chief Justice Tindal, Mr Baron Gurney, and Mr Justice Patteson. The prosecution team numbered four, led by the Attorney General, while the sole defence counsel was Mr Clarkson. John felt dejected in the face of the forces ranged against him, showing no sign of the jaunty appearance he had managed when first interviewed. When asked how he pleaded, he replied 'not guilty' in a feeble and low tone. As the Attorney General delivered his opening address, John was much affected by the accusations and listened attentively to every word.

John Francis was indicted:

For that he, feloniously and traitorously, did compass, imagine, devise, and intend to bring and put our Lady the Queen to death; and in order to fulfil, perfect, and bring to effect his most treasonable compassing, device and imagination, he, on the thirtieth of May, maliciously and traitorously did shoot off, and discharge a certain pistol loaded with gunpowder, and a certain bullet, which he in his right hand held, at and against the person of our said Lady the Queen, with intent thereby and therewith, maliciously and traitorously, to shoot, associate, kill, and put her to death; and thereby he then and there, traitorously and maliciously made a direct attempt against the life of our said Lady the Queen.

This was the first count, the second held that the pistol was loaded with 'other destructive materials and substances unknown', and the third made no reference to what the gun contained.

Colonel Arbuthnot and Private Allen both testified that the prisoner fired directly at the Queen, and the latter stated that he could tell that it was loaded with a ball from the noise that it made; a damning statement. The prosecution advanced no evidence of Francis having purchased or obtained a bullet for the gun, but instead argued that it could have been loaded with all kinds of deadly material such as stones or marble. The defence, they said, would not try and prove insanity, but instead hold that the pistol was only loaded with powder, and it was just the frolic of a young man with no evil intention. The Attorney General acknowledged that if there was any doubt whether the gun had a potentially lethal charge, then the prisoner should be acquitted, but then contradicted himself at great length on the monstrousness of the defendant being released and what that would imply for the future health of the sovereign.

Despite having nearly twenty years' experience, William Clarkson's defence of the accused was decidedly lacklustre. He started his address by saying that he regretted the interests of the unfortunate prisoner at the bar were not confided to someone more competent to defend him than he was, and that he had a very difficult task to undertake in defending the prisoner. After such an inauspicious opening, how much weight could his words carry? He called no witnesses, but threw doubt on whether the pistol was loaded with any missile. Rather than dismiss it as a 'frolic', he accurately assigned the action to that of a desperate and penniless young man looking for notoriety and hoping to be provided for in the same manner as had happened two years earlier to Edward Oxford. John tried to follow all that was being said, but it was rather bewildering.

In his summing up, Chief Justice Tindal said that the jury had to be convinced that the gun was loaded with a bullet or some material intended to cause the sovereign severe bodily harm in order to find him guilty of high treason, otherwise they should acquit him. It was still only mid-afternoon; the trial had not even lasted a full day. The jury took just twenty-five minutes to reach a verdict. They found the prisoner guilty of the second and third counts (that the pistol was charged with a destructive substance other than just powder and wadding), but expressed doubt on the first (that it was loaded with a bullet). John turned pale.

The Chief Justice then pronounced sentence, finishing with the words:

> Nothing now remains for any human tribunal but to declare the sentence of the law, which
> is that you, John Francis, be taken hence to the place from whence you came, that you be
> drawn on a hurdle[6] to a place of execution, and there be hanged by the neck until you are
> dead, and that afterwards your head be severed from your body, and your body be divided
> into four quarters, and be disposed of as Her Majesty may think fit, and may Almighty
> God have mercy on your soul.[7]

John fainted into the arms of the gaolers, and was removed supported by two turnkeys,
sobbing most piteously. For the first time, he confronted the consequences of his crime.
Instead of being looked after in an institution, his fate was too terrible to contemplate.

Public debate on John Francis's guilt did not stop with the verdict. The following Monday,
the *Morning Chronicle* wrote in an editorial:

> It is evident that the public mind is greatly interested about this man's fate, not from
> anything remarkable in him, for, from all that appears, he is a mere drivelling assassin,
> with scarce mind enough to conceive the enormity of his crime, but from a doubt whether
> it was the intention of the man to commit murder.

The concern arose from the lack of motive, but the paper dismissed its importance, saying
that 'this man was possessed either with a deliberate malice or the desperate recklessness of
a murderer' and the punishment should be carried out.

While John languished in Newgate awaiting his sentence, he came into contact with another
felon condemned to death, whose crime and behaviour were in stark contrast to his own.
Armed with a pair of cavalry pistols that fired a bullet as large as a musket ball, the highwayman
Thomas Cooper had robbed several people in Highbury. Cornered by the police, he first shot
PC Moss in the arm, then PC Daly in the shoulder. When Daly continued to come at him, he
shot him fatally through the heart with the second pistol. Disarmed by a crowd of civilian
pursuers, he was also found to be carrying a foot-long dagger, hidden in his fob pocket. After
Cooper had been condemned to death, he continued to act violently in Newgate, raging that
he wished he had done more to harm the police and those who were witnesses against him.

John and his family behaved quite differently. Later that week, his father submitted a petition
to the Queen, which outlined the respectability of himself and his family, and how his wife:

> is most ardently attached to her ill-fated son and on hearing of the horrible crime he had
> committed, she was seized with the most alarming illness, and has ever since remained in
> the utmost bodily and mental distress, so much so that her life is wholly despaired of; and
> your petitioner dare not intimate to her the most melancholy fate that awaits her son.

He held that it was not his son's intention to cause her serious harm, and begged for his life to
be spared. Hoping to make the best impression possible, John Francis Snr used a professional
scribe and directed the petition through the Secretary of State, Sir James Graham. John's
sister, Jane, took a more personal approach, and wrote in her own hand to Baroness Lehzin,

asking that the letter be placed before Victoria. She spoke of her brother's awful fate, and that 'we are all labouring under the most painful mental affliction'. Petitions also rolled in from other quarters unconnected with the family; for example, from a retired solicitor in Bradford, a Gloucestershire gentleman, and the people of Hartlepool and Margate.

The law stated that executions should be carried out within twenty-one days of sentence being passed, and in late June the sheriffs and the chaplain informed John Francis and Thomas Cooper that they would be executed on Monday 4 July at the usual hour. John was filled with dread and became more and more anxious and despondent as the day of his execution approached. He was visited daily by the chaplain, the Revd Mr Carver, who was little help, merely exhorting him to repent of his atrocious crime.

John knew what to expect from reading the papers and his expedition to watch the hanging of Daniel Good, little more than a month earlier. He couldn't stop his mind from going over and over the awful scene. Good had pleaded his innocence until the very last, but, at five minutes before eight o'clock, his hands were tied, his neckerchief removed, and he was led in solemn procession along the gloomy passage to the scaffold, the minister reciting the burial service, while the chapel bell tolled. He ascended unaided, at which 'he was assailed by the most hideous yells and long-continued execrations of the mob'. Good turned pale and trembled, but said nothing. The noose was secured, the black cap pulled over his face, and a few seconds later the bolt was withdrawn. A gasp left the lips of the crowd watching the fatal drop, the man's body struggling violently as the soul departed. An hour later he was cut down.

John gradually became more and more distraught as he contemplated his fate. Worse than Good, he knew full well that afterwards his body would be desecrated, not even available to his family for decent burial. The long hours dragged by painfully slowly. On Thursday 30 June he was visited for the last time by his relations, and the whole family parted in great distress. When he awoke from a restless sleep the next morning, he quickly remembered that he had only three days left until his execution. On Saturday morning at eight o'clock, there were only forty-eight hours remaining before he would go before the baying mob. His hope had vanished and he gave himself up to despair, repeatedly saying to the turnkeys who watched over him that he was totally lost.

Then, at 2 p.m., the resolution of the authorities faltered. Whether through compassion or for other reasons, after consulting with the Privy Council, the Queen sent a reprieve. John Francis's sentence was commuted to transportation for life and hard labour in the most penal of settlements in the Australian colonies. When the governor told him the news, John burst into tears and slumped down onto a chair, overcome with joy and astonishment. Cooper received no such reprieve, and at eight o'clock on the Monday morning, the sentence was duly carried out before a vast crowd.

* * *

John Francis's initial euphoria soon gave way to renewed despair. Transportation for life was an awful future to contemplate. He would be taken to the other side of the world to live in the most appalling conditions of slavery, and would most likely never see his family or homeland ever again. A similar feeling of relief and horror gripped his parents, especially his mother, who was still gravely ill. The terribleness of his perceived fate was summed up by a letter writer to *The Standard*, who praised:

> the wretched state in which he will now be doomed to drag out the remainder of his miserable existence and natural life in this world; that he will be sent to one of our most penal settlements and worked in chains; that the labour and work will be severe and hard in the extreme – a thousand times worse than death itself; that he will be [...] entirely shut out from the world for ever hereafter; that he will be debarred from communication whatever with his friends; [...] and the only relief will be [...] death itself, a miserable exile on a foreign shore!!!

His parents probably saw him one last time and gave him money and food to help with his journey. Two days after he had been due to die, he was taken to the station terminus at Nine Elms[8] and escorted aboard a train of the London & South Western Railway. John's first journey by railway was full of foreboding and very different from Victoria's pleasurable experience of a year earlier. After arrival at Gosport station, he was taken to the Railway Hotel and given dinner. Whilst eating, he suddenly burst into tears, crying, 'Indeed! I never meant to hurt the Queen.' His meal finished, he was taken to the prison hulk *York*, beached on the mudflats of Haslar Creek, and was there incarcerated with hundreds of other inmates. Conditions on board were awful in the disease-ridden, damp, and overcrowded hold, and it was with some relief that five days later he and 120 other convicts were brought up from the gloom and conveyed to the *Marquis of Hastings*, anchored at Spithead[9], the vessel that would take them to the other side of the world.

The Admiralty used private contractors to transport convicts to the penal settlements, and always accepted the lowest bid for any ship classed as seaworthy. This was a relative term, and the *Hastings* had sprung a leak on her journey from Gravesend to Portsmouth, and put into harbour for repairs to the forward caulking.[10] It was a twenty-three-year-old barque, a three-masted, square-rigged sailing ship of 452 tons. The *Hampshire Advertiser* described the vessel as 'reported to be much too old for so long a voyage, and to be nearly rotten'. At least it was fast, and if it managed to reach Australia in one piece, then the journey should take less than four months. Still an extremely long time to be incarcerated at sea.

The *Hastings* had a crew of around thirty, consisting of the master, Captain John Biddle; first, second and third mates; carpenter, steward, cook, and boatswain; and about twenty other seamen and boys. Before the prisoners were embarked, the guards arrived, consisting of Major Raitt, Ensign Holditch, and twenty-nine men of the 80th and 99th regiments. Major Raitt brought with him his wife, three children, and a servant, and four other women and children accompanied the remaining soldiers. Also present on board was the surgeon superintendent, Dr Alexander Bryson, who worked for the Admiralty and was responsible for the care and conduct of the convicts. In the early days of transportation, the death toll amongst convicts was very high, and the surgeon superintendent role was introduced not so much for the good of the prisoners, but rather to ensure that they did not escape their punishment by expiring on the journey.

John, his legs in irons and chained to the next man, was herded onto the ship under the watchful eye of the redcoats. A total of 240 convicts boarded the vessel, half from the *York* hulk and half from the *Leviathan* in Portsmouth harbour. They were driven below, where the deck was divided by a strong, gated barricade to form a large prison cell. Down each side as far as the bow were rows of bunks, each 6 foot square, designed to provide sleeping accommodation for four or five men, so each convict had around 15–18 inches of space. To some of the long-term inmates of the hulks, the new accommodation seemed almost luxurious compared to their previous home. The prospect of leaving for Australia also seemed attractive, as they had heard stories of prisoners finding a new life and becoming wealthy.

But John was in despair as he adjusted to his new environment. Still wearing his heavy leg irons, which made every step an effort, he was given a bedding roll, pillow, and blanket, plus two wooden bowls and a wooden spoon. He was issued with two sets of trousers and shirts, labelled 'A' and 'B': the A suit to be used one week, and the B the next. They were all numbered so as to prevent pilfering, but some prisoners later threw their worn and dirty garments over the side and stole a better pair.

Provisioning of the ship continued apace, with hundreds of barrels of water, wine, flour, salt beef and pork, and some livestock, including chickens for the eggs and at least one cow for its fresh milk. A week later all was complete, and on 18 July the *Marquis of Hastings* set sail for Van Diemen's Land, making its way out from the Solent and down the English Channel. Their route would take them down through the Bay of Biscay, past the Canaries and Cape Verde, and out into the Atlantic. Just one stop was foreseen, at the Cape of Good Hope. For the remainder of the time, 300 men and a handful of women and children would be cooped up on two decks, crammed into a total surface area not much larger than a tennis court.

Once at sea, the convicts' leg irons were removed, and it was easier to move around the prison. John Francis found he had little in common with his fellow prisoners. Almost all were transported for larceny, for stealing anything from clothing to silver goblets. Some were professional pickpockets or highwaymen, and liked to talk of their exploits. They were mainly poor, illiterate, and used to rough ways, and John's mild manners and conversation did not fit easily with them. Lonely and isolated, at one point John tried to talk to the crew, one of the many things that were forbidden, and he was put back in irons for a day or two as punishment.

The convicts were divided into 'messes' of six men, and each instructed to elect a mess captain, who would be responsible for the tidiness and good behaviour of his messmates. Some of these captains were also given wider responsibilities, as deck captains, constables, or hospital attendants. In this way the authorities encouraged the convicts to police themselves in return for minor rewards. Others with skills might help as cooks or barbers, and perhaps John later found favour as a carpenter, a key skill on a wooden sailing ship.

As the ship left Land's End behind, life on board began to follow a regular pattern, and John gradually became used to the daily routine. At 5 a.m., those selected as cooks were called on deck, and at sunrise the prison's doors were opened. When the time came for John's division to go up, he followed the other men to the bathing tub positioned on deck, waiting in line for sea water to be thrown over him. Water and biscuit[11] or gruel were issued to each mess captain for breakfast; all bedding was rolled up and stowed on deck. One man was assigned from each mess to clean and dry-holystone[12] the prison deck, followed by prayers for all. Dinner was at noon and supper at 5 p.m., and in between some of the convicts were brought on deck to work at their trades or perform other tasks such as picking oakum[13], while others attended school below, where they learnt reading and writing. At 6 p.m. or dusk, John and the other convicts were again locked up below, and prayers were said around 8 p.m. The men were shaved twice a week, and their hair was cut fortnightly. Two days each week were allocated to laundry, when John was required to wash one set of his clothes. Seawater was used, fresh water being far too precious, which left a film of salt on the garments. This wasn't too bad for the seamen and prisoners with their loose-fitting clothes, but the officers' breeches caused a terrible itching in the groin.

John's food ration was set at two-thirds of the navy standard, a higher level for many than their normal meagre diet, provided that none of the supplies were filched by members of the crew intent on profiteering. A typical amount per week was 3 lb bread, 2 lb flour, 2 lb salt beef, 1 lb salt pork, 2 pints pease[14] and ¼ lb butter. There might also be rice, oatmeal, suet, raisins, and sugar, but when provisions ran low, the main meals might just be skilly (thin soup) and duff (flour pudding).

As the weeks passed, John found that the main problem was boredom. When on deck there might be something to look at, such as strange birds, dolphins, or flying fish, but the long hours in prison were terrible. Although forbidden, gambling was rife, in a desperate attempt to relieve the tedium, with convicts betting their clothes, rations, or anything. Little light fell through the bars on the hatches, none when they were battened down during storms, and John found the smell below suffocatingly rank. The sweat of 240 men mixed with the stink of bilge water and the mouldy aroma of rotting timber. On deck, near the bowsprit, were the 'heads', holes suspended above the sea used as toilets, but down below buckets were employed, which added to the stench. In addition, seasickness was commonplace, as the vessel, designed to hold the maximum in cargo, rolled drunkenly in rough weather.

Then, as the ship headed south, it became unbearably hot. Little air filtered down below, and even this disappeared as they reached the doldrums, and melting pitch dripped from between the timbers. Rats, cockroaches, and body lice were all that seemed to prosper. Lying in pools of sweat, with the temperature still 90–100 degrees at night, John yearned for the sound of flapping in the sails and the creaking of the rigging to show that the wind had returned. All he could think of was cool water to parch his thirst. The ration was just 2 pints a day, and this was now brackish, green, and at blood heat. Even so, it tasted like nectar.

To make conditions worse, dysentery was rife. Dr Bryson put the outbreak largely down to the change in the diet and the noxious atmosphere in the cells at night, and prescribed magnesia and rhubarb mixture. Most responded well to this treatment, but some cases required opium, chalk, or catechu.[15] The surgeon superintendent appears to have been conscientious and diligent, something not true of all in his position, and kept extensive notes on each patient. Happily, John was not one of them.

But despite his duty of care, Bryson had been instructed to carry out a scurvy experiment on the prisoners during the voyage. It was common practice to commence a regular course of lemon or lime juice three weeks into a voyage as a prophylactic, but the Admiralty wanted to test other approaches.[16] The supplement was therefore denied the convicts in order to encourage the development of scurvy, an act which Bryson justified to himself by imagining that when reintroduced it would be all the more powerful, because otherwise 'it might like many other remedies have lost in some degree from long use its peculiar action on the system'. But for John and the other men, it was another affliction to worsen their sorry state.

Around the middle of August, the first symptoms of scurvy started to show themselves, with hemeralopia[17], and later, diseased gums. Bryson waited until 12 September before taking action, dividing the sufferers into three groups for treatment with lemon juice, citric acid, or nitrate of potash.[18] Selection for a safe or risky group was a lottery, and we do not know how John fared. The medicine was administered in draughts of wine, water and sugar, and increased in potency depending on the severity of the symptoms. Those on lemon juice and citric acid began to improve, but the final group quickly developed ashen skin, poor digestion, and accelerated scurvy, with loose teeth, boils, and rigidity of the tendons. Nevertheless, Bryson persisted with the experiment until they reached the Cape of Good Hope, when he was forced to bring their medication to a close by the severe decline in health of the third group.

The ship anchored on 24 September and spent three days in Table Bay, taking on water and other supplies. A stock of oranges brought relief to the third group, and seven days' worth of fresh provisions improved the health of the ship's company generally. The sight of land, and the ability to exchange news, was a welcome relief after two months at sea, although the prisoners were probably kept manacled and locked up below. But they soon learnt of a terrible disaster that had struck a similar prison ship, also heading for Van Diemen's Land, less than a month earlier. The *Waterloo*, its timbers rotten, had been wrecked in Table Bay with the loss of 189 souls, both convicts and crew. The surgeon superintendent had survived, saved, in a twist of fate, by a prisoner whose irons he had knocked off earlier. That same month, a troop ship with 700 soldiers bound for China had also been driven ashore, and the *Sabina*, a Manila ship, had struck a reef with the loss of twenty lives.

With these losses in mind, John contemplated the last and most dangerous leg of their journey, the run through the Roaring Forties and the Southern Ocean. Although winter was just drawing to a close, the seas could be mountainous, and by now the ship was no doubt leaking terribly. With the hatches battened down, and almost no light, the water collected on the prison deck and rolled in waves from side to side as the boat wallowed through the sea. Everything was damp, the weather was now cold, and the men shivered in their flimsy convict suits. Everybody concentrated on pumping out the water, trying to keep warm, and surviving.

Disaster did not strike, and the ship made reasonable headway. Six weeks later the cry came from aloft that land had been sighted. The *Marquis of Hastings* sailed into Hobart harbour on 8 November and dropped anchor. The passage had taken 113 days, only a couple of weeks longer than the fastest clippers. Dr Bryson's care had ensured that only two convicts had died, one early on through suffocation caused by a piece of biscuit in the larynx, and one from severe, untreatable diarrhoea. Many men were suffering from the lack of fruit and vegetables, with sores around the mouth and their teeth dropping out, but they had survived. They longed for dry land, but John was also fearful of what awaited them.

* * *

It took a long time to disembark. After what seemed an age, the prisoners were brought on deck and lined up. Each was presented individually to an officer of the convict department, but when not all were processed the first day, they were sent below again. Finally, John was cross-questioned over his crime and sentence. Each convict was encouraged to declare his offence, confession being seen as part of the process of reform. John admitted that he had shot at the Queen, but held that the gun was only loaded with gunpowder and paper. Minute details of his appearance were noted in large volumes by convict clerks, including the tiny scars on the knuckle of his right forefinger and the thumb of the left hand, and the red stain above his right elbow. The aim was to be able to identify an escaped prisoner. This whole process took several days.

Finally, early one morning, the prisoners were issued with fresh clothing: shapeless yellow smocks and trousers printed with black arrows and identification marks, and woollen caps in the shape of a fez. They were rowed ashore. Stepping onto solid ground, John found that the land would not stay still, and he rocked back and forward, barely able to keep his balance until he relearned his land legs. They were lined up and addressed by the Lieutenant Governor, John Franklin. He exhorted them to good behaviour, the rules were explained, and the severe penalties for disobedience were dwelt on. The system, set up by the previous governor, was like a game of snakes and ladders. Especially good behaviour, such as informing on a fellow prisoner, took a convict up a ladder towards earlier release; bad conduct resulted in a slide down a snake to experience even worse conditions.

The first stage was called 'probation' and involved hard labour, normally lasting for between one and four years depending on the length of the sentence. But, because of his heinous crime, the authorities varied the rule, and ordered that his term should be five years. Along with others destined for the empire's most penal establishment, John was re-embarked for the voyage to join the gang at Port Arthur. Situated in the south-east corner of the island, about 40 miles from Hobart by sea, escape from Port Arthur was virtually impossible. It was located on the Tasman peninsula, connected to the rest of the island by a narrow isthmus of sandy wasteland that was always guarded by soldiers. Trying to escape by swimming in the shark-infested seas was equally daunting.

Chained down below, John felt the waters calm as the ship sailed from Maingon Bay past West Arthur Head and drop anchor. Brought up into the light, John's first view of the settlement was of a beautiful sloping green cove surrounded by giant forests, with an impressive flour mill, hospital, church, and the numerous other buildings of a well-ordered township. But soon the severity of the punishment awaiting him became clear. Convicts chained up along the roads broke rocks, others yoked together were pulling ploughs on the land, while those in the special punishment units dragged heavy chains or balls of iron attached to their legs. Different uniforms identified the different classes of convict: those in the higher grades were dressed in a short high-buttoned jacket of grey or yellow topped with a scarf, while those in the chain gang wore coarse wool outfits that were a patchwork of yellow and black. The jackets had the prisoner's number and their barracks printed on the back, and all the garments were covered with the broad black convict arrows. A tramway from Port Arthur ran the whole length of the peninsula and gangs of convicts were assigned to push the tram-cart that carried officials. On the hilltops, semaphore stations were used to warn of escapes into the surrounding bush, where mantraps were hidden to catch the 'bolters'.

John was offloaded with the other new arrivals and taken to the prisoners' barracks, a weather-board structure 190 feet long by 30 feet wide. Inside were ten passages with seven cells on each side, each 7 feet long by 4 feet wide by 8 feet high. The bed was a shelf 2 feet 3 inches wide; there was practically no light; and a draught blew from the perforated panel in the door up to the foul air vent in the ceiling. During the winter it was very cold, with little or no bedding. In the year that John arrived, 5,300 new convicts had to be accommodated, and even the inadequate clothing was in short supply. This was especially true of the leather boots, and many were forced to walk with their feet bound in cloth, referred to as 'toe rags'.

Luckily, John's arrival was in the spring, and it would be six months before the bitter weather returned. He was provided with a tin plate and a ramekin, each marked with his number, and was given his daily allowance of 6 oz of bread and 2 oz of flour. The work he was immediately assigned to was gruelling: clearing the forests, constructing roads, or mindless tasks like rock breaking. The prisoners were treated like slave labour, and the chief superintendent proudly claimed that the work was 'the most incessant and galling that the settlement could produce'. Any disobedience was instantly punished with the lash, the worst offenders held over until daily assembly, when they were tied to 'triangles' and whipped with a cat-o'-nine tails until their backs ran with blood.

John's first months in the colony were extremely tough. He later described the period as being doomed in an 'abyss of wretchedness and misery to perpetual bondage and slavery', and he depicted Port Arthur as a 'depraved and contaminated place'. According to an official report, 'unnatural crime'[19] was prevalent, and John was a handsome young boy. He did all he could to rise out of the misery and was obedient at all times, anxious to offer his skills in carpentry and with the pen. John was a changed man from the lazy and arrogant youth of a few months earlier. It would appear that he fared better than most, and after a period of backbreaking toil, he was put to work on more constructive tasks, although the life would still have been severe. Just a couple of months after his arrival, he began teaching in the convict school, a task that he took to readily. Carpentry was at the heart of the settlement's work, as gangs of up to a hundred men felled the huge blue gum trees, carrying them down to the sawpits on their shoulders. The timber was cut up by convict pairs, with the man on top referred to as the 'top dog', while the one below, who quickly drowned in sawdust, was known as the 'underdog'.

In January 1844, after little more than a year of his sentence, John petitioned the Lieutenant Governor for a reduction in his probation. However, the response just confirmed that he would serve five years from the date of his arrival in Port Arthur. Another petition in March was sent to London, but produced the same response. He continued to be well behaved, and two years later he was rewarded with a six-month reduction in the probation period after raising the alarm over a fire in the settlement. Two months later, he was moved from Port Arthur to Launceston, where he was set to work with the gang based in the Royal Engineer's Yard. The prisoners' barracks was originally built as a store, and subsequently converted to accommodate twenty-five men in each of the four 34-foot by 20-foot rooms.

But when John was there, 100 were crammed into each ward by using triple-tiered sleeping berths. Unsurprisingly, 'unnatural crime' was even more widespread. The superintendent, Captain Gardiner, was dismissed later for suspected criminality and immoral behaviour with the female convicts.

For those not put to the treadmill, most of the work was also with timber, so perhaps again John fared better than most. Then, two and a half years later, in October 1846, to his great relief, he was removed entirely from the gang. His punishment probation period had been just under four years. He became a Probation Pass Holder (PPH), which meant that he was put out to work as the servant of a settler in the colony or assigned to work for the government. The former was preferable, as the convict was paid in addition to his accommodation and food, although masters could abuse and ill treat their servants. The rate of pay had been set at £9 per year, but recently this had become negotiable between master and servant, and depended on demand. John's diet also improved greatly, with the daily ration laid down for servants being 1 lb of meat, 1½ lb bread (or 1 lb bread and 2 lb vegetables), 1 oz sugar, 1 oz roasted wheat, ½ oz soap, and ½ oz salt.

John was labelled PPH 3rd Class, the highest ranking, which meant that he was allowed to keep all his wages. Lower classes had money kept back and placed in a savings account against good behaviour. He had to attend a muster on the first Sunday of each month, and was required to go to a divine service at least once every Sunday, but otherwise was free at times when not needed by his master. As a carpenter, he may well have been used to provide services to other settlers for the profit of his employer. Passholders were euphemistically called 'Government Men'.

Australia was treated as an open prison. Convicts might be free to wander about, but they were not free men, had to carry their pass at all times, and were subject to prison discipline. Misdemeanours could mean the lash or being returned to the chain gang. Corrupt officials could also threaten to fabricate misbehaviour unless bribed, but it was in the interest of masters not to report their servants, as they might lose them. Instead they preferred to administer punishment themselves.

Launceston was Tasmania's second city, a thriving town of several thousand people when John arrived. Situated in the north of the island at the end of the Tamar river, it was established as a garrison town in 1806 by Lt-Col William Paterson, and later named after the governor's Cornish birthplace.[20] It gradually grew into a trading port, with strong links to the mainland.

John Francis initially spent six months in Launceston in the service of a Mr Turner, and then was with William Tyson for two and a half years. Mr Tyson, a building contractor, was a member of the Scottish Presbyterian community in Launceston, and seems to have been a lenient and kindly master. He was responsible for the construction of a new church for the faith, and John was probably involved in this work. The foundation stone for St Andrew's Kirk was laid by the Lieutenant Governor in October 1849, and the stylish modern building opened a year later. It was probably Tyson who widened John's knowledge of the building trade, as well as helping him obtain permission to marry.

John's wedding to Martha Clarke, a free woman, took place on 12 October 1848, at the Independent Chapel in Frederick Street. He was just coming up to his twenty-sixth birthday, but his bride was only sixteen years old. She was the illiterate daughter of John

Clarke, a butcher and farmer, who had also been a convict, transported in 1811. Her mother, born Maria Kirk in Launceston in 1809, was one of the first white Tasmanians, being the daughter of Matthew Kirk, a soldier and member of the first northern island settlement, and Elizabeth Edwards, an early convict.

As a married man now successfully plying his trade as a carpenter, John must have felt that he had passed through hellfire and come out the other side. In November 1850, he graduated another point up the convict scale, and was granted a Ticket of Leave. This allowed him to work for his own benefit rather than being controlled by a master, but he was still under convict law and had to attend the musters and church services. Two years later, he applied for a pardon, which was refused by the Lieutenant Governor. By May 1853, the latter felt he was eligible, but decided to send the documentation to London for approval. Viscount Palmerston, Secretary of State for the Home Department, wrote, 'I cannot consent to any mitigation.'

The Lieutenant Governor tried again in October 1855, on this occasion directing the petition to Lord John Russell, the Prime Minister. By then, John was a respected member of the community, and the application was supported by both the Protestant and Catholic bishops of Tasmania, the mayors of Hobart and Launceston, and magistrates and councillors from Launceston town. This time, the new Secretary of State, Sir George Grey, responded favourably. A conditional pardon was finally granted on 12 August 1856, which meant that he was a free man provided he did not return to England.

During the 1840s and '50s, settlers campaigned to end transportation; indeed, William Tyson was a leading light in the movement. Although a source of cheap labour, around a third of the island's population were convicts and that type of immigrant was thought to account for the high level of crime. The last transport arrived in 1853, and the following year, Van Diemen's Land was renamed Tasmania. For those who had escaped from the system in good health and not too psychologically brutalised, Tasmania proved a land of opportunity. Wages were higher than in Britain, employment opportunities abounded, land was cheap, and class divisions were not so great as at home.

During the latter half of the 1850s, John prospered as a builder, his success culminating in November 1860, when he was awarded the contract to build Launceston General Hospital in Mulgrave Square. Construction, at a price of £10,122, took the best part of three years, but the end result was described as 'an admirable structure'. Meanwhile, his young wife proved very fecund and produced an annual succession of babies, with ten children born between 1850 and 1863: seven girls and three boys. All survived infancy, except for the third daughter, who died of dysentery when eight months old.

For the majority of the 1850s, the family rented a house in Canning Street, not far from the site of the hospital. But then, in 1858, they bought a substantial plot with a house and workshop on the corner of York Street and Charles Street, closer to the town centre. In 1860, the family moved out and John Francis, working with his partner Mr Galvin, built a new auction mart on the site, which he then leased to the Cohen brothers. The substantial new building opened on 2 June 1864, and featured large plate glass windows, an iron tramway for deliveries, and an American wheel[21] for lifting goods to the upper store. Meanwhile, John Francis bought another plot, not far away in Paterson Street, containing a house and workshop for his family and business.

No doubt John wrote home to his family in England, telling of his growing wealth and the opportunities in Australia. At some point, his mother and at least one of his brothers and one of his sisters came out to join him. But 1864 turned out to be the peak of John Francis's good fortune. He was to have no more children, as the succession of babies born to Martha Francis every twelve to eighteen months abruptly stopped in 1863, when she was still only thirty-one years old. Whether this was associated with an abstinence from sexual intercourse, a better understanding of how to avoid pregnancy, or the result of some medical condition, is not clear.

An economic depression also set in. The gold fever that gripped Victoria and New South Wales in the 1850s had filtered across the Bass Strait, and small quantities were found in 1852 in Tullochgorum, not far from Launceston. This find helped to increase the prosperity of the town, but the seams were soon worked out, and with the growth of Melbourne across the water and the decline in government work too, a downturn followed in the 1860s. No longer was Tasmania a centre for immigration; now the young were leaving to seek their fortune in Victoria.

In October 1864, John Francis attended a meeting organised by William Tyson and others to discuss further gold prospecting in Tasmania. The meeting resolved to invite Mr Hargreaves of New South Wales, who had been the first to discover gold there, to come to Tasmania to lead the search. The very presence of such a man with his renowned reputation would encourage hundreds of others to follow, bringing prosperity back for all. Hargreaves would require an initial investment of close to £1,000, and John Francis was one of those chosen to form a committee to raise the funds.

But the diggers did not come, and gold in appreciable amounts was not found until nearly twenty years later. Work dried up for John Francis, and he watched with consternation as his hard-earned wealth slowly seeped away. Three years after the gold-mining meeting, in 1867, he gave up waiting, sold his properties, and moved with his family to Melbourne. Property prices were depressed, so he got less than he hoped in the sales, and they could only afford to rent a six-room, one-storey house in the city, albeit in the fashionable area of Emerald Hill.[22] Not long after John arrived, a painter and decorator landed in Victoria. It was John Freeman, aka Edward Oxford, who had completed his ordeal in the lunatic asylum and was now seeking a new life in Australia. As they were both in the construction industry, they may well have met, but it seems unlikely that Edward would have given away his true identity, although he may have recognised John Francis.

Work was more plentiful in Melbourne than Launceston, but the competition was also much fiercer. He first found employment as a clerk of works, and then set up again as a building contractor. But his luck seemed to have run out and, in 1869, he was forced into bankruptcy by contract losses of £165 for building work. His assets amounted to only £5 for furniture and £7 for wearing apparel, plus he was owed £21 for the building of a double cottage in Emerald Hill. His declared debts, however, amounted to £244, mostly for building materials and £49 in loans, but also including £11 for the doctor and £7 to the baker.

In the end, the sums involved were not huge, as only £84 of the money owing was proved (including £8 for the hire of a pianoforte), and on 28 May of the same year, John Francis was discharged from his debts. The family moved to the cheaper suburb of Carlton, just to the north of the city, where they never stayed for more than a year or two in the same rented house. His petition for insolvency had also mentioned illness in the family, and John's mother passed away in 1870. Two years later his wife Martha died suddenly, on 23 March 1872, at their home in Charles Street, Carlton, just a short step from Melbourne General Cemetery. The doctor recorded on the certificate that death was due to 'sudden derangement of the stomach – convulsions – 12 hours'. Poisoning could well have been the cause, perhaps from contaminated food or drink, although something more sinister is always possible. We will never know, as there was no post-mortem or inquest. She was thirty-nine years old.

John was left with nine children aged from eight to twenty-one, but did not remarry. He probably had help from his sister, Catherine, who had remained a spinster and lived not too far away. Their unmarried brother Henry Burdett Francis was also in Melbourne from time to time, when he was not engaged as a sea captain on passenger steamships. Another family tragedy involving Henry occurred much later, after the captain had retired. At that time he was living with his sister, and niece Maria, one of John's daughters, and suffering chronic pain from an aneurism of the aorta.[23] One Saturday in March 1886, he went into the outside water closet, sat on the seat, put a revolver in his mouth, and pulled the trigger. Maria heard the shot and was the first to find the bloodied body.

John Francis continued to work as a builder and remained in the Melbourne suburb of Carlton, moving eventually to Fenwick Street. He did not rise in Melbourne society like Edward Oxford, but remained a tradesman to the end. Eight years after his wife died, when he had just turned sixty, he developed tuberculosis. The illness took hold, and over the next two years, he gradually wasted away. He died on Thursday 12 March 1885. The formalities were carried out by his son John, and he was buried that very same day, aged sixty-two. His fine grave in the General Cemetery also holds his brother Henry, and nearby lie his mother, wife, and daughter Martha.

John Francis's life had followed a rollercoaster, through the depths of despair, up to the heights of respectability and wealth, and down again. Many times he must have regretted his actions as a rash youth, and at others praised the fortune that brought him to Australia. But he did enjoy plenty of good times during his life, something which seems to have completely eluded the Queen's next assailant.

3

The Diminutive Newsvendor, 1842

Less than twenty-four hours after the Queen had shown clemency to John Francis there was another attempt on her life, but the act played out more like a comedy than an incipient tragedy.

Victoria was on her way from Buckingham Palace to her regular Sunday service at the Chapel Royal, travelling in the last of three carriages. She was accompanied by Albert and her uncle, the King of the Belgians, a male servant, and a lady. It was a closed landau[1], but it was a hot day so the window was drawn down. All along The Mall were lines of well-wishers two or three deep, numbering perhaps two to three thousand.

About halfway down, near to the pump which served as a watering place, stood a strange-looking youth. He was a cripple, only 4 feet or so high, with a pronounced stoop and a large hump on his right shoulder. His spine was crooked in two places, and his arms were no thicker than walking sticks. Beneath his dark cloth cap, his face was long, pale, and haggard. With his brown surtout coat[2] trailing along the ground, he shuffled along twisted to the right. His deep-set eyes moved restlessly beneath a low brow.

As the carriages approached, the boy elbowed his way to the front. He pulled a pistol from under his coat and held it out at arm's length. When the third carriage was only two or three yards away, he pulled the trigger. There was a click, but no explosion. The royal procession rolled on, unaware that anything had happened.

Seeing the little man, many in the crowd thought it was a joke. They were reminded of the freak shows they had seen and the clowns at the circus, and some thought it was just a child playing. But one, Charles Dassett, an oil and colourman[3], took it more seriously and grabbed the youth, saying, 'How dare you shoot at the Queen!' He took the gun and, with the help of his brother, dragged his prisoner off in the direction of two constables who stood lower down The Mall.

A crowd followed them in good humour, pushing and calling on them to let the man go as the gun was unloaded. Some shouted, 'Give the pistol back to the boy', and others called to the lad, 'Put it into your pocket and run away with it.' When Dassett reached constables Hearn and Claxton, he said, 'Here is a boy who wants to have a pop at the Queen.' But Hearn, who had been only three months in the force, just laughed and said it did not amount to a charge, while Claxton said, 'Pooh, pooh, it's all nonsense', and walked on.

The pressure of the crowd forced them to let go of their prisoner, and the hunchback made off across Green Park. Dassett, still holding the pistol, walked on down The Mall with his brother and uncle, pursued by a mob of 300 or more interested bystanders. As rumours spread that there had been an attempt on the Queen's life, they wanted to see the gun and the perpetrator. Further down the road, Dassett encountered PC James Torrington Partridge, an officer of seven years' experience, who took a dimmer view of a man with a firearm in the royal park. He arrested him and took him off towards Gardener's Lane police house. Dassett protested that the gun was not his, but belonged to a crippled dwarf. The constable looked doubtful.

At the police house, he was questioned by Inspector Hickman and the full story emerged. The gun was inspected, and when turned upside down, two small pieces of tobacco-pipe fell out, a less than lethal charge. But the authorities now took the event seriously, and an alert was put out for the hunchbacked youth. A circular containing the lad's description was read out to those going on duty that evening in all the Metropolitan Police districts. Gradually, as the night progressed, numerous constables came across possible culprits and the station houses across London began to fill with hunchbacks. One Inspector apprehended two deformed brothers, and in another case, a whole family who suffered from distortion of the spine were suspected.

In Holborn, around midnight, a little hunchbacked gentleman was crossing the street. As he reached the middle of the road, which separated the districts of 'E' and 'F' divisions, he was spotted by two constables on their respective beats. They both rushed upon the poor fellow, each saying that they had seen him first. They pulled him backwards and forwards into their respective districts, to the great distress of the little man. After some considerable mishandling, they compromised and took him to Gardener's Lane. But he, like most of the others, was not the man they sought. In fact, by this time, the culprit had already been apprehended. His name was Mr Bean.

* * *

For John William Bean, it was not a comedy at all, but another unfortunate event in his unhappy life. He was seventeen years old when he committed the crime, but in many ways, still a child. He was born on 12 July 1824 in Clerkenwell, and still lived in the same part of London, at 14 St James's Buildings, Rosoman Street, with his parents and four brothers. His father, also called John William, was a gold chaser and jeweller, but hired himself out to others as a journeyman in what had become a crowded profession, and the family were poor. John's brothers, Frederick, Henry, Edmund, and little Alfred, were aged from fourteen down to just five months old.

Although John was the eldest child, he was often tormented by his brothers because of his deformity. From the age of four he lived apart from them with his uncle Jabez and aunt Charlotte in Southwark, but returned to the family fold when he was ten. He was a studious boy and reading was his favourite pastime. Conscientious in his religious studies, he went to the Sunday School of Claremont Chapel, Pentonville, where he received several books bound in Morocco leather as rewards for merit. On a Sunday afternoon, if he could obtain the loan of a newspaper, he would devote the entire time to reading.

When he was about eleven years old, he wrote the following lines in a clearly legible hand in a pocket book:

This book belongs to Jack Bean,
As deep a boy as ere was seen;
If you were to say go forward Jack,
And shut your eyes, he'd walk straight back.

On another page he wrote, 'May 24th. Our blessed Queen's birthday, long may she live.'

When he was sixteen, John joined a temperance society and was given a medal for sobriety. But although he tried to behave like a normal upright citizen, his deformity preyed on his mind, and he worried about the difficulty of finding employment. He frequently cried to his father about it, saying, 'I shall never be like anything else, now I am getting near a man.' He had already had several part-time jobs: for a cheesemonger; as an errand boy for a watch finisher; a reading boy in a printing office; and a regular job on Sundays for Mr Hilton, a newsagent.

His father tried to teach him his own trade, but John repeatedly said that he did not like the work. On one occasion he disappeared from home for a few days, but was seen and persuaded to return. His parents urged him to learn what he could of the jewellery trade now, and when he had chosen another profession, he could move to that. Later, he was placed with a Mr Hackson, a lacquerer near Oxford Street, who said he would teach him his business provided his father paid for an apprenticeship indenture. But John would not stick at it, and left soon after.

He read a lot about the fate of Edward Oxford, and remarked to Mr Hilton, 'How well Oxford is provided for.' To his father he said that he'd read that Oxford was allowed a pint of wine a day and somebody to teach him French and German. His father replied that it was nonsense, Bethlem Hospital had denied the claim, and he should pay no heed.

But John did pay heed and, in June 1842, he decided to sell some of his precious books. On Tuesday 21 June, he walked to nearby Exmouth Street and bought a pistol for 3s 6d from William Bird, a pawnbroker and general dealer. A common pocket pistol, very old and rather rusty, Bird nevertheless claimed it was capable of being fired. John knew no better, but the gun was a joke compared to the weapons of the previous two royal attackers. It was an old flint lock, about 9 inches in length, and the lock was fastened with a common nail rather than a screw. Unscrewing the barrel was difficult because of the rust. The pistol was inlaid with silver wire to create a scroll as decoration, but the stock was worn, with a piece broken off on the left side.

John attempted to fill the pistol with gunpowder in the shop, but did not really know what he was doing, and Bird told him to be careful or he would do himself a mischief. Later that day, he tried to make the gun fire, without success. He went back to the shop and asked Bird to look at it, but the dealer put him off. Obstinately he returned on the following days, until finally the shopkeeper agreed. Bird pointed out that of course it would not work without a flint, and put one in for a penny.

On the Saturday, John had the idea that a neighbour, George Whitmore, might be able to help improve his purchase. He took the pistol to the man, an apprentice to a steel polisher, who agreed to oil the pistol, but could not clean it. Whilst he had possession of the gun, he tried it with a new flint, but the spark was not strong enough to light the powder. He gave the gun back to John on the Monday. Seeing it as just a child's toy, the neighbour attached no importance to it.

That same day, John was asked by his parents to go and pay an outstanding bill. He did as he was told, but, with the gun in his pocket, he wanted to show his parents and the world that he was more than just a deformed and pathetic child. He decided now was the time to make the break and leave home.

When their son failed to return from his errand, his parents became increasingly worried. On the Tuesday they contacted the police and gave his description to Constable Henry Webb of 'G' division. In fact John was in Islington, where he spent two cold and damp nights in the fields at Barnsbury Park, before finding an unfinished house to sleep in. He was hungry, but managed to subsist on the few pence he earned: 4d for holding two horses; 3d from a gentleman on Hungerford Pier, for whom he fetched a glass of ale. During the day he roamed around Regent's Park and the West End of London.

Despite his desire for independence, he did think of his parents at home worrying. He sent them a letter, which his father received on the Wednesday:

Half-past two, Tuesday.
Dear Father and Mother,

Thinking that you might feel surprised at my prolonged absence, I write these few lines to acquaint you that I am seeking employment, which, if I do not obtain, I will not be dishonest, though I may be desperate. It will be useless to seek for me, as I am determined never to be at home again. Please give my love to my brothers, though they never used me well as such. I have little more to say, excepting, remember me to my aunt and uncle and thank them for what they have done for me. I should have written to you sooner, but I did not like. Hoping you are well, excuse this scribbling, nor think no more of me. I can chide myself;

your unhappy and disobedient Son,
J. Bean.
PS I took the money safe yesterday.

Conscientiously, he also sent a note to Mr Hilton containing a list of customers. His erstwhile employee did not expect to be there to help with the Sunday newspapers. On that day, John was in The Mall, making a name for himself.

After he escaped from Dassett and the crowds, John went straight home. He reached the house at two o'clock and begged his mother's forgiveness. He was confused and shaking, and asked for food, saying that he hadn't eaten for twenty-four hours. His mother provided him with a substantial dinner before she went out.

When Constable Henry Webb came on duty later that afternoon in the new Clerkenwell station house, he listened intently to the description of the hunchback that was read out by Inspector Penny. It sounded very familiar. As soon as he could he walked to Bean's house and was surprised when the young lad, who was supposed to be missing, opened the door. He was in his shirtsleeves and without his cap, but the description definitely fitted. When John saw the policeman, he was horrified and slammed the door. But then, when Webb kept knocking, he decided he had to open it again.

John expected to be accused immediately, but instead the policeman asked if his parents were in. He said that they were not, and the constable then asked where his father was. John said that he did not know. Webb said, with surprise in his voice, 'Why, you had absconded from home,' and John replied, 'Yes, I had, but I have returned and am sorry for it.' But he felt it necessary to lie that he had returned at 11.30 a.m., and added, as if to counterbalance the untruth, 'I hope I shall turn out a good boy.' Webb did not want to scare the boy into running, and suggested they go to look for his parents together. When he touched John's arm, he noticed that it was trembling. At that point, John's mother happened to return, and Webb persuaded them both to go to the station house. It was 9 p.m.

Once in custody, John was taken to Gardener's Lane, where his identity was confirmed. He was searched, but nothing was found on him but a comb and a piece of string. As it was late, he was locked up for the night in the same cell that had earlier held both Oxford and Frances. Despite the alarming events of the day, John managed to sleep soundly, only waking once before the constable watching over him finished his shift at 8 a.m. On seeing the hour, John remarked in a despondent tone that Thomas Cooper must just have been hanged at Newgate. He could see clearly now that he had probably exchanged one life of misery for something much worse.

Nevertheless, he was ravenously hungry, and ate a filling breakfast of coffee and rolls. Later, John was taken to the Home Office, where the Privy Council was due to meet that afternoon. A large crowd had gathered outside Gardener's Lane station house, and as a diversion, one of the witnesses was brought out, escorted by two policemen. Most of the crowd fell for the ruse and followed them. When John emerged, escorted by Inspector Hughes and a police sergeant, there were few to observe their passage through the park and in by the garden gate. He was placed under guard in one of the rooms of the Home Office while they waited. He could not stop his lips from quivering, and his eyes twitched from side to side.

When John was brought before the august assembly in their ornate and intimidating surroundings, he refused to answer questions or give the reasons for his actions. The Privy Council interviewed the witnesses in his presence until 3.45 p.m., when they remanded him in custody until Wednesday. On his way down the stairs, John admitted privately to Inspector Martin that he had bought the gun in a pawnbroker's. He was taken by cab, accompanied by Inspector Hughes, to Tothill Fields bridewell, and delivered into the custody of Lieutenant Tracy, the governor.

When he was stripped for his bath, his small stature became even more embarrassingly apparent. Although he measured around 4 feet 6 inches from the sole of his foot to the top of his head, with his stoop he was only about 3 feet 6 inches tall. He looked even younger than he was. John felt very low and depressed. He told them that he had absconded from home, because 'he was tired of his life', and he claimed that he knew the pistol would not go off. Nevertheless, the surgeon at the prison, Mr Lavie, reported to the authorities that the prisoner secretly rejoiced at his notoriety and could barely conceal the emotion.

On the Wednesday, he returned to the Home Office by Hackney carriage, accompanied by Inspector Hughes, and came before the Privy Council again. He still felt dejected and, on being brought into the room before the Council, he looked around in considerable alarm at the assembled dignitaries. They now included Sir Robert Peel, the Duke of Wellington, the Chancellor of the Exchequer, and many other noblemen. Throughout the examination, he remained sullen and reserved.

At the end of the session, he was indicted for a misdemeanour, the capital charge having been dropped. Bail was allowed, given two sureties of £250, something patently well beyond the means of his family. He was taken back to Tothill Fields to await trial.

* * *

With the increasing frequency of attacks, there was renewed interest in the Queen's security, with larger crowds at her afternoon outings watching in case of another attempt. After John Francis had struck, one wag even suggested that Constitution Hill should exchange names with a thoroughfare in South London: Shooter's Hill. Parliament moved to reconsider the law. Since 1800, the trial of those who had clearly meant to kill the sovereign had been changed to the same procedure as a normal trial for murder. But for those crimes where only an attempt to wound or alarm the sovereign could be proved, the law of high treason made it difficult to secure a conviction, and gave much power to the defendant.

On 12 July, Sir Robert Peel introduced a bill in Parliament to amend this part of the treason acts. Under the new terms, the trial could be conducted in the same way as for larceny, and the penalty would be up to seven years' transportation and 'personal chastisement'. The aim was that this degrading punishment would dissuade those just looking for notoriety. The new act came into force a few days later.

But John Bean would not face this charge, only that of a simple misdemeanour. His incompetence with the gun was now a joke, not even worthy of an indictment for treason. The newspaper *The Era* published a short editorial under the heading, 'The Hunchback of Newgate':

> The fiend, miscreant, monster, Bean, has sadly vulgarized treason. His thimble-full of powder and broken 'bacco pipe have killed all the importance of the petty traitor, who is henceforth not to bare his neck for the rope, but his back for the whip. From this time the Arms of England admit to a new supporter; in addition to the Lion and Unicorn they take the Cat! *Honi soit qui mal y pense* may henceforth be freely translated by the Beans and Francises as follows:
>
> A rod is in pickle,
> Your toby to tickle.[4]
>
> The traitor sinks from the hero of the scaffold to the vagabond of the cat's tail. He is levelled down to an apple stealer; and his hopes for a 'provision for life' terminates with the application of a whip-cord. This is a wise measure; it is smiting the evil that generates traitor-fools, *at the proper end.*

The trial was not fixed until the end of August, and the defence had some time to consider its approach. On 16 August, Bean's father wrote to the commissioners of the Metropolitan Police asking for the names and addresses of the two constables who had refused to take his son into custody, and who had subsequently been dismissed from the force for incompetence. The aim was to underline the lack of seriousness of the so-called attack.

On 25 August, John was taken from Tothill Fields to Newgate. At nine o'clock, he was led through the dimly lit underground passage and up the steps to emerge blinking into the dock of the Central Criminal Court. The room was not large, only about 40 feet square, but it was filled with people. Opposite, running the length of the wall was the raised bench for the judges, currently the only space unoccupied. Above the chief seat was a canopy surmounted by the royal arms and beneath it a gilded sword upon the crimson-draped wall. On the right side of the bench was the jury box and witness box; on the left were the seats for privileged witnesses and visitors, and also for the reporters and jurymen-in-waiting. The space bounded by the bench on one side, the dock on another, the jury box on a third, and the reporters' box on the fourth, was occupied by counsel and attorneys, the larger half being assigned to the counsel.

In this crowded environment, the participants stifled in the lifeless air as the day wore on. Slumber was an ever-present risk, especially in summer. Above the dock was the public gallery, with seats for about thirty at any one time. A fee was payable to the warder for admission, despite the fact that spectators could see nothing of the prisoner except his scalp, and hear very little of what was going on. Nevertheless, for exciting trials, the corridors were always blocked with people trying to get in. But on this occasion, there was less public interest, and the gallery was not even full. Even the notoriety that John expected was greatly inferior to his two predecessors.

John was as decently dressed as possible, and he tried not to show alarm. But he knew he looked pale and cut a rather pathetic figure, with his head barely reaching above the edge of the dock. He could not sit down, as he would have disappeared from view completely, but leaned on the front of the dock as he grew tired. The proceedings began, the public expecting entertainment in return for their price of admission, and the officials intent on carrying out their respective roles, seemingly little interested in the outcome. Amongst the players, only the accused was desperately concerned about the result.

John was described as eighteen years old and a 'chaser'. The charges were read out. The first long-winded count said that he,

> being a person of a turbulent and seditious mind, and greatly disaffected to our said Lady the Queen, and unlawfully and wickedly continuing and intending to vex, harass, and alarm our said Lady the Queen, to disturb and break the public peace of this realm, and to terrify the faithful liege subjects thereof [...] with force and arms, in and upon our said lady the Queen [...] did make an assault [...] did point, aim and level [...] the said pistol [...] and did attempt to fire off and discharge, by pulling the trigger of the same [...]

At least the man formulating the indictment had put some effort into the case. The second count omitted the reference to assaulting the sovereign, but specified an attempt to harass and alarm the Queen and her subjects. The third lengthy count was essentially for common assault, and the fourth for attempting common assault.

John pleaded 'not guilty' in as firm a voice as he could muster. At 10 a.m., the judges swept into the court: Lord Abinger, Mr Justice Williams, and Mr Baron Rolfe. The Crown was represented by a team of five lawyers led by the Attorney General, while the counsel for the defence was Mr Horry.

The Attorney General gave the opening address, but, after a short while, Mr Horry rose and requested that the witnesses be excluded from the court, which was done. The Attorney General particularly emphasised the fact that the firing of the pistol would have caused great alarm and a breach of the peace. In a flight of fancy, he said that in former times, when most carried a sword, each would have drawn their weapon and caused great 'alarm, confusion and tumult'. He also claimed that the act of pointing a pistol that might have been loaded was in fact an assault.

The Attorney General quoted an extract from the letter that John wrote to his parents when he was absent, which he misread slightly, perhaps deliberately:

> Thinking you will be surprised at my prolonged absence I write these few lines to you to tell you that I am seeking employment, which if I do not succeed in obtaining, you may depend on it that I will do nothing that is dishonest, although I may do something desperate, but I shall never return home again.

By substituting 'I will do something desperate' for 'I may be desperate', he was able to claim that the letter showed the prisoner's intention. John, perhaps confused by the whole charade, made no sign that he had recognised the error, and his counsel made no objection.

The prosecution then called numerous police officers and witnesses to the attempt, and those involved in John's acquisition of the gun. The evidence of William Bird, the Exmouth Street shopkeeper, was particularly important. Under cross-examination, he said that, despite its old condition, the pistol was able to cause harm, but that it had not been loaded with sufficient powder. There was enough to go off, but insufficient to carry a ball a great distance, although it would carry three or four yards. The pieces of tobacco pipe would cause no harm.

When Mr Horry rose to open the defence, he first questioned the indictments. He said the first amounted to high treason and could not be classed as a misdemeanour. The second he dismissed, as there was no alarm caused to the Queen, in fact she was completely unaware of the attempt. There were similar objections to the third and fourth counts. Their Lordships acknowledged the comments on the first count, but said that the trial should proceed, and the judges would decide on the points of law later in their instructions to the jury.

Mr Horry then addressed the jury and said that the first count should be dismissed, even though the pistol was pointed at the carriage, it was not necessarily the Queen who would feel assaulted as there were two or three other individuals within. The second count, that it would cause terror and alarm amongst Her Majesty's subjects, was negated by the fact that it actually caused much mirth. He also questioned whether Dassett's evidence should be believed, as it was not corroborated in every particular. Only he had heard the click.

Mr Horry then called two witnesses associated with the events. The first said that, contrary to Dassett's evidence, he did not see the accused aim the pistol. The second, Thomas Bosphor, a journeyman painter, concurred, and also said that for a full ten to fifteen minutes before the carriage passed he had watched the accused holding the gun in his right hand pointed towards the ground. He said that he did not do anything because he hadn't the presence of mind and wanted to see what would happen. He had only offered to give evidence after he had met the prisoner's uncle, John Gray, outside the Home Office the next day.

Character witnesses were also called. David Hilton, the newsman, said that he knew the prisoner well and that he was very mild and inoffensive in his behaviour. John Bickley, the watch finisher, described him as a very good boy, always mild, trustworthy, and inoffensive. Two of his uncles, John Gray and Jabez Elliott, also testified to his character. The prisoner's father was called and said that his son was mild-mannered, and he had never heard him say anything against the Queen, indeed the reverse. He mentioned their limited resources and that he had been unable to employ an attorney to defend his son. John, who had been following the proceedings as closely as he could, at this point started crying.

In his closing speech, the Attorney General threw doubt on the truth of the defence witness statements, which he said contradicted all those who had come forward immediately after the event. The judge was also harsh with regard to Thomas Bosphor, saying that if his account was true, he would be guilty of misprision (the deliberate concealment of knowledge of a crime) of treason. Following his summing up, Lord Abinger ruled out the first count and directed the jury to just consider whether or not the prisoner was guilty of the second count.

After the long-winded indictments and the lengthy defence, the jury were almost perfunctory in carrying out their duty. They did not need to retire, but immediately found the prisoner guilty of the charge. John showed no further emotion at the verdict.

After a brief consultation with his colleagues, Lord Abinger then proceeded to pass sentence. He spoke of the awfulness of the crime and asked:

> what shall be said of a man who, on his own wanton, wicked, or if you like, capricious view, should aim at something mischievous in order to attain a kind of ignominious notoriety, or an asylum for the rest of his days, and should make an attempt which was calculated to strike the bosom of every loyal subject with alarm, terror and obligation?

He regretted that, because the offence had been committed earlier, Bean had to be sentenced under common law, and not the new statute, which would 'gain him another species of notoriety, by being publicly whipped at a cat's tail'.

John William Bean was sentenced to be confined for eighteen months in the penitentiary at Millbank. He was taken down, while the spectators rushed for the door, desperate for fresh air.

* * *

Millbank prison was built in 1821, following the so-called 'Panopticon' design of Jeremy Bentham, famous for his utilitarian principles. The largest penitentiary in London, the huge brooding mass was constructed in six spokes that radiated from a central hub like some gigantic, grey starfish. The centre housed the governor and turnkeys, giving them rapid access to any wing, and the end of each spoke terminated in a fortress-like tower. Situated on marshy and unhealthy land on the north side of the Thames between Vauxhall and Lambeth bridges[5], the whole was enclosed by high walls in the shape of an irregular octagon. Steps down to the river made for the easy embarkation of the many convicts who were awaiting transportation to the colonies.

Soon after his trial, John was taken in through the forbidding gates and incarcerated in an individual cell, just like all the other inmates. The prison was organised using the 'separate system', where the prisoners were isolated and forbidden to talk to each other, giving them plenty of time to contemplate their wrongdoings. The aim was reform and to provide a more humane and less brutal environment, but the prisoners found the regime far worse.

John's cell was a bare cubbyhole furnished with a small table, a slop bucket with a lid, a hammock, and a rug. In the wall at the corridor end was a narrow slit, through which he could poke the stick he was given. One end was black, indicating that he was ready to work, while the other end was red, indicating needs of a more personal nature. John was put to tailoring, for which he could earn up to 8*d* a week. But it wasn't rewarding work, and he soon found the environment dreadfully depressing, with the gloomy walls, gloomy faces, and above all the gloomy silence.

John was known only by his number, and his name was never spoken. Every time he was taken from his cell, he was made to wear a cap pulled down across his face with eye-slits cut in the peak, so that no inmate could recognise another. Once a day, unless it was raining, he was taken from his cell for exercise in the yard. Fifty or more convicts walked briskly in a circle, each holding onto a rope knotted at fifteen-foot intervals, which was the closest approach allowed. Silence was also maintained in chapel and at school, with only the priest and teacher allowed to speak. Any talking by the prisoners was immediately punished, although many became adept at communicating without moving their lips.

By mid-October, John was ill and suffering on account of his weak constitution. According to the prison regulations, his relatives could only see him once every four months, and if he ever wrote to any friends, the interval extended to once every eight months. Not for the first time, he wished that he was dead. Unsurprisingly, the authorities were finding that the separate system seemed to be increasing the suicide rate, but they persevered with the method. At some point the regime for John may have been lightened. He might have been allowed to work in the kitchens, cap peak up, but still in silence, or he may have been transferred to another prison to labour at public works. But with the comparatively light sentence of eighteen months, he was eventually released back into society.

Little is known of the remainder of his life as he sank back into obscurity, his moment of fame passed. Despite his looks, he married a few years after his release, in 1846. His bride was Esther Martin, four years his senior and the daughter of a Thames lighterman[6] and a laundress. On the marriage certificate, he gave his profession as jeweller, but it seems that he made his living mainly by selling newspapers, an occupation he had learnt earlier from Mr Hilton. He listed his occupation variously as a newsvendor, newsman or newsagent, but whether he just sold papers on the street corner or managed a shop is unclear.

John's father died two years after his son's marriage and his mother moved to Rotherhithe with her remaining children, where she worked as a shopkeeper. John and Esther Bean settled in the area near Fleet Street and Covent Garden, where they had two children: Samuel in 1849 and Esther Ann in 1852. His wife died not long after, and the children were looked after elsewhere, so that John then lived alone for many years. He married for a second time in 1869, this time to Catherine Tryphena Watson, a widow ten years his junior, who was born in Penzance. Her father was a fisherman who captained a boat out of Newlyn, and she had been born at sea, on a day when her mother had been out in the boat with her father. Catherine was illiterate and her surname was even spelt wrongly on the marriage certificate. John's son, Samuel, who was also a newsvendor, came to live with them for a while.

Sometime afterwards, they moved south of the river to Camberwell. John had difficulty finding work and, in 1877, spent seven weeks in Wandsworth County Lunatic Asylum. He was probably suffering from depression, made worse by the fact that his wife had to go out to work to support them, a shameful situation for a Victorian man. Catherine sometimes worked as a monthly nurse[7], and it was probably in this capacity that she was away from the house on the fateful day of Wednesday 19 July 1882.

At a quarter to two that day, she left her husband sitting on a chair reading the newspaper. When she returned at eight o'clock, she knew immediately that something was wrong. John was lying on the bed and nothing she did would wake him. She called to the landlady, and they sent for a doctor, who put his state down to the effects of poison. With the aid of a constable, a cab was called, and John was taken to St Thomas's Hospital. One of the house physicians examined him and made every effort to revive him, but he died forty minutes later without regaining consciousness.

A phial labelled 'poison' was found close by the bed. It was laudanum, a tincture of opium, which was widely used as a painkiller. The coroner recorded a verdict of 'suicide by poison, being deranged'. John William Bean was fifty-eight years old. All that remained to console Catherine was the letter that he had left for her:

Dear Wife

Good-bye. The end has come at last. I can bear up no longer. What I suffer no tongue can tell. I am sure you will sooner see me as I am than between four walls of an asylum, for it drives me mad to see you trying to get a living for two. You may find friends when I am gone, so do not fret for me as I have been an incumbrance to you long enough, although you have never complained.

Thank those who have been kind to us and avoid those who have done us harm, and I leave the rest to Him from whom no secrets are hid, and to whom all hearts are known. I have been more sinned against than sinning, and my whole life has been one of trouble and worry from my very infancy.

My dear, if I could in any way have worked for you it would have been a pleasure; but I will not die in a workhouse, where honest poverty is treated as a crime; and I know you will do as I have done sooner than be a pauper.

So good-bye, and God bless you, and with my last breath I think of you, hoping you will be better without me than with me.

Once more, good-bye, your ever loving and affectionate husband,

John

4

The Irish Navvy, 1849

It was seven years before Victoria faced another attack, a period when her personal life underwent radical changes. First of all, much to her distress, she found herself in conflict with her beloved husband, with their first really serious arguments in 1842. The underlying cause was money and power.

The Queen knew little of costs, entertained often and lavishly, and gave expensive gifts. Over 100,000 dinners were served at Windsor Castle in 1839, not including the grand ball suppers, and the christening of the Prince of Wales had cost just under £5,000. Ordered goods for the royal household had a habit of going missing, expenses were paid for those only tenuously connected to the court, and every day, every single candle across the palaces was replaced, regardless of whether it had been used, the discards going to the servants as 'palace ends'. The Privy Purse was under pressure.

Albert set about reforming the household and gaining better control of expenditure, but that created enemies. In particular, Baroness Lehzin, who held considerable power even though she had no official position, felt threatened. She had been Victoria's governess and had remained close to the Queen, her confidante and advisor. Despite her marriage, Victoria had insisted that Lehzin keep her bedroom next door to the Queen's. There was a connecting door, and Victoria enjoyed their intimate conversations, when they often discussed the latest household gossip.

Lehzin had privileged access to the sovereign's finances and, in 1842, she tried to take charge of the Duchy of Cornwall revenues, the right of the infant Prince of Wales, to use for nursery expenses. As Albert struggled to gain more control over management and expenditure, Lehzin tried to undermine the Prince's position. He was appalled at the lack of control, the influence that Lehzin exerted, and the threat to his own position.

His increasing concern led to an outburst of anger in June, when Albert railed about the 'crazy, stupid intriguer' who was 'obsessed with the lust of power'. At this time the Princess Royal was ill, and he told Victoria that he thought that Lehzin, the appointed nursery nurses and the doctor were all incompetent. Victoria took this personally and flared up; accusing him of trying to drive her from the nursery and crying that he could murder the baby if he wanted to. But later she felt miserable and wrote in her diary, 'There is often an irritability in me which [...] makes me say cross and odious things which I don't myself believe and which I fear hurt A.'

Although Victoria felt she still depended on her old governess, she relented, and the nursery was placed in the hands of a new superintendent. Later that summer, the split with her confidante came, and the baroness left the Queen's service in September. After breaking the tie, Victoria gradually became used to being without Lehzin and achieved greater independence as a result. Albert steadily brought the royal finances under control, and Victoria slowly regained her confidence in him.

The Queen was not at this time particularly interested in the daily business of government, whilst Albert found the work satisfying. He gradually became, unofficially, her private secretary, and the country grew to be governed by something like a dual monarchy. Everything was done in the Queen's name, but Sir Robert Peel knew it was best to consult Albert on any fresh issue. Technically, royal assent was needed for all Acts and many government appointments. In practice, the constitutional monarchy gave the sovereign just the right to be informed and to be heard. The Queen remained vigilant that these rights were not eroded.

As the succession of royal babies continued, it is indeed a wonder that Victoria managed to devote as much time as she did to the process of government and the many formal and informal contacts with dignitaries and her subjects. Much to her horror, the Princess Royal and the Prince of Wales were swiftly followed by Princess Alice (1843), Prince Alfred (1844), Princess Helena (1846), Princess Louise (1848), and Prince Arthur (1850). In the midst of all this procreation, Victoria became disillusioned with Buckingham Palace, and longed for somewhere more comfortable by the sea, away from the dirt of the city and the constant public gaze. She did not like the Pavilion in Brighton, which was sold to pay for repairs to Buckingham Palace, but the huge savings made by Albert in the Privy Purse provided them with the opportunity to purchase their own property.

Osborne House on the Isle of Wight was bought, and the royal family paid their first visit in the spring of 1845. Victoria was entranced: 'It is impossible to see a prettier place,' she told Lord Melbourne, 'with woods and valleys and *points de vue*, which would be beautiful anywhere, but all this near the sea [...] is quite perfection.' Two summers later, she drove down to the beach and used a bathing machine. 'I undressed and bathed in the sea (for the first time in my life),' she wrote in her journal. 'I thought it delightful till I put my head under the water, when I thought I should be stifled'. Victoria loved the views, the comfort, and the seclusion, and would spend time there as often as possible. With the train to Gosport and the steam packet, the journey was not arduous.

The only thing it lacked was Scottish air, which the Queen had become addicted to on earlier visits to the country. In 1848, she took out a lease on Balmoral, an isolated, castellated country house in the Highlands. Victoria thrived in the cold mountain air and the solitude, while her retinue, including the government minister who always accompanied her to ensure communications with London, just had to put up with being chilled to the bone and miles from anywhere. For the Queen, 'all seemed to breathe freedom and peace, and to make one forget the world and its sad turmoils.'

One such turmoil was the question of import tariffs, where opposing views were causing conflict in Parliament and the country. Peel had been making significant progress towards free trade, so as to make imported goods cheaper and encourage other countries to reduce tariffs to allow in British goods. By 1845, he had removed duties on 600 items and reduced tariffs on 500 others, but he was about to meet resistance which would split his party and finish his career. He wanted to repeal the Corn Laws, which protected grain famers and kept the price of bread artificially high. But Parliament largely consisted of landowning gentry and aristocracy, and refused. Thus, that December he resigned, but the opposition could not form a government and, in May 1846, Peel finally got the measure through with support from the Whigs.

It was Peel's last success, and he resigned definitively less than two months later. He was never in office again, and died tragically three years later, when his horse slipped in the rain on Constitution Hill and fell on him. From the summer of 1846, the Whigs ruled in a coalition with the 'Peelites' against the protectionist Conservatives. They were led by Lord John Russell, a weak Prime Minister, who was dominated by his Foreign Secretary, Lord Palmerston. Palmerston was loved by the people for his jingoist policies, but hated by Victoria, as he frequently took action without consulting her, or even the Prime Minister. An example of this behaviour came after a Jewish British subject in Greece, Don Pacifico, had his house destroyed by an anti-Semitic mob. When the Greek government rejected his application for compensation, Palmerston despatched a fleet to blockade Piraeus and seize Greek vessels of sufficient value to settle the claim, much to the displeasure of the French and Russian ambassadors. The Queen belatedly warned Palmerston, 'that for the sake of one man the welfare of the country must not be exposed'. But the Foreign Secretary vehemently defended his actions and his popularity grew further.

The expression of British power abroad may have been popular, but the demands for wider suffrage were not diminished; indeed they received a boost in 1848, the year of revolutions in Europe. That year, Louis Philippe was replaced by a republican government in France, and uprisings occurred in Greece, the German states, and the Habsburg Austrian Empire. In Britain, the Chartist demonstrations became larger and noisier, and the lamps outside Buckingham Palace were smashed to shouts of *Vive la République*! Two months after the French rebellion, a mass meeting was called for Kennington Common. In a *quid pro quo*, the Chartist leaders were released from prison in exchange for the promise of a non-violent demonstration. To further ensure peace, the government called up reserve troops to patrol the streets, and over 100,000 special constables were appointed.

On 8 April, Waterloo Station was cleared and the Queen and her family left for Osborne House. For once, she did not object to the show of apparent cowardice. It was just three weeks after Princess Louise was born, and Victoria was suffering again from post-natal depression; sometimes crying, and not a little frightened. At dawn on the day of the Chartist meeting, the bridges across the Thames were sealed by troops, and the river was patrolled by gunboats. In fact, the demonstration only attracted 20,000 supporters, according to the government, and on being told that no deputation would be allowed across the Thames, the Chartist leader Fergus O'Connor asked his disappointed followers to disperse and took the petition to the Home Office by cab, alone.

In July 1848, there was an uprising in County Tipperary over the situation in Ireland, instigated by a real organisation called 'Young Ireland', which had been in existence for a decade and was probably the inspiration for Edward Oxford's fantasy. However, the band of ill-fed and poorly armed peasants was no match even for the local police, and the organisers were soon arrested. Their leader, William Smith O'Brien, was charged with high treason and sentenced to be hung, drawn and quartered, later commuted to transportation. He and other Irish 'gentlemen' revolutionaries were soon to be found in Port Arthur in Van Diemen's Land. Sporadic resistance continued through 1849, and it came as no surprise to anyone that the next attempt on the Queen's life should be made by an Irishman.

Saturday 19 May 1849, the Queen's thirtieth official birthday, saw London thronged with people in a holiday mood. It was a fine morning, and Prince Albert inspected a large muster of the household guard and watched the trooping of the colour. The shipping in the river hoisted their flags, and the Honourable Artillery Company fired a double royal salute. It should have been a happy day, free of troubles.

Victoria and Albert drove to St James's Palace at 2 p.m., escorted by a squadron of the Life Guards, to hold a drawing-room.[1] The Queen displayed all her majesty, wearing a train of green and silver silk, trimmed with red roses and violets, and *tulle d'illusion* in silver. Her headdress was composed of diamonds, feathers, roses and violets. In the royal closet[2], the archbishops and bishops delivered a congratulatory address and prayed for her continuing health and wellbeing. The royal couple then entered the throne room for the reception.

After returning to Buckingham Palace, the Queen went out again in the late afternoon for her traditional airing. She was accompanied in the open landau by Princess Helena, the Prince of Wales, and Princess Royal (aged two, seven, and eight) with three attendants, and a single mounted equerry. Prince Albert rode on horseback alongside with his usual entourage. They returned from the park around six o' clock, with Albert riding some distance ahead. He was already dismounting in Buckingham Palace as the carriage passed beneath the triumphal arch between Hyde Park and the palace. The Queen acknowledged the cheering crowds as they proceeded down Constitution Hill, unaware that her life would soon be in danger once again. In a few moments, they reached the spot chosen by Oxford and Francis to fire at the sovereign. After a gap of seven years, history was about to repeat itself.

* * *

In 1826, at the age of three months, little baby William was left at the Foundling Hospital in Cork. Perhaps it was because his mother had died, maybe he had been born out of wedlock, or it could just have been that his parents were too poor to feed another mouth. To reduce infanticide, some institutions had taken to leaving cradles outside their doors so that babies could be left anonymously, but in William's case some information was available, as it was known that his father was George Hamilton, a mason. Any contact that was made with his parents, however, did not last, and as an adult, William did not know if his father was alive or dead.

William grew up in the orphanage with over 400 other children. The Cork Foundling Hospital was linked to the house of industry – the Irish euphemism for the workhouse – and was supported by a tax on imported coal and by charitable donations. The objective was to clear destitute children off the streets; to care for them was secondary. The regime was tough and the healthcare crude. Even years later, on average over sixty children were carried off to the cemetery every year, more than double those that left on their own two legs. The governors at least saw that their souls were looked after, ensuring they were well educated in the Protestant faith. William, of course, like most of the other inmates, was Catholic.

But William survived. His first language was probably Gaelic, although he was also taught English, the language of the country's rulers. At that time, he was reportedly a reasonably intelligent boy, but the world in which he grew up was characterised by poverty, hunger, and violence. The early part of the nineteenth century had seen a large growth in the population, but unlike in the north and elsewhere, south-west Ireland saw virtually no industrialisation. The cottage industry of weaving was gradually rendered uneconomic by mechanisation elsewhere, and subsistence farming was virtually the only way to survive. As the population grew, the sole crop that would prosper in the climate and could provide enough sustenance and nutrients was the potato. When the harvest was poor, those at the lower end of the social scale went hungry; something that happened repeatedly in Cork after William turned five.

Social unrest was common. Disraeli later claimed that Ireland was ungovernable because of 'a starving population, an absentee aristocracy, and an alien Church'. The island had become part of the United Kingdom in 1801 following the Act of Union, something designed to give the people representation in Parliament, but seen by the disenfranchised poor as further consolidation of the grip of foreign landlords. Church tithes, a tax that fell on any who possessed land, also went to pay for the occupier's heathen religion, the so-called Protestant Church of Ireland. Violent resistance was initiated by a succession of secret societies, such as the 'Whiteboys', named after the colour of the shirts they wore on midnight raids, and the 'Oakboys', identifiable from the sprig of leaves that adorned their caps.

In the years just before William was born, Cork witnessed many arson attacks and murders by the 'Rockites', led by the mythical leader 'Captain Rock', directed against Protestants, landlords, and unwanted tenants. Five regiments were drafted in from England, and night-time curfews and trial without jury were introduced to quell the rebellion. The 'tithe wars' of the early 1830s continued the violence, and when William was nine, armed police and the British Army allegedly killed seventeen people in Rathcormac, 15 miles north of Cork, in the course of collecting a tithe of just 40s.

A year later, on 19 August 1836, William left the orphanage. Barely ten years old, he was apprenticed to a farmer, Phillip Rynard, at Graigue, a hamlet near Adare in County Limerick, about 50 miles north of Cork. He became an agricultural labourer, learning the basics and working long and exhausting days for his master. Even with such cheap labour, Rynard could not make a good living and decided to immigrate to America four years later. William moved to Adare to become a land servant for John Barkman, who kept a shop in the town.

William had learnt to read and write at the orphanage, if somewhat imperfectly, and it was either through a newspaper or word of mouth that he heard at this time about Edward Oxford. Because of his experiences, William was fiercely anti-royalist, and his sympathies were with the attacker, adding 'that it was not right to serve under a petticoat government'. His employer was amused by the young rebel, and from time to time he would taunt his employee that he was 'still serving under petticoat government'. William seethed and longed to escape from the confines of the backward and oppressed region.

The population was also still growing, and the harvests had not improved. Then, in 1845, came the arrival from Europe of *phytophthora infestans*, potato blight. That year half the crop was lost, and the following year three-quarters. Over the next five years, a million people died from starvation or related diseases, and another million emigrated.[3] The government in Westminster did little to help, and during the crisis absentee landlords continued to export food to England and evict unprofitable tenants.

But William was gone. The year before the blight arrived, he left for England, to seek a livelihood and better his condition. No doubt he sailed from Cork, where the passage could be bought for a few pence. Those with more money, perhaps £5 in steerage class, were heading for America, and the docks were thronged with people. Already, before the great famine, around 100,000 Irish were emigrating every year, but the number doubled or trebled during the years of terrible hardship.

William went to live in London, lodging with an Irishman, Daniel O'Keefe, who hailed from Adare and was a slater and bricklayer. O'Keefe supplemented his living by taking in paying guests, and there were ten lodgers as well as his wife Bridget, two sons, two daughters, and a servant living in the modest house at 4 Eccleston Place, Pimlico. The whole household, apart from the children, were born in Ireland. With his experience gained in building farm walls and ditches, William bound himself to O'Keefe as an apprentice and worked as a bricklayer's labourer. But London did not meet his expectations in terms of earning a good living. The labour was hard, for little pay, and in any case William was often out of work. The following summer, when he was twenty years old, he took off for France, where revolution was in the air.

Ever since the defeat of Napoleon I in 1815, the French monarchs had tried to forget the earlier revolution and impose the old ways. Louis-Philippe was more moderate, but favoured the middle classes over the mass of the proletariat. The heir apparent of the republic, waiting in the wings, was Louis-Napoléon Bonaparte, the nephew of Napoleon I and next in line in the Bonaparte dynasty. He was imprisoned by the King, but in May 1846 he escaped from the Ham gaol dressed as a workman. Bonaparte crossed to England, for exile in Southport, about the same time as William was travelling in the opposite direction.

William found employment on the Continent, first in the construction of the Belgian railways, and then working for Le Compagnie de Chemin de Fer de Tours à Nantes. But, for whatever reason, William had had enough by November and returned to England and Eccleston Place. Again he couldn't find work until O'Keefe secured him a job in Bow, by which time he was in arrears on his rent by £4 10s. He managed to pay some of the debt off, but remained only intermittently employed through 1847 and 1848. In June of that year, he again went to Paris, where the revolution had finally arrived, and he became embroiled in the uprising known as the 'June Days'.

In February 1848, the King had been deposed; the Second French Republic established. Many democratic reforms were introduced, but in June an insurrection blew up over the closing of the National Workshops, which had been providing the unemployed with work. The barricades were thrown up on 23 June, and over the next three days 4,500 soldiers and protestors died before the rebellion was put down. Democratic presidential elections were held, which were won by Louis-Napoleon, but three years later he staged a *coup d'état* and declared himself Emperor of France, Napoleon III.

William fared better than many in the June fighting and suffered only a short period of imprisonment in Paris. After his release, he returned once more to Eccleston Place. Again work was intermittent through the winter, and William talked about committing some crime so that he would be taken by the police and could find a billet in prison for the season. Daniel O'Keefe kindly allowed him to stay on rent free, and William managed to get some food to eat through the generosity of his landlady and of Ellen Tooney, another lodger, who was a milk seller and collected leftover food from her clients.

In the first five months of 1849, William managed perhaps only seven weeks' work. His support for the revolutionary cause intensified, and he took to attending meetings of the People's Charter Union in the lecture rooms in nearby Sloane Square. The society met three nights a week, and the meetings were crowded with working people. On 11 May, he went to a discussion discourse on 'What form of government is most compatible with liberty'. The intellectuals led the debate, but William's feelings were more basic.

By then he was twenty-three years old, but perhaps still rather juvenile in his outlook. The day after the meeting, a Saturday, William asked O'Keefe's eleven-year-old son Edward whether he had ever had squibs or crackers. The boy answered yes, saying that they could be bought in a nearby shop. William said he was going to have a bit of fun and could make them fire through the trees. He showed Edward a device made from a piece of wood in the shape of a pistol stock and an old kettle spout. Edward bought a halfpennyworth of squibs, and William demonstrated the device, which the young boy agreed to buy from him for a penny.

A week later it was the Queen's birthday. Bridget O'Keefe was arranging things in the room where William was sitting, when she turned out a small pocket pistol. It was an old flintlock of her husband's with a screwed brass barrel, which the children sometimes used as a toy. William asked her to lend it to him and said that he would clean it. He had an idea.

At about a quarter to three that afternoon, he asked Edward to run and fetch a halfpennyworth of powder. The lad said that they would not sell him gunpowder, but William was sure they would. Edward indeed managed to buy some lower quality powder from a woman in nearby Elizabeth Street. When he returned, William went into the yard behind the house and satisfied himself that the pistol would fire. He then went out, saying he was going to the park – St James's and Green Park were both about half a mile away – to shoot some sparrows. Edward wanted to go with him, but William refused to take him.

He made his way to Green Park and thence to Constitution Hill, passing throngs of people in a festive mood, still celebrating the Queen's birthday. Alongside the roadway, beside the trees now in bright green springtime leaf, a crowd had gathered hoping to see the sovereign. Amongst the better-dressed onlookers, William stood out as a labourer, dressed in a shabby flannel jacket, old corduroy trousers, black moleskin waistcoat, white stockings and blucher boots[4], with a greasy cap pulled down over his brown hair. Around half past five, he took up position by a tree, just across the railings from the roadway, and walked about on the spot for some time. Another bystander, Daniel Lamb, a huntsman with the Warwickshire and Northampton hounds, thought it strange that William never withdrew his hand from his pocket.

After a while, William spoke to Lamb and asked whether the Queen had already passed by. He said no, but a few moments later a carriage approached and William asked again, 'Is this the Queen?' On hearing Lamb's affirmative, William said, 'I'll let the — know it!' He pulled the pistol out of his pocket and raised his right hand, just as the carriage went past. A second later there was a flash and a loud bang.

William was immediately seized by one of the park keepers. Another man, who had been so close to the pistol that his cheek had been singed by the explosion, also grabbed him. He tried to put the pistol away in his pocket, but it was taken from him. Constable Topley, who climbed over the railings from the road, then arrested him. A cry went up that the Queen had been shot, and the mob turned their attention in an instant from the royal cortège to the perpetrator. The crowd began chanting, 'Kill him at once! Kill him at once!'

But the Queen was not hit. On hearing the loud report, Victoria immediately stood up, and said to one of the footmen, 'Renwick, what is that?' He replied, 'Your Majesty has been shot at.' Seemingly satisfied with the response, she resumed her seat and leaned forward to reassure the children. The equerry, General Wemys, wheeled his horse and rode towards the source of the commotion. Seeing a gentleman of about fifty raise his fist to strike the would-be assassin, the general grabbed his arm. A large body of police soon reached the melee and William was hustled away to Buckingham Gate, where a cab took him to the police house.

By then, the Queen was already inside Buckingham Palace, where Albert greeted her on the steps with great emotion, saying, 'Thank God, you are safe.' They walked for a few minutes in the grounds, discussing the events. The children gave their accounts of the drama, and even 'Lenchen', the two-year-old Princess Helena, managed, 'Man shot, tried to shoot dear Mamma, must be punished.' Word of the attempt spread, and the nobility and gentry converged on Buckingham Palace to enquire after the Queen's health. *The Times* later listed over 300 of their names, from His Royal Highness the Count of Syracuse to the Duchess of Roxburghe, before running out of space and adding, 'and numerous others'.

In the vicinity of the great clubs in Regent Street and Pall Mall there were shouts of 'long live the Queen', and along The Mall people sang snatches of the national anthem. At Her Majesty's Theatre, the performance of *The Barber of Seville* was interrupted to give the news that the Queen was safe, and the audience insisted on 'God Save the Queen' being sung, not once, but three times. The routine of a royal birthday had received a vast and visible stimulus.

* * *

William decided not to cooperate with the police. When he was interviewed by the inspector at the Gardener's Lane station house, he at first refused to answer any questions, and only reluctantly gave his name and address. He then said that the pistol was only loaded with powder and that he had no intention of harming the Queen. He did it to get into prison, as he was tired of being out of work. They searched him and found in his pockets the bowl of a pipe, a small quantity of powder, and a few halfpennies. Inspector Otway and Sergeant Langley of the detective force went to his lodgings. They found little in his room except for two shirts, lent to him by his landlady, and a few scraps of paper with writing unrelated to the attack. William was locked up in the cells for the night. He commented to the turnkey that he was pleased to see that they were much cleaner than those in Paris.

The witnesses to the attack were questioned by Superintendent May of 'A' division and Commissioner Mayne. Lord John Russell, Sir George Grey, and other ministers were informed at their various celebrations in honour of the sovereign's birthday. Lord Russell was entertaining a dozen or so noblemen and gentleman at his private residence in Chesham Place, while Sir George Grey was hosting a state banquet at the Clarendon Hotel.

The Privy Council met in the Home Office the following day, Sunday, at two o'clock. Present were Sir George Grey, the Secretary of State for the Home Department; Mr

Waddington, the Undersecretary; the Attorney General; Mr Hall, the Bow Street chief magistrate; and the two commissioners of police. Also there were Sir Charles Wood, the Chancellor of the Exchequer, and Mr W. G. Grey MP, private secretary to Lord John Russell.

William was brought into the room escorted by Superintendent May and Inspector Otway. At the sight of the assembled dignitaries, he turned ashen and started to tremble. Three-quarters of the twenty witnesses in attendance were examined by the Council, and throughout William stood silent, his eyes cast down at the floor. When specifically asked if he had any questions for the witnesses, he mumbled that he did not. His landlord and wife appeared, and their son showed the Council the wooden stock and spout that he and William had played with. He then turned to William and said, 'Here, Hamilton, I can pay you the penny now, for I did not have one on Saturday.'

The examination lasted three hours, and at the end Mr Hall asked the prisoner whether he had anything to say in reply to the charge, but warned him that anything he did say would be taken down and used in evidence against him. William muttered that he had nothing to say. He was then charged with a misdemeanour under the Act of seven years earlier, and remanded to Newgate prison. Being unable to meet the bail terms, he was immediately taken there by Inspector Otway in a cab.

William spent three weeks in Newgate, that dark, dismal labyrinth of wards, courts, and corridors, teeming with prisoners and visitors. The prison was now almost exclusively occupied by people awaiting trial, and as the next session approached, the cells filled with men and women on remand. Although the building was kept scrupulously clean, foul smells predominated and little light or air penetrated from the deep wells of the courtyards. Locked gates at intervals along the corridors separated the different sections, men and women, suspected felons and misdemeanants. William was no doubt confined in one of these crowded wards, the maximum capacity of which was set by the warder in charge to a level of misery that was just bearable. By night, the prisoners slept on the floor using prison mats and blankets, and by day they huddled around the fire or ate the meagre fare at the table.

But William's stay in Newgate did not last long. A Grand Jury[5] sat on Monday 11 June at the Central Criminal Court under the chairmanship of the Recorder to consider the law relating to the charges on the 200 or so cases to be heard in the current session. Most of these were straightforward, but considerable time was spent on Hamilton. The Recorder elucidated the detail of the Peel Act of 1842, which laid down a penalty of seven years transportation beyond the seas or up to three years imprisonment, with or without hard labour, accompanied by up to three public or private whippings. The following evening, a true bill[6] was issued against William Hamilton for shooting at Her Majesty.

The trial took place at 10 a.m. on Thursday 14 June before Lord Chief Justice Wilde, Mr Justice Patteson, and Mr Baron Rolfe. The prosecution consisted of the Attorney General, Mr Welsby, Mr Clarkson, Mr Bodkin, and Mr Clarke, instructed by Mr Hayward. William, with no relatives to support him, was left with no counsel to defend him. He was charged with five counts. The first was that he unlawfully, knowingly, wilfully and maliciously, did discharge a pistol at the Queen with intent to injure her. The second that he discharged it near to the Queen with the intent to harm; the third with discharging it at the Queen with intent to break the public peace; the fourth near the Queen with the same intent; and the fifth was an intent to alarm the Queen.

William, who was still dressed poorly in his labourer's clothes, pleaded 'guilty' in a subdued tone. The Attorney General did not present the case, instead saying that all was before the court in the depositions and he was sure the learned judges were well acquainted and in a position to decide on the punishment. William was asked if there was any reason why the judgement of the court should not be passed upon him. Not knowing what to say in mitigation, and with no lawyer to advise him, he made no reply.

After a short consultation, the Lord Chief Justice summarised the facts and concluded that the prisoner did not mean to cause any serious harm and his motive was only to gain notoriety. He said that, 'It is highly important that persons influenced by the same motives should be taught that the notoriety is short lived, and that it is speedily followed by suffering and degradation.' The court sentenced William to be transported for the term of seven years. Apparently, the Queen had expressed the wish that he should not be flogged.

William showed no emotion and was taken down, back to Newgate and the further misery that awaited him. He did not hear Daniel O'Keefe apply for the pistol to be returned to him, saying that he had been offered £40 for it. The court, amid much laughter, ordered the 'valuable' article to be restored to him.

* * *

Three weeks later, William Hamilton was moved from Newgate to Pentonville, a new 'model' prison that had been constructed five years earlier. It housed young prisoners awaiting transportation; the individual cells had toilet facilities and good ventilation, but the daily regime was soul-destroying. William was introduced to the 'separate system' and spent most of the day in isolated silence. For a few hours he was put to solitary work, and he spent an hour or two in the chapel, standing in a closed booth in the raked auditorium whilst he was harangued by sermons, prayers, and scripture readings. When moving through the corridors or in the exercise yards, he had to wear a mask, as at Millbank, to prevent any visual communication. Breaking of the ban on speaking was punished by a spell in a 'refractory cell' in pitch-black solitary confinement.

Pentonville was also finding that the regime, designed to make the malefactor consider his wrongdoings, was rather driving the prisoners insane. The plan was that inmates would spend eighteen months in such conditions and then be transported to the colonies as Ticket of Leave men. But by the time William arrived, the spells had been reduced as so many had ended up in Bethlem instead. He spent just two and a half months in the prison, where his conduct was described as 'good', but his character as 'indifferent'.

On 25 September, he and sixteen other prisoners were taken to board HMS *Hercules*, which was moored at Greenhithe, near Gravesend. The warship was a seventy-four-gun, third-rate ship of the line, launched in 1815. The day before, a company of 166 officers and men of the Royal Artillery had embarked, bound for Gibraltar. On board also were thirty-three convicts from Millbank Penitentiary, thirty-five other passengers, mainly the families of the officers, plus the crew, making almost 300 persons in total in the small ship. William was not sure which was worse: to be isolated in his solitary cell or crammed with others in the damp stinking hold.

The vessel made slow progress. The following day saw dense fog, and on the twenty-seventh they set sail, but then anchored not far away. Five days later, they made all plain sail, and over the following two days, wallowed down the Thames through a storm with force 9 gales, which added to the plight of William and the other prisoners incarcerated below. The first convict died as the storm abated, and a second passed away four days later.

Another week was spent at anchor in 'the Downs', near to Deal, and they only reached Spithead on 12 October, where they anchored again for four days to take on more supplies. At last, on 16 October, three weeks after William had joined the ship, they hoisted all sail and headed down the English Channel, through the Bay of Biscay. They anchored in Gibraltar Bay on 2 November, but again were forced to languish in quarantine, and only on the seventh did they start to disembark. William had to wait while a full description of each prisoner was recorded, and eventually the clerk noted his birthmark and the many minor scars resulting from his occupation and adventures. Under 'Relations and Next of Kin', he wrote, 'No Friends'.

William was assigned to the prison hulk *Euryalus*. Named after one of Jason's mythical Argonauts, the ship was formerly a thirty-six-gun frigate that saw action at the Battle of Trafalgar and in the war of 1812 with the United States of America. A small vessel of 130 feet by 38 feet, she was converted into a hulk in 1825 and served as a juvenile prison in England, before being moved to Gibraltar in 1847. William was taken to one of about forty 'bays' that lined the three decks. About 18 feet by 15 feet and enclosed by iron bars, each housed eight to ten convicts during the nightly lockdown. Another hulk in Gibraltar, the *Owen Glendower*, was used more as a hospital ship. William listened occasionally as its bell tolled, a warning that another convict had escaped.

William was assigned to a construction gang that worked on the dockyards or the fortifications. The more amenable convicts were allowed to sleep in barracks on land, but William was not well behaved. The conduct of each prisoner was assessed each quarter in a muster involving the chaplain, the officers, and quartermasters, and assigned to categories: very good, good, indifferent, suspicious, bad or very bad. Convicts of the same category were housed together and, unsurprisingly, those in the lower bands were the most disruptive and violent. A pecking order developed in each bay, as the warders made no attempt to control behaviour, and the weakest were victimised ruthlessly. During the day, misbehaviour was dealt with by flogging or the wearing of chains whilst working, eating, and sleeping.

Over the first quarter of 1850, William's conduct was recorded as 'suspicious', and over the next four years the rest of his scorecard read: six 'very bad', one 'bad', one 'indifferent', and seven 'good'. Only in the quarter before he quit Gibraltar did he achieve a 'very good'. The idea was that model inmates could be given a pardon, or serve a much reduced sentence, and those whose behaviour was tolerable would find a seven-year sentence reduced to three years before reaching Ticket of Leave status. But William served nearly five years in Gibraltar, and he must have been counting the days until his release. Then, only two years before his full term was up, he was transported to Australia.

William embarked on the SS *Ramillies* on 17 May 1854, along with 156 others from Gibraltar. They replaced 160 convicts from England, who disembarked for a spell of work on the Rock, and joined 120 other convicts who were bound for Australia. Also on board were sixty-nine pensioner guards[7] and their families, plus a few other warders and the crew, making 412 in total on the small 757-ton barque. They sailed three days later.

The captain was Charles Hodder and the surgeon superintendent was Daniel Ritchie. The latter had to deal with a few cases of measles amongst the children, which luckily did not spread to become an epidemic, and several instances of ophthalmia, but in general, the ship's complement were quite healthy. He remarked on the particularly well-developed muscular systems of the Gibraltarian convicts, for individuals of their class, caused no doubt by the heavy labour. William was thankful that, on dry days, he and the other prisoners were allowed on deck from sunrise to sunset. He had to attend school, either in the morning or afternoon, and there was a library for reading. The surgeon's intention was to prevent slothful apathy, which was 'so often the precursor to disease'.

Quite a few of William's fellow prisoners came from the south-west of Ireland, so no doubt they talked of the old country and the perfidy of the English. Of the 216 convicts on board whose offences were recorded in the criminal registers, more than half were for stealing of one type or another, but there were also sixteen assaults, nine killings, fourteen arsons, fourteen rapes, two cases of sacrilege, one of carnal knowledge, and eight convictions for bestiality, sodomy, or unnatural acts.

There were plenty of stores and provisions, but William found the diet boring. Many of the convicts rejected the oatmeal, but by the time the ship reached colder latitudes, some complained of hunger and took it again for breakfast. The surgeon had greater success when he started to add an ounce of wine to the breakfast gruel. 'So great was the effect this produced in rendering the meal popular,' he wrote, 'that in a few days every man on the lower deck had applied for and received their full ration.' Two gallons of wine per convict were stored for the voyage, and there was a surplus after allowing for the daily ration after dinner of half a gill.[8] The surgeon used wine as a reward, withholding it after bad behaviour. Half a gill was deemed a good quantity: less would not be a reward; more could 'produce an amount of excitement which might lead to some infraction of order'.

Many of William's fellow prisoners from Gibraltar also complained about the unpleasant biscuit. The surgeon agreed to replace the allowance of ¾ lb of biscuit with ½ lb of flour, which seemed to go down well. But this success led to further demands and agitation, and the surgeon re-imposed the old ration, saying that there would be no more changes. At latitude 33.23°N and longitude 9.48°W (off the coast of Morocco), they began to issue lemon juice and sugar. The Admiralty instructions said to combine the mixture with wine to make a kind of sherbet, but the surgeon decided not to do this, as the withdrawal of the wine ration as a punishment would lead to health consequences, and he was loath to let the convicts take the intoxicating wine mixture below, where it might be traded or stolen. The lemon juice ensured that most stayed healthy and there was little sickness during the voyage.

The *Ramillies* reached Fremantle, Western Australia, on 7 August, after a journey of seventy-nine days. Over the following week, William and all the other convicts were disembarked in the Swan River Colony, and William was officially granted Ticket of Leave status on 31 August. Western Australia was still sparsely populated by white people. The colony had been established in June 1829 exclusively for private settlement, and two townships were built: Fremantle as a port at the river mouth, and Perth as the capital halfway between the port and the fertile lands to the east. But settlers arrived only slowly, and by 1850 there were only just over 5,000 whites, with more than half of these in the townships rather than out on the agricultural lands. The colony was still dependent on the Crown financially, and the decision was taken to establish a penal settlement to provide additional labour. Over the next twenty years, nearly 10,000 arrived.

The idea was to take the better-behaved criminals who could immediately work for the settlers as Ticket of Leave men. But most were unskilled and not inclined to hard work, while the pay at Ticket of Leave rates depressed the income of other free men. Apart from a prison, few important public works were completed, and the economy of Western Australia did not really take off until gold was discovered over thirty years later. It is not known what work William was put to, but probably it used his skills as a bricklayer and mason. He finally received a conditional pardon in February 1856, only four months short of when he would have finished his sentence anyway. Presumably this was because of his continuing bad behaviour.

What happened to William after this date is largely unknown. Nothing has been found in the records until twenty-four years later when, on 22 January 1880, he was discharged from Geraldton Hospital. What could have happened in the intervening years? In 1853, convict hiring depots were established outside of Perth so that settlers did not have to travel so far to hire the men they needed. Two were established near Geraldton, a town on the coast about 400 kilometres north of Perth, one at Greenough to the south, and one at Lynton to the north. The latter was established to provide labour for the Geraldine lead mines, about 40 miles north of Geraldton, and was a popular destination for Ticket of Leave and free men. But the work was tough, and a miner's health often suffered.

William might have been one of them, returning to the town with his health broken. Although his hospital discharge record confirms that he arrived in Western Australia aboard the *Ramillies* in 1854, it gives his age as seventy, rather than his actual fifty-three. He might have looked much older than he actually was, or perhaps he lied in order to get charitable support. From Geraldton Hospital, William was transferred to Mount Eliza in Perth, where the convict station had been converted into an invalid depot for indigent and aged men, relieving the load on the poorhouse. He survived another four years, but died in 1884. His death certificate put his age at seventy-five, but in fact he was less than sixty.

Born deprived, William Hamilton tried to better himself in London, but made no progress in escaping his lowly station. His imprisonment and further anguish arose directly from his desperation and anger at the ruling classes. The next of the Queen's attackers was starkly different; he actually came from that world of wealth and privilege.

5

The Gentleman Dandy, 1850

The next attack on the Queen happened barely a year later, and it was the first to cause Victoria actual harm.

The attacker was not Irish, as some had feared. Less than three months after William Hamilton struck, Victoria began a state visit to Ireland, starting in the town of Cork where the Irishman had been born. Many were concerned for her safety and the reception that she might get in such a lawless and afflicted country, while others felt the display of wealth would be an effrontery and she should be shown the poor in their hovels. But in fact the preparations brought much-needed employment, and the reception was generally rapturous. They toured the town in an open landau, and later, in Dublin, Victoria wrote that, 'a more good-humoured crowd I never saw, but noisy and excitable beyond belief, talking, jumping, and shrieking instead of cheering'.

Back in England, Albert threw himself into an exciting new project, which was to become known as the Great Exhibition. For her part, Victoria discovered, much to her displeasure, that she was pregnant again. Their seventh child and third son was delivered on 1 May 1850, a year to the day before the Great Exhibition was due to open. He was christened Arthur, after the Duke of Wellington, who had been born on the same day eighty-one years earlier. Wellington became one of the boy's godparents at the christening towards the end of June.

As her newborn was welcomed into the world, the Queen's elderly uncle, the Duke of Cambridge, was seriously ill and approaching the end of his life. Five days after the christening, she went to visit him. Having become used to assassination attempts on Constitution Hill and in the vicinity of Buckingham Palace, nothing prepared Victoria for an attack just outside her uncle's residence.

On Thursday 27 June, she set out in an open barouche and four from Buckingham Palace, accompanied by Viscountess Jocelyn, lady-in-waiting, and three of her children: the Prince of Wales, Prince Alfred, and Princess Alice. Robert Renwick, the sergeant footman, was seated in the rumble behind Her Majesty. Cambridge House was not far away in Piccadilly, just opposite Green Park and about a quarter of a mile from Hyde Park Corner. They arrived just before six o'clock, and the visit was to last about half an hour.

While the carriage was waiting at the gates, a crowd of around 200 people gathered hoping to catch a glimpse of Her Majesty. Amongst them was a gentleman, fancily dressed in an open blue frock coat, top hat, and carrying a short partridge cane with a brass ferule. He was about 6 foot tall and slender, with a light, delicate complexion, very light brown hair, and he wore mustachios like a military man. A premature baldness over the crown of his head made him look older than his thirty years, and his high forehead revealed a few wrinkles, which twitched in a strange fashion.

The gentleman stood for a few minutes, taking in the scene, a serious expression on his face, and then turned and strode off down Piccadilly. He walked strangely, his head thrown back, kicking his heels up and swinging his arms and cane. He had not gone far when he turned and went back to Cambridge House.

He moved through the crowd on the left side of the exit gate from the courtyard, pushing in front of a bystander, to reach the edge of the kerb. The displaced man was annoyed, but said nothing, respecting the intruder's rank as a gentleman. Soon afterwards, the Queen and the rest of the party emerged and got back into the carriage. At twenty past six, the cortège moved off. Two outriders went first, followed by the barouche steered by the postillions. Lastly, on horseback, came the equerry-in-waiting, Colonel the Honourable Charles Grey. The carriage moved slowly and as the outriders cleared the road, came to a temporary stop exactly opposite the gentleman.

Suddenly the man sprang forward and struck the Queen with his cane. Victoria fell to one side and the children cried out. Renwick, seated behind the sovereign, leapt forward and grabbed the man's collar. The postillions, in the act of turning into the road, looked back and pulled up the horses.

The Queen said, 'Go on, Renwick, I am not hurt', although her bonnet was stove in and blood showed on her forehead. She rearranged her hat. As the carriage drove up Piccadilly towards Buckingham Palace, she tried to show no outward signs of alarm and acknowledged the cheering of the crowds.

Back outside Cambridge House, someone shouted, 'The villain has struck the Queen.' The first to lay hold of the attacker was a shop assistant who worked nearby, followed quickly by the man he had pushed in front of, who took him by the arm. Several others grabbed him, and one man hit him with his fist, drawing blood. Worse would have followed if the police had not then arrived. Sergeant Silver had heard the cry and ran to the spot to find the attacker in the hands of the crowd. With the assistance of other constables, he managed to wrest the man away from the mob, and took him off in the direction of Vine Street police house.

At Buckingham Palace, Sir James Clark, the Queen's physician, was sent for and arrived soon after eight o'clock. He examined Her Majesty's forehead and found a livid mark on the outer angle of the right brow and a small cut, which had been bleeding, although by then it had stopped. He was surprised that so small a weapon had broken the skin, but assumed it must have been used violently as it had sliced through her bonnet. By the next day, the bruise had become a bump the size of a walnut.

After being seen by the doctor, the Queen decided to continue with her evening schedule despite her wound. She was due to take christening guests to a production of Meyerbeer's *Le Prophète* at the Covent Garden Italian Opera, and she entered the royal box part-way through the performance. The first act was over and the skating divertissement of the second act was proceeding, when a loud cry came from the pit: 'The Queen! The Queen! God Save the Queen!' All eyes turned to the royal box, where Victoria stood alone. The audience and musicians rose to their feet as one, and a chorus went up for the national anthem. In seconds, the cast appeared on the stage, the band struck up, and all three verses were sung, led by the opera's soloists. The cheering continued for a long time afterwards, as the Queen continued to stand, saluting the audience.

The Times wrote the next day:

> It was, indeed, a sight that must have moved every breast capable of manly sentiment. A young and defenceless woman, a Royal lady, [...] had been attacked in the streets by a scoundrel or madman [...] Yet, in spite of this, scarcely three hours later [...] she came, as though nothing had happened, the mark of the ruffian's violence plainly visible on her forehead.

During the evening, the Queen met with the Prime Minister, Lord John Russell, and remarked to him, 'I know the man who struck me perfectly well by sight; I meet him oftener in the Parks, and he makes a point of bowing more frequently and lower to me than anyone else.' Albert wrote the next day to Baron von Stockmar:

> Victoria, thank God, is well, although her forehead is much bruised, and her nerves are still somewhat shaken by the shameful occurrence of yesterday. The perpetrator is a dandy, whom you must often have seen in the Park, where he had made himself conspicuous. He maintains the closest silence as to his motives, but is manifestly deranged. All this does not help to make one cheerful.

In a letter to her uncle the King of the Belgians, on 2 July, Victoria wrote:

> I have not suffered except from my head, which is still very tender, the blow having been extremely violent, and the brass end of the stick fell on my head so as to make a considerable noise. I own it makes me nervous out driving, and I start at any person coming near the carriage, which I am afraid is natural.

* * *

The attacker's name was Robert Pate, and several episodes in his youth and later should have warned of his mental instability. He came originally from the fenlands in the north of Cambridgeshire, a world away from the smart streets of London. His father was a man of property in Wisbech, where he had carried on a business as a corn factor[1] and merchant, but now lived the life of a gentleman. He was a self-made man who came from humble and unhappy origins.

Robert's grandfather was born around 1751 in Cambridgeshire, and married when he was twenty-two years old. The couple moved to Thorney, an important ecclesiastical centre in the fens, where the monks of the abbey had, in olden times, supervised the maintenance of the drainage waterways. There followed a succession of deaths. The couple produced three children, all of whom died young, and then their mother died too. Robert's grandfather remarried less than two years later and sired another eight children. Of these, four died as infants, and one at six years old, leaving just three survivors from the total of eleven children. Robert Francis Pate, the attacker's father, was the eldest, baptised in 1786, followed by his sister Mary in 1793, and brother William in 1794.

This litany of deaths reflected the low life expectancy in the fens. The dreary, foggy, and boggy wastes caused rheumatism, neuralgia, and fevers, and in summer most people contracted fen ague.[2] The brackish water gave off a sulphurous odour, and the disease was supposed to result from inhaling the miasma. Opium was used widely to suppress the first stages of the ague, and many gardens cultivated a patch of white poppies. Indeed, general consumption of the drug was great, and Ely was said to be a city of opium-eaters. Poppy tea was also a widespread sedative given to babies, and infant mortality was probably worsened by the resulting suppression of appetite and other deleterious effects.

But the fen drainage in the area created fertile lands, and Robert's grandfather prospered as a farmer. By 1800, he owned around 60 acres of land in Murrow Watch in Wisbech Hundred, a few miles from Thorney, which he worked himself. He died in 1809, by which time his eldest son was twenty-two. Sometime afterwards, Robert's father moved to Wisbech and went into business with his brother, William, as a corn factor and merchant. Both brothers married during the course of the 1810s, only for the high mortality rate to cause further sorrow. Robert's father married Maria, and a daughter, Sarah, was born in 1818, but died three months later. Two healthy babies followed, with Robert born in 1819 and his sister Mary two years later. But their mother died soon after and their unhappy father buried her in Wisbech St Peter, beneath a memorial plaque placed in the floor of the nave.

Robert Pate was born on Christmas Day, 1819, and baptised on Boxing Day, but his childhood was not blessed by his birth on that joyous day. Losing his mother when he was sixteen months old, he grew up without maternal influence as his father did not remarry until much later. But he did become very close to his sister Mary, fifteen months his junior, who became a steadying influence later in life. Materially, he also lacked for nothing, as his father was becoming wealthy.

They owned and lived in a large three-storey house on the Old Market, on the far side of the River Nene from Wisbech town centre. The Old Market was so called even in the thirteenth century, and probably dated from Saxon times, before being replaced by the New Market alongside the Norman castle in the 1100s. The Pate warehouses were just across the road from their house, bordering on the river where the ships could tie up. The Nene was a navigable river and Wisbech was the port for Cambridgeshire and the main town for the surrounding area at the north end of the fens. North 12 miles down the Nene lay the vast expanse of the Wash, while 18 miles across the flatlands to the south, the stone galleon of Ely Cathedral sailed above the watery fenland.

As a boy, Robert must have enjoyed the bustle of the port and grown used to the damp world of the surrounding countryside. Drainage of the marshland continued apace, but as the peat dried out in the south of the fens, it shrank. The whole area had been barely above sea level, but the effect was to make the land lower than the Wash. Dutch engineers helped build banks, and hundreds of windmill pumps were constructed to raise water on the way to its outfall. But often, in the winter, high tides created floods in the north of the region, and heavy rains did the same in the south. The fiercely independent fen men, who had not profited from the drainage, saw the works as a curse against the natural order.

Robert grew up in a privileged environment, playing with the children of the merchant class and probably afraid of the local ragamuffin children of the fen men. In 1830, the River Nene was deepened between Wisbech and the sea. The town was already an important port, but the lessening of the flood risk and the improved ship navigation saw prosperity grow further. The windmill pumps were gradually being replaced by steam, so Robert's father's business of importing coal and exporting corn prospered. Until the railways changed the economics of distribution, the best way to send corn to London from the region was via Wisbech. By the 1840s, the corn market was one of the largest in the country.

When he was about ten, Robert was sent away to board at a small private school in Norwich run by the Revd Thomas Currie. It must have been a shock for the young lad, taken away from the town he knew, his friends, and his adored sister. The Revd Currie was also probably not a very proficient or dedicated teacher; he had been a master at the grammar school in the town, but resigned when he was passed over for the headmastership, and instead made a living by taking six pupils into his home at Upper Close. This was obviously not his preferred occupation, as, while Robert was his pupil, he tried several times to secure a senior position at a school elsewhere or a living in a parish, but without success.

Robert's father was gradually moving up the social scale from being just a merchant to a highly respected member of the community and a gentleman. He was a magistrate and a member of the town council and, in 1831, he was appointed as a Deputy High Lieutenant of the county by the Lieutenant, the Earl of Hardwicke. The appointment was approved by King William IV under an act of George III, and his responsibilities were particularly associated with the militia.

While Robert was away at school, his father remarried. In 1834, after thirteen years alone, he married Mary Anne Orton, the wealthy widow of a fellow magistrate of the town. Her former husband had died while administering justice from the bench, barely twelve months earlier. She should still have been in mourning, but perhaps they could not wait. As well as the wealth that she brought to the marriage, his bride was rich enough to put over £5,000 into a pre-nuptial trust for her own use. Robert's father was then forty-seven and his bride one year younger; unsurprisingly, there were no more children. Perhaps, also, the union was not as close as with his first wife. When she died twenty years later, he did not have her name added to the inscription on the church memorial plaque.

His father's second wife arrived too late to have an influence on Robert's upbringing, and it seems unlikely that he warmed to his new stepmother. In 1836, the partnership between Robert's father and uncle in 'Wisbech, Peterborough and Ely' was dissolved, perhaps because Robert Francis wanted complete ownership of his prospering enterprise. Around 1840, he moved around the corner from the Old Market to North Brink, a street of fine houses overlooking the river and the town. He bought a large three-storey house next to his friend, the solicitor Edward Hugh Jackson. The next mansion beyond was both the home and the bank belonging to his two friends William and Alexander Peckover. Increasingly, Robert Francis was in competition with the bank, lending money in mortgages to members of the church community.

Around 1837, Robert returned from his schooling in Norwich, and the question of his future profession arose. It would have been natural for him to be groomed to take over the corn factor business, but this did not happen. Perhaps his father did not think his son was intelligent enough, or perhaps he was already behaving strangely. Much later his father said, 'I was always uncomfortable about him.' An alternative explanation is that his father was already set on retiring from business and wanted his son to follow a gentleman's calling rather than a trade.

The army was chosen as a suitable occupation, which Robert went along with, and expressed an interest in joining the 10th Hussars, a prestigious regiment. It would be a way to make connections with the sons of aristocrats, although no doubt they would never allow him to forget that his wealth came from trade. An approach to purchase a cornetcy in the regiment was made in 1838 by a friend, Mr Thomas Charles Harrison of the Treasury. He attested that Robert was a fine gentlemanly youth of eighteen, and that his father was a gentleman of considerable property at Wisbech, who would allow his son £400 or £500 a year, in addition to his pay.

The 10th Hussars, also known as 'The Prince of Wales's Own', was a cavalry regiment, and can trace its origins back to 1715 and the Jacobite rebellion. The official price for a commission in the cavalry was £840 for cornet and £1,190 for a lieutenant, but often a premium was paid to the previous incumbent or the regiment. The 10th was a prestigious choice, with many well-connected officers, so the premium would have been quite high. A system of commission purchase ensured that officers belonged to the higher social class, had a financial stake in the regiment, and were less likely to encourage looting. It did mean that gentlemen took positions of command over the more experienced lower ranks, but the worst of the incompetents could be weeded out through the commanding officer's veto and an obligatory period of training.

While he waited for a vacancy, Robert's father ensured that his son prepared for life as a young officer. In late 1838, he was to be found in Edinburgh, where he may have been undergoing military training. At some point, he also travelled to Malta, perhaps to broaden his horizons. On 5 February 1841, he was finally selected and appointed to a cornetcy by purchase in the 10th Hussars. Soon after that, his regiment was sent to Dublin, to join the large military force in Ireland that was keeping a lid on the unrest. The following year, they moved to Ballincolig, a few miles west of Cork, and then to Cahir in Tipperary. The regiment was not involved in any major action, and the existence in Cahir was pleasant enough. The town boasted an ancient castle situated on an island in the salmon-filled River Suir, and was enclosed by the rolling Irish countryside and the nearby mountains of Galtee and Knockmealdown. Robert became a lieutenant by purchase on 22 July 1842.

* * *

Two years later, a personal disaster befell Robert. Initially, the commanding officer, Lieutenant-Colonel John Vandeleur, had thought Robert a gentleman of mild demeanour who carried out his duties rather well. He was also quite liked in the regiment, according to colleague and friend Captain Frith, and was temperate in his habits. But all this changed in 1844.

Robert owned a fine Newfoundland dog and two favourite horses, which he adored and was closer to than any of his colleagues. One day, the animals were attacked and bitten by a mad dog, the property of Captain Wallington. A few weeks later, all three started to display the symptoms of rabies, and the commanding officer took the decision to destroy them. Nothing that Robert said would dissuade Colonel Vandeleur from carrying out the sentence of death. After his horse 'Ottoman' had been shot, Robert lay down beside it and cried. He was inconsolable, and it tipped him over the edge.

Robert became reserved and morose, and started to behave strangely. He ceased to take any pleasure in the discharge of his duties and cut his hair very short, so it often appeared shaved. Sometimes he would stare into the distance, lost in thought, and then walk away quickly.

He soon acquired the nickname 'cracked pate'. He avoided company and took long solitary walks. Sometimes he was reserved and sometimes wild and excited, without any apparent cause. He often complained of being ill, saying he had bricks and stones in his stomach and bowels, and that the surgeon could give him no relief. He fancied that the cook and the mess man intended to poison him.

In correspondence with the Duke of Wellington, his father claimed compensation from Captain Wallington for the loss of the horses. Robert was upset that such a claim should be made, and felt further estranged from his fellow officers. The following year, the colonel sent him in charge of a detachment from Newbridge to Dublin, with orders to return the next day. But he left them in Dublin, and returned to England without leave, taking the boat to Liverpool. He made his way to his father's house, where he explained that he had to escape because persons were conspiring to take his life. He said he had been hunted through the Dublin streets by various people, who he had also seen at the barracks and in hotels in London. His father was astonished and hurt by his conduct, and warned his son that he could be shot for the offence. Robert was past caring and said that it could not be helped. His father ordered him to return, and Robert left the next morning, catching the first boat to Dublin.

He returned to the regiment ten days after his abrupt departure, looking wild and giving no explanation. The colonel informed General Wyndham, but court martial proceedings were not taken. The following year, 1845, the regiment returned to England after four years in Ireland, and were stationed in York. An unpleasant surprise came soon afterwards, when they were told to prepare for service in India. Early in 1846, the colonel wrote to Robert's father advising him to take him out of the regiment because of his erratic behaviour. Robert duly resigned, but as it was just a short time before his regiment was to embark for India, his action was taken as a sign of weakness or cowardice. In March 1846, Robert travelled to London, where he sold his commission without his father's knowledge, for £1,800. After payment of his debts, he was left with £1,200.

That same month, Robert took lodgings in Jermyn Street in London, the parallel street to fashionable Piccadilly. Charles Dodson, who had been his servant in the army, accompanied him to act in the same capacity. Robert liked to have a regular pattern to his day, and he always rose at seven o'clock, first putting his head into a large basin filled from two pails of water. He then took a bath, in which he put half a pint of whisky and two-thirds of an ounce of camphor. While in the bath he liked to shout loudly and sometimes sing. Every day at 11.45 a.m., he would go and dress, meticulously selecting from his fine wardrobe. But he didn't like change and always wore the same sort of clothes, winter and summer, and he kept a fire going whatever the season.

Robert lived the life of a recluse, never mixing with society and keeping his blinds drawn down. During eighteen months, he received only one guest. When Captain Frith called once, Robert said that he did not want to receive anyone, so his erstwhile friend never visited again. He paid his bills regularly, filing the receipts away, but never went to church or studied the Bible. Instead he read the newspapers and books, including a compendium of nursery rhymes and a study of the works of Hogarth.

He also liked to go for walks, and from November he took a regular outing by cab. Precisely as St James's clock chimed a quarter past three each day, he would go down, brooking no delay. He would generously pay the cabbie 9s for the ride, which Dodson always had to supply as nine shilling coins, with a sixpence and a penny to pay the gates and the bridge. No other coins would do, and Pate paid the coins to the cabbie with the heads uppermost.

He always used the same cab driver, a man called Edward Lee, and they always took the same route: down the Brompton Road and over Putney Bridge to a particular spot on Putney Heath. Robert would then get out and walk through the thickest furze bushes and gorse, rain, hail, or snow, and meet up with the cabbie by a pond ten minutes later. Sometimes he was wet through as a result, but he didn't mind. After staring at the water for a while, he would jump into the cab, and they would proceed to a spot on Barnes Common. Again he would walk through the furze bushes, and then they would return via Hammersmith Bridge. Sometimes he would ask to go at a gallop, and sometimes at walking pace. These outings continued for fifteen to eighteen months every day, including Sundays.

While he was living in Jermyn Street, he caused something of a sensation by printing handbills laying claim to the throne as a descendent of Henry VIII. The tract contained lengthy quotations from the scriptures and was posted on the Temple-bar gates. He would also sometimes grab respectable females, ask their name, stare vacantly at them for a few moments, and then dart off. He was well known at the opera, where his conduct drew attention, and he was ultimately refused admission.

Robert's expenditure was greater than the allowance he received from his father, and after a year or so, the money from the sale of his commission ran out. He was not on good terms with his father, and his repeated requests for a higher allowance were refused. He never went home to Wisbech, except once in 1847. That was the year Robert's father received the honour of being appointed High Sheriff for Cambridgeshire and Huntingdonshire, a position that required him to obtain a coat of arms. By then, he had retired from active business and was viewed as a member of the gentry. As High Sheriff that year, he was one of the dignitaries who received Her Majesty on the occasion of the installation of Prince Albert as Chancellor of Cambridge University.

In December 1847, he was forced to intervene to pay off his son's debts. Regardless of the expense, Robert then moved round the corner to an elegant suite of apartments on the third floor above Messrs Fortnum & Mason's premises, on the corner of Duke Street and Piccadilly. He hung his cap and sword from the Hussars on one of the walls, kept his possessions and extensive wardrobe orderly, but continued to shrink from society. He would sit for hours at the window without reading or occupation of any kind. Some of his time was spent writing, and later, some of the manuscripts were described as 'very curious lucubrations'.[3] He never drank spirits or wine, and for long periods, retired to bed at eight o'clock every evening.

The cab rides stopped, perhaps due to lack of funds, but he walked extensively. He would leave home at midday, usually not returning until dinner time. He mostly went to one of the royal parks, but he was often also seen in the West End, where he attracted attention by his strange gait. His hat was pushed far back on his head, his face elevated towards the sky, causing such a curve in his back that his coat hung and swung about him like a sack. He kept his countenance extremely serious, while swinging his legs and arms and flourishing a light cane. A spectator seeing this burlesque might wonder whether it was an ostentatious fool, or a wag performing some absurdity for a wager.

Walking did not cost him money, but his expenditure continued to exceed his income. In 1849, he was expelled from the Army & Navy Club for non-payment of his subscription, where, in any case, he was much disliked because of his strange behaviour and suspected cowardice. But later that same year, his beloved sister came to live in London, and he broke his reclusion to visit her on several occasions. She was living close by in Savile Row with the family of a friend of their father's, James Startin, who was a consulting surgeon.

In the autumn of 1849, when Robert Francis met his son in London, he was shocked by his extraordinary appearance. He consulted a medical friend, who put him in touch with Dr John Conolly, who had been the head physician of Hanwell Lunatic Asylum and had given evidence at Oxford's trial, but who now had his own private practice. Dr Connolly offered advice, but did not meet with Robert for fear of alarming him and making his condition worse. He said that he thought Pate had 'a very small share of mental power, without object or ambition, and unfit for all the ordinary duties of life'. He hoped that Robert's sister's presence would be a stabilising influence and might gradually bring him out of his reclusion.

But the following January, she married the brother of her host, William Startin, who was a widower, architect and engineer, twelve years her senior. William needed to travel for his work, and, not long after their marriage, they left for Jersey in the Channel Islands.

No further attempt was made to tackle Robert's mental problems, and in the spring the keeper of a livery stable on the corner of Park Lane and Piccadilly, Charles Mason, noticed a change in his appearance and behaviour. Robert had used the stable to keep some horses until he had given them up after being thrown in November 1846, but he continued to acknowledge the man as he passed on his walks. The keeper would call out a greeting, and Robert would reply in a gentlemanly and friendly fashion, 'How do you do, Mason?' But by the middle of May, his appearance had become wild and he would say nothing, shaking his cane in irritation.

Later, on the fateful day in June when the Queen visited her sick uncle, Robert encountered Captain Frith at about three o'clock, halfway between Duke Street and Hyde Park Corner. The swinging of his arms and stick seemed even more excited than normal, and although he acknowledged the captain, he did not stop to talk.

His route to and from Hyde Park took him past Cambridge House. By chance, the Revd Charles Driscoll, who had met Robert at the Startin's residence, was travelling on an omnibus[4] down Piccadilly at about six o'clock, on his way to dine at the Army & Navy Club. As the omnibus struggled with the traffic, he saw Pate outside the Duke of Cambridge's house, standing on the west side of the east gate. He stood for two or three minutes, and then strode away westwards, his coat flung back and throwing his heels up as he walked.

Then the omnibus moved forward, and Robert Pate disappeared from view. Revd Driscoll neither saw him return nor what happened twenty minutes later.

* * *

Sergeant Silver of 'C' division took the Queen's attacker into custody and escorted him to Vine Street. At the station house, Robert Pate gave his name and address, describing himself as a retired lieutenant of the 10th Hussars. James Summers, the man who was one of the first to take hold of the assailant, gave his witness statement, as did many others from the crowd: Lieutenant Charles William Doherty; Daniel Farrar (carpenter); Samuel Cowling (bookseller); William Gower (builder); William Phillips (porter), and Thomas Harrison (cab driver).

When asked what he had to say to the charge, Robert said that it was true that he had struck Her Majesty a slight blow with a thin stick, 'but those men cannot prove whether I struck her head or her bonnet'. He refused to give his motive, and was taken to the cells. On being searched, two keys and a pocket handkerchief were found, but no money or weapon. Robert did not feel sleepy, just restless, and he passed the night chatting to the two officers assigned to watch over him. He did not talk about his action, but frequently asked about the ordinary night-time cases that were brought to the cells. Later, he said it was the result of a momentary impulse which he was unable to control.

The following morning, another inspector at Vine Street who came from Wisbech recognised the prisoner. He said to him, 'I wish to heaven I had been at your right hand yesterday, and then this should not have happened.' Robert replied, 'I wish to heaven you had', and added that 'he had felt very low for some time past'. But he remained determined to avoid actually talking about the crime. Mr Otway, the newly promoted superintendent of C division, sent Inspector Field, the chief officer of the detective force, to search the man's lodgings. A great many papers and documents were seized.

At noon the next day, the prisoner was brought out, to the hooting of the gathered crowd, and taken by cab to the Home Office, accompanied by Superintendent Otway and Inspector Whall. Robert was quite the dandy, wearing a loose blue frock coat, a white double-breasted waistcoat buttoned closely up to the throat, a blue neckerchief, a pair of tweed trousers, and buttoned boots. He was put in an anteroom and sat nonchalantly in a chair, with his right arm over the back and hands locked together. On being summoned a few minutes later into the main room, he picked up his hat and walked to the door with a careless and somewhat lounging gait.

At the Home Office were assembled the Home Secretary, Sir George Grey; the Chancellor of the Exchequer; the Military Secretary; the Attorney General; Mr Hall, the Chief Police Magistrate; and others. Robert, who showed no emotion, was introduced, and stood at the end of the table while the charge was read by Mr Mayne, the Chief Commissioner of Police. Immediately afterwards, Mr Hardisty of Great Marlborough Street, solicitor to the Pate family (and a cousin once removed of Robert's stepmother), entered the room, accompanied by Mr Huddleston, barrister, who would represent the prisoner.

The witnesses were then questioned: Colonel the Honourable Charles Grey, equerry to the Queen; Robert Renwick, the sergeant footman; Sergeant Silver; and Samuel Cowling, the man Robert had pushed in front of. The latter witness, who had lost his hat in the subsequent melee, asked for recompense as he was very poor. The Attorney General assured him that his claim would be liberally satisfied. Robert was told that he could ask questions of the witnesses, but he declined. However, when the Attorney General asked for an adjournment until Tuesday next, his barrister asked that it be delayed until the following Friday. This was agreed to.

The committal was made out, and at this point Robert asked for some books to be brought from his library, including Guizot's *History of Civilization* and *Palace of Architecture*. He was taken by cab, accompanied by Superintendent Otway to the House of Detention at Pentonville. As they emerged from the Home Office, the hissing and hooting by the crowd was fearful. There were cries of 'scoundrel' and 'rascal', and it was with some difficulty that the police protected the prisoner from summary vengeance.

Robert's father arrived in town during the course of the afternoon, but was unable to see his son. At Pentonville, the prisoner was given over to the care of the governor, Lieutenant Hill, and put in an ordinary cell by himself. He asked about food, and was told he could buy his own, but opted for the prison allowance and ate most of it. He was visited by Mr Wakefield, the surgeon, who pronounced him healthy and apparently sane. Over the next few days, he appeared content with his situation, spending his time in reading and study, although he missed his normal daily exercise.

Robert appeared again before the Privy Council at the Home Office on Friday 5 July. He did not feel well and was more anxious than previously. He was dressed as before, but his eyes were vacant and he felt more dejected, casting thoughtful glances at those present. Six witnesses were interviewed, and then Robert was committed to Newgate prison. On 9 July, the Grand Jury issued a bill against Robert Pate, and the hearing was fixed for just two days later, Thursday 11 July.

The Old Bailey was full. At ten o'clock, the learned judges entered the court: Mr Baron Alderson, Mr Justice Patteson, and Mr Justice Talfourd, accompanied by the Lord Mayor and several other dignitaries. The Attorney General and three other gentlemen represented the Crown, while Mr Cockburn QC and Mr Huddleston acted for the defendant. Robert was brought up, walked to the front of the dock and bowed slightly. He was very well dressed and maintained his erect military appearance. He was charged with 'having an offensive weapon, that is to say a stick, and unlawfully and maliciously striking at the person of our Lady the Queen with the intent to injure [her]'. The second count was the same except the intent was to alarm her, and the third count was intending to break the public peace. Robert pleaded 'not guilty' in a loud voice.

The Attorney General began his speech by saying it was with great regret that he found himself prosecuting this case. On the one hand, the object of the attack was a lady and a sovereign who had endeared herself to her subjects by her great virtues, and on the other, the person charged with the offence filled the position of a gentleman and a man of education, and had at one time held Her Majesty's commission. He felt these were circumstances which very greatly aggravated the offence. He called upon Colonel Grey, Robert Renwick, Sergeant Silver, and Samuel Cowling to establish the facts of the attack, and Sir James Clark to detail the injuries.

Mr Cockburn rose for the defence and also spoke of his abhorrence of the attack, 'Upon a sovereign who is revered and loved by all classes of her subjects [...] perhaps more than any other who had filled the throne of these realms.' But he planned to show that the man in the dock was in a state of mind that rendered him not responsible for his actions. He first argued that no sane man would commit such an act. The motives of a desire for notoriety or escape from poverty could not be construed for his client. It could not be a political act with such an inadequate weapon, but was the motiveless act of an insane mind.

Mr Cockburn called many witnesses to attest to Pate's strange behaviour in the army, particularly the episode concerning the horses: Colonel John Vandeleur, Captain Frith, Captain Sir Thomas Munro, Corporal Thomas Venn, Sergeant George Pitt, and Trumpeter Thomas Martin. He also called the prisoner's father; Charles Dodman, his servant; Edward Lee, Pate's cab driver; and Charles Mason, the livery stable keeper. James Startin spoke about how he had written to Robert's father concerning the prisoner's behaviour, and his strange antics were described by George Gardner, the beadle of the Burlington Arcade, and Inspector Squire of the Metropolitan Police. Because of the way that he wielded his cane, he was known by one witness as 'cut and thrust'. Two witnesses who had known the defendant through the Startins, the Revd Charles Driscoll and the flamboyant Irish MP O'Gorman Mahon, said that they considered him not right in the head.

Dr Connolly gave evidence that he thought him of unsound mind, someone who would know the difference between right and wrong, but was subject to sudden impulses of passion. Dr Munro agreed with the diagnosis, and concurred that there was no specific delusion. When he said again that he was sure he was of unsound mind, the lead judge Baron Alderson asked him to 'be so good as not to take upon yourself the functions of judge and jury'.

The Attorney General delivered his closing speech, saying that it was freely admitted that the prisoner had struck the Queen, but the defence were asking for a lenient sentence on the grounds of a weak mind. They did not claim insanity, which would lock him away for life. Baron Alderson summed up. He said that the intention 'to injure Her Majesty was apparent from the fact that he actually did injure her'. It was clear that, at the present time, the prisoner was sane, and the onus fell on the defence to prove that he wasn't at the time the offence was committed. Further, he said it had to be a delusion that drove him to commit the act, 'It was not because a man was insane, that therefore he was dispunishable – that was a grievous delusion under which medical men laboured.' The question came down to whether the man knew it was wrong to strike the Queen. 'A man might say that he picked a pocket from some uncontrollable impulse; and in that case the law would have an uncontrollable impulse to punish him for it.'

The jury retired at 3.20 p.m., and was out for nearly four hours. When they returned at 7.05 p.m., they found the defendant guilty. Baron Alderson said there was no doubt that the jury had come to the right conclusion. He admitted to the prisoner that 'it has pleased God to visit you with some mental affliction', but then railed about the awfulness of the offence. He said that 'considering the station of your family and your own position, the Court will not inflict the disgraceful punishment of whipping upon you', but he did sentence Pate to be transported beyond the seas for the term of seven years.

Robert listened to the sentence without showing any emotion, and when the judge had finished, he bowed to the court, immediately turned round, and without uttering a word returned to gaol. The trial had lasted nearly nine hours.

The next day, his father wrote to his friend and banker William Peckover: 'Although the Sentence is dreadful it is considered the best of the three.' It would appear that the defence thought that the alternatives – incarceration in a mental hospital indefinitely, or imprisonment for up to three years accompanied by the disgrace of public whipping – were worse outcomes, even though the latter was classified as a lesser sentence. Perhaps gentlemanly dignity was more important than the actual punishment. Nevertheless, Robert Francis was much affected and continued, 'Such a day to me it was as I shall never forget, if I get over it [...] It is a heart-breaking affair but it must be borne, and I hope Providence will enable us to stand up against it.' He also asked in the letter for the transfer of £200 to a local bank, presumably as funds to alleviate his son's condition.

The judge's comment on whipping being an unsuitable punishment for people of their station became the subject of a question in the House of Commons two days later. Mr George Thompson inquired of Sir George Grey whether he would make any representations on the remark, which was 'likely to materially affect public opinion as to the administration of justice'. The Home Secretary replied that it was not his duty to call the judge to account.

Why did Robert Pate make the attack? One speculation at the time was that it was as a result of a bet – he mixed with high Tories and Orange supporters in the regiment and probably lost money gambling with them. The suggestion was that he was told that he would have a gambling debt cleared if he dealt the Whig-sympathising monarch a lesson. But this seems very unlikely, years after he had started living as a recluse.

The Zoist, a journal of cerebral physiology and mesmerism, said that he came across the Queen by chance while out walking and, presented with the sovereign before him, he just acted irrationally. The publication raged about the conduct of the trial. In particular, it described the Solicitor General's ethics as 'at variance with practical medicine, and so strongly opposed to the knowledge and experience of so many excellent physiologists'. The judge's summing up was felt to be even more inaccurate, and that only when Mr Baron Alderson has 'studied cerebral pathology [...] shall we receive his dictum'. The defence counsel, Mr Cockburn, the article said, gave but 'a feeble exposition of the law of lunacy', but then, perhaps that was his intention.

In fact, the legal profession was following the definition in the 'McNaghten Rules' of 1843, that specified that an insanity defence must show that 'at the time of the commission of the acts constituting the offense, the defendant as a result of a severe mental disease or defect, was unable to appreciate the nature and quality of the wrongfulness of his acts'. But *The Zoist* stated that 'neither consciousness nor the ability to distinguish right from wrong constitutes anything like a test of either the sanity or responsibility of an individual', and that this truth could be attested to by a visit to any lunatic asylum. The journal was in no doubt that Pate 'was clearly insane, and that his last act was merely the termination of an absurd series of movements, the promptings of a diseased brain'.[5] If he had been cared for properly earlier, the whole affair might well have been avoided.

* * *

After one more night in Newgate, Robert Pate was taken to Millbank Prison, but he was treated altogether differently to the other prisoners. After a spell in the infirmary because of the delicate state of his health, he was assigned to a room belonging to one of the prison officers, rather than a common cell. His hair was not cropped, and he was allowed to wear his own linen, while a tailor visited him to take his measurements for custom prison dress, rather than the standard bulk issue. He exercised in a separate yard, ate food specially prepared for him, and was visited by the governor on several occasions.

The newspapers heard of this special treatment and questioned the apparent leniency. But his father was grateful, and a few weeks later, he wrote to Sir George Grey saying that he was 'well aware that my son has been most indulgently treated in his confinement', but that he feared for the rest of his sentence and pleaded to Her Majesty for further indulgence.

Three weeks later, Robert Pate was seen off by the governor and, accompanied only by the infirmary warder, taken to the sailing ship *William Jardine* at Portsmouth. Sir George Grey, mindful of the impression of favouritism given by the newspaper reports, made it known to the commander of the *William Jardine* that Pate should not 'be in any way excepted from the Regulations applicable to persons in his condition'. Nevertheless, a certain amount of money accompanied Robert that was probably used to buy favours.

Robert was one of the last to join the boat, which set sail on 12 August. There were 261 male convicts on board, most of who had already served much of their sentences and would be Ticket of Leave men in Australia. There were just seventeen convicts headed for incarceration, of which Robert was one. He was depressed and fearful of what awaited him, but some privileges remained. Rather than being confined in the communal cells, he was allowed a berth in the hospital, because of 'his low and despondent state'.

The *William Jardine* was a ship of 670 tons, lofty between the decks and recently refurbished. It was a fast passage, just ninety-four days, but Robert's mood did not improve. The surgeon superintendent thought his manner absent and peculiar, saying that he was not disposed to enter into conversation with anyone. He even declined the use of books, claiming that 'reading made his head ache'. It was an uneventful passage, with the convicts unwilling to endanger their Ticket of Leave status by bad behaviour.

The vessel docked in Hobart on 14 November, and in the more egalitarian society of Australia, his special privileges largely came to an end. His period of probation was set at twelve months, and after a few days he was taken to join the gang at Cascades Punishment Station. Named after a waterfall in the freshwater stream, the station was situated in Norfolk Bay, about 6 miles west of Eaglehawk Neck, the strip of land that isolated the peninsular containing Port Arthur from the main part of the island. The sheltered waters of Norfolk Bay were now increasingly used to unload cargo, which was taken to Port Arthur using the convict-powered railway, which followed a 4-mile switchback route over the hills through the gum and fern forest.

The 400 or so convicts at Cascades were crammed into cells in a self-contained community beside the bay. Much smaller than Port Arthur, there was nevertheless also a hospital, chapel, convict mess hall, workshops, and all the necessary accommodation for the officers and the commandant. Most of the free labour was used in felling trees, and rails were laid to help bring the timber from the forest to the sea, where a steam engine had recently been installed to drive a mechanical saw. Some of the convicts were also put to work in the fields and in construction, while the particularly recalcitrant were forced to labour 100 feet down in the coal mine that had been dug nearby.

After a life of idleness, Robert must have found the work desperately arduous. Living amongst the hardened lower classes, it is likely that his fellow convicts added to his misery and compounded his mental problems. A few months after his arrival, a friend of Revd Charles Driscoll saw Robert toiling in convict clothes in a gang working on the public roads. The friend wrote back to England, and the Revd Driscoll wrote to the Home Office from where he was then living in Vichy, France, asking for a remission of Robert's sentence. He said he had heard from a friend in Hobart that Lieutenant Pate had 'not obtained a Ticket of Leave like other convicts' and that the hard work and convict life meant 'that his mind is now completely breaking'. The letter showed a lack of understanding of the Ticket of Leave system, but nevertheless the Home Secretary took the precaution of enquiring of the Lieutenant Governor as to Robert Pate's health. Of course the turnaround of all these letters was slow, so the answer to the Revd Driscoll's enquiry came a full thirteen months after the sighting. The Lieutenant Governor reported that, during his probation, Robert Pate's health was uninterruptedly good, and he never required medical attention.

In fact, Robert's probationary period had been reduced by eighty days because of 'task work', that is, extra work voluntarily undertaken. On 24 August 1851, he was transferred to the prisoners' barracks in Hobart, becoming a Pass Holder Class 3, before being assigned to Mr Abbott of Davey Street five days later. John Abbott was the registrar of births, marriages and deaths, so probably the work was of a clerical kind, and Robert's life must have improved immensely.

A year later, Robert applied for a Ticket of Leave, but was refused. Back in England, in April 1853, his father sent a petition, also signed by six other Justices of the Peace of the Isle of Ely, asking for a conditional pardon once half his son's sentence had expired. Viscount Palmerston, who was by then the Secretary of State for the Home Department, wrote, 'I can see no reason for interference in this case.' But in September of the same year, Robert was granted his Ticket of Leave and he left Mr Abbott's employ. In December, he made his own application for a conditional pardon, supported by John Abbott, but although he was eligible, the Lieutenant Governor thought it wise to ask London. Palmerston again refused.

In the event, Robert was never granted a pardon and completed his sentence. But once he had obtained his Ticket of Leave, he no doubt led a life of leisure that was pleasant enough. He would no longer have been forced to have some kind of employment, just to keep to the discipline of attending weekly church services and the regular musters.

While he was serving his sentence, many of his relations back in England reached the end of their lives. His uncle was the first, dying in 1851 in Peterborough, then Robert's stepmother passed away in 1854. From her personal monies, she left £100 to her stepson, but rather more to her cousins, servants, and friends. Finally, his father Robert Francis Pate died of a 'decline of digestive powers and general atrophy' on 5 August 1856, at the age of sixty-nine. He died a wealthy man. As well as his freehold house and 6 acres of land elsewhere, he was worth about £6,000 in cash and life insurance policies and nearly £50,000 in mortgages, promissory notes, and bonds. But if Robert, when he eventually heard of the death of his father, expected to inherit substantially, he was to be severely disappointed.

His father had left a complicated will which stretched to ten pages plus a codicil. He left his personal possessions equally to his son and daughter, and gave substantial bequests to his nephew, William Pate, and various servants. The remainder of the money was put into trust under the care of his friends William and Alexander Peckover, bankers, and Edward

Hugh Jackson, solicitor. The trust covered the cost of an annuity of £300 per annum to his son and £200 to his daughter, increasing to £300 after ten years. Further sums were to be paid under certain circumstances for the education and maintenance of the children of Robert, Mary and William, and the capital passed to those offspring after the decease of these three.

So Robert's father did not pass his wealth to his only son, either because of his mental problems or because he never forgave him for his actions. His daughter, Mary, as a married woman, was not a suitable heiress, so instead he decided to skip a generation. His son would only benefit from an annuity which, although five to ten times a working man's wage, was at a level that Robert had found difficult to survive on in London. What's more, Robert had no children to benefit. His sister already had three, but even she had to take the trustees of the estate to court in order to obtain proper maintenance for her offspring.

* * *

On Tuesday 18 August 1857, Robert Pate married Mary Elizabeth Brown in the Church of the Holy Trinity, which stands on Potter's Hill with a grand view across Hobart to the sea. His sentence had come to an end the previous month and, as a free man, he no longer needed to seek permission to marry. His bride was the only daughter of William Clavey Brown, a free settler in the wool and cloth line. Robert was thirty-seven years old, and Mary claimed on the marriage certificate that she was a couple of years younger. She was actually nearly a decade older than that, at forty-four. She was still a spinster, unusual given the gender imbalance in Tasmania at the time, and what's more, she came from a wealthy family. It's not clear why she did not marry earlier; perhaps she was prevented from marrying by her father, or just extremely unattractive.

The ceremony took place by licence, and Robert gave his occupation as 'gentleman'. The witnesses included Lieutenant Robert Clements, who had joined the 10th Hussars just after Robert resigned, but left after being wounded in the Crimea in 1855, and Captain James Duff Mackay, who was the barrack master in Hobart. It is clear that Robert had regained some of his respectability, at least amongst part of the township.

His new wife, Mary, was born at the end of 1812 in Stonehouse, Gloucestershire, where her father carried on his trade in the sheep-grazing hills of the Cotswolds. His business was not always successful, and he went bankrupt three times whilst they were still in England: once as a clothier in 1816, and twice after they moved to London as a wool and cloth merchant in 1824 and 1826. Perhaps for this reason, the family emigrated to Van Diemen's Land in the late 1820s or early 1830s, and in 1833 he was recorded as a fellmonger[6] near Hobart.

But his business acumen must still have been wanting because, in 1835, he was to be found in the debtor's prison, and was subsequently declared insolvent. After that, his fortunes improved, and at some point in the 1840s, he was working 2,560 acres at Kangaroo Bottom, near Hobart. By the 1850s, he was a respected gentleman, attending the levees of the Lieutenant Governor. Mary's father died in 1853 at the age of seventy-four, leaving all his wealth to his wife, Elizabeth. Subsequently the ownership of ten tenements in Murray Street, known as 'Brown's Terrace', was passed to Mary, together with four other houses and shops in the same street.

After marriage, Robert moved into Mary's family home, a large brick-built house at 46 Patrick Street, which consisted of nine rooms with a coach-house, stable, brewery, detached cottage, outbuildings, and a huge garden stocked with fruit trees. It is likely that the newly-weds occupied the cottage, but then, three years later, Robert's mother-in-law died and Mary inherited the main house. Although she had an elder brother, he appears to have died nearly twenty years earlier, and Mary seems to have been the sole heir. Unsurprisingly, Robert and Mary had no children.

Robert exhibited no more extreme signs of mental instability, at least none that brought him into conflict with the law or led to any spells in a lunatic asylum. Perhaps this was down to the calming effect of married life and the watchful eye of his wife. He clearly had friends in Hobart, as indicated by the witnesses at his wedding, but his crime was known to society in the town. They were not, for example, invited to the Lieutenant Governor's levees. They must have lived quietly, as no mention of Robert is recorded in the local newspapers of the time, except for one slightly bizarre incident.

In December 1858, Robert appeared in court as a prosecution witness in a crime concerning the theft of a flowerpot valued at 6d. The accused was a little ragged girl, Margaret McKay, who was just eleven years old and illiterate. She had been sent out early in the morning by her mother to visit her sister, who was about to give birth, but was found at 4 a.m. by a constable, holding a pot containing a pretty flower. The girl, shivering and crying, said she had taken it from a garden in Patrick Street where the gate was unlocked. The constable woke the owner, and Robert Pate said the flowerpot was indeed his, and accompanied them to the watch house[7], where he signed the charge sheet. He told the court that he had pressed charges because he had lost several flowers lately, but he trusted the court would be lenient. The magistrate expressed considerable surprise that he had taken the strange decision to prosecute such a young girl who had never done wrong before, and instructed him to keep his gate locked in future. Robert meekly said he would. The accused was discharged and told to be a good girl from now on.

After six years as a free man, perhaps because of homesickness, Robert and his wife decided to sell up and return to England. Much of their property was put up for auction, including fourteen tenements in Murray Street and a small cottage and allotment in Brisbane Street. Although the properties provided a steady income, they were not worth as much as earlier since more than half of them were vacant. Their effects up for sale included a rosewood pianoforte, a Chinese desk, a collection of paintings, some of which had been exhibited in the museum, a 'capital family phaeton'[8], and all the accoutrements of a gentleman's residence.

The auctions were held on 27 April 1863, but in the end they didn't leave until two years later. Their main residence was finally auctioned in March 1865 and they left Tasmania for ever a month afterwards. The steamship *Robert Morrison* docked in London on 14 August 1865. Robert had been absent from England for exactly fifteen years.

They settled in Hammersmith, to the west of London, at 12 St Peter's Square, where they lived for more than fifteen years, mostly alone, apart from one or two servants. Robert was reunited with his sister, Mary, who lived at Hereford Lodge in Brompton, West London. But three months after Robert's return, Mary's husband died and she had to move out. Her husband had not done well in business and his effects amounted to less than £100.

Mary went to live with her brother, much to his pleasure, although she still had an independent income from the annuity bequeathed by their father. Her children, aged five to fourteen, now needed a male guardian, and Robert was proposed. In an affidavit of February 1866, Robert's wife produced evidence to his good character and a supporting letter from the previous Bishop of Tasmania, who was 'fully aware of all the circumstances which led to the residence of my said husband at Hobart Town'. It appears that the court did not think a retired felon was a suitable person, and instead appointed an older man from the legal profession, Richard Edward Arden.

By 1871, Mary had moved back to Kensington, where she lived alone with two servants. She married again in 1874, but the following year her firstborn son, Robert Francis Pate Startin, died while serving with the 10th Hussars in India, brought on by an accident whilst pig-sticking.[9] Robert's sister's own life came to an end three years later in June 1878, when she was living with her second husband in St John's Wood. She was fifty-seven years old and her estate was valued at under £1,500.

Following her death, Robert's only connection with his late sister was through his two surviving nephews, Henry and James, and niece Florence. They all did well in life, but it is not known how much Robert was involved in their success. Henry went to Oxford University and later became a vicar, and Florence married the son of a rector in Devon. James Startin was the star of the family, eventually becoming acquainted with the royal family. He joined the navy as a cadet, and later, when he was a lieutenant on the *Victoria and Albert*, a steamer that functioned as a royal yacht, he married the daughter of a Liverpool merchant. It was a fashionable London wedding: the guests included Her Royal Highness the Marchioness of Lorne, and expensive gifts were received from all manner of illustrious people, including a pair of silver candelabra from His Royal Highness the Duke of Edinburgh Prince Alfred and a claret decanter from Prince George of Wales.[10] They took their honeymoon at his brother Henry's chateau on the Loire. In the new century, James rose to the rank of rear-admiral and became *aide-de-camp* to King Edward VII. He was knighted, the new King presumably unaware that his aide was the nephew of the man who had struck his mother.

In the 1880s, Robert Pate and his wife moved south of the river to South Norwood, where they lived at 1 Ross Road until their deaths many years later. They called the house 'Broughton', after Mary's mother's maiden name, the source of their wealth. Robert lived to a greater age than most of his blood relations. But at the end of January 1895, he suffered a stroke and became paralysed. James came up from Devonport, but his uncle died on 6 February, aged seventy-five. He was buried in Beckenham cemetery, and his grave was marked with a large Celtic cross. He left £22,464 to his widow. The proof of his will was widely reported in the press, and, unlike the previous royal assailants, his attack on the Queen was remembered.

His widow died five years later on 17 November 1900, aged eighty-two according to her death certificate, but actually she was almost eighty-eight. Her estate was valued at £35,296 and the considerable increase probably indicates that either she retained wealth in her own name during the marriage or received further bequests after Robert's death. Their wealth was finally distributed in dozens of individual bequests to friends and charities, with Mary's beloved fox terrier dogs being left to the care of her erstwhile servant, called, appropriately enough, Kate Fox.

So ended the strange story of the gentleman who struck the Queen. The trial and punishment showed up the different rules for the higher classes, although Robert's spell in Cascades Punishment Station must have been all the harder for his soft early life. It was also another case where the court's deliberations over the sanity or insanity of the accused probably reached the wrong conclusion. Those attackers who were not right in the head were often found 'guilty'; while those who understood what they were doing were sometimes pronounced 'not guilty on the grounds of insanity'.

But it was a long time before the courts were faced with having to make another such decision. It would be a generation, all of twenty-two years, before the Queen faced another assailant. The intervening period would see great change in the fortunes of her country, but also great sadness in Victoria's personal life.

1. Queen Victoria's marriage to Prince Albert.

2. A contemporary engraving of Edward Oxford's attack. Reproduced by kind permission of the London and Metropolitan Archives.

3. The grave of John Freeman.

4. John Francis shooting at the Queen.

5. John Francis's interrogation by the Privy Council.

6. The ruins of the Port Arthur Convict Settlement.

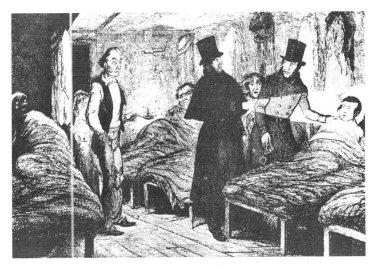

7. Police making an arrest in a boarding house.

8. The Central Criminal Court.

9. Exercising under the Separate System.

10. The Chartist demonstration on Kennington Common.

11. William Hamilton's attack.

Left: 12. Victims of the Irish famine.

Right: 13. A prison cell at Pentonville.

14. Robert Pate's assault on the Queen.

15. North Brink, Wisbech, in the nineteenth century.

Left: 16. Queen Victoria as painted in 1845.

Above: 17. The remains of the convict mess room at Cascades.

18. The Great Exhibition.

19. John Brown and Queen Victoria.

20. Arthur O'Connor being apprehended.

21. Crossing sweepers in London.

22. Roderick Maclean shooting at the Queen's carriage.

23. The trial of Roderick Maclean.

THE FENIAN GUY FAWKES.

Above left: 24. The House of Commons chamber after 'Dynamite Saturday'.

Above right: 25. Punch's view of the Fenian bombing campaigns.

6

The Wily Clerk, 1872

The Great Exhibition of the Industry of All Nations opened on 1 May 1851. The driving force behind the event was Prince Albert, and it was his crowning achievement, only realised against considerable opposition. The idea was to hold an ambitious international trade show that would show off Britain's arts, crafts, and industries, but both finance and location were major problems. Protectionists saw it as propaganda for free trade, gainsayers saw it as a waste of money, and there were fears that the innovative design would collapse in a gale.

But on the day it opened, Victoria wrote in her diary, 'It was the *happiest, proudest,* day in my life [...] Albert's dearest name is for ever immortalized with this *grand* conception, *his own*.' The exhibition was held in Hyde Park in a monumental edifice of glass, dubbed the Crystal Palace, more than a third of a mile long with 293,655 panes of glass. It was one of the greatest engineering achievements of the century. The attractions were astonishing, from every corner of the globe, with over 17,000 exhibitors and more than 100,000 exhibits. In the centre was a crystal fountain carved from four tons of pink glass that shot water high into the air, catching the sunlight of that particularly hot summer. Everywhere there were new marvels: the electric telegraph system, new photographic processes, the eight-cylinder *Times* printing machine, and the latest in railway technology. From abroad came French textiles and fashionable garments, an American reaping machine and Colt revolver, and from India a gold-and-silver throne and a howdah displayed on a stuffed elephant. Another innovation in a public place was the 'retiring rooms and washrooms' available to the visitors for a penny, which were used by 827,000 people, not counting the free urinals for men.

Over six million visitors came during the 140 days that the exhibition was open, with no damage or violence, and Victoria described it as 'a complete and beautiful triumph'. But by the end, Albert was exhausted and ill with severe stomach cramps. He was only thirty-two, but balding and looking prematurely old, and the period following the Great Exhibition was something of an anticlimax for him and the country. The respect that he had earned slowly melted away.

Eighteen months after the doors closed, the Queen gave birth to her eighth child, Prince Leopold, who was diagnosed as a haemophiliac.[1] The birth had been relieved, Victoria felt, by the assistance of 'blessed chloroform [...] soothing and delightful beyond measure', but she again suffered from postpartum depression. She brooded over the injustice of a woman's lot and sent vicious notes to Albert, complaining about trivialities. Later she would regret her outbursts, 'I feel how sadly deficient I am, and how over-sensitive and irritable, and how uncontrollable my temper is when annoyed and hurt.' During her rages, the Prince would retreat, but Victoria would follow him from room to room, continuing to upbraid him. Later, harmony would return.

In the wider world, war threatened in the east as Russia sought to profit from the declining Ottoman Empire and gain free access to the Mediterranean from its warm water ports in the Black Sea. Prussia supported Russia, while Napoleon III in France supported the Turks and was anxious for a foreign military victory. In England, rumours spread that Albert was a Prussian spy, not helped by the fact that he still spoke and wrote in German privately, and the right-wing press, possibly encouraged by Lord Palmerston, printed hints that the Prince was about to be arrested on treason charges.

Fearful of Russian influence in the region, the British fleet was ordered to Constantinople. The Turks attacked the Russians in October 1853 and, after the French fleet sailed through the Dardanelles, the British followed. After months of indecision, the combined British, French, and Turkish armies landed at Gallipoli in May 1854. Offensives in the Crimea took place in the autumn, and after severe losses and a bitter winter, Sevastopol fell to the French in September 1855. The campaign suffered from poor communication between the allies, and revealed serious shortcomings in the British military system: an army that had not fought for forty years, commanded by gentlemen generals who preferred parades and champagne to action, was shown to be woefully inadequate.

Throughout the conflict Victoria thought of 'her beloved troops' day and night, and worried when there was no news from the front. For the first time, she personally presented medals at the Horse Guards to returning soldiers, and was delighted to meet her brave soldiers, many of whom were severely maimed. She wrote, 'Many of the privates smiled, others hardly dared look up [...] all touched my hand [...] I am proud of the tie which links the lowly brave to his Sovereign.'

Victoria was upset by a conflict she felt was unnecessary, but amongst the populace the war was unbelievably popular. Eventually, though, the military mismanagement became clear, and after a motion for an enquiry into the condition of the army was passed in the House, the Prime Minister, Lord Aberdeen, resigned. While the country clamoured for Lord Palmerston to be instated, Victoria called first on every other possible alternative, from Lord Derby via Lord Lansdowne to Lord John Russell, but without success. Palmerston, seventy-one years old and with failing eyesight, was installed in Downing Street. But after the success of the Treaty of Paris, which finally ended the conflict, she magnanimously expressed her satisfaction at the way the war had been brought to an end by bestowing on him the Order of the Garter.

In April 1855, Emperor Napoleon and the Empress Eugénie paid a visit to England to cement cooperation. Much anti-French feeling persisted in the country from the earlier wars, but Victoria was charmed by Napoleon. In August, the Queen returned the favour, and visited Paris with Albert. The crowds were rapturous, although the dowdiness of the sovereign's wardrobe was remembered for a long time. Victoria's ninth and final pregnancy came the following year, and Princess Beatrice was born in April 1857. Tired of so many pregnancies and still only thirty-seven, she asked for advice on birth control. On being told that abstinence was the only legal and moral solution, she reputedly said, 'Oh doctor, can I have no more fun in bed?'

In June 1857, news reached England of the Indian Mutiny. The rebellion had started over a rumour that the grease for new cartridges was made from beef or pork fat, against the Hindu or Muslim religions, but was then exacerbated by the inappropriate official response. The cabinet vacillated over what to do, and Victoria wrote to Palmerston 'that the Government incur a fearful responsibility towards the country for their indifference'. Using her experience of the Crimea, Victoria took a leading role in cajoling him into taking urgent and effective action. Many lives were lost during the ensuing campaign before the final relief of Lucknow towards the end of the year.

Palmerston's popularity grew with the military successes abroad. On dubious grounds, Britain launched an assault on the Chinese mainland with French help, and captured Canton in 1858 and Peking in 1860, forcing the country to fully open up to trade. The British fleet also supported Garibaldi in the unification of Italy and helped prevent Austria from regaining Lombardy, much to the delight of popular opinion and to Victoria's private disgust. The American Civil War broke out in 1861, and Britain announced its neutrality, even though the blockade of Confederate ports cut off the provision of cotton and led to half a million unemployed in the northern textile industry. An incident in which a Yankee cruiser intercepted a British ship to seize two Confederate agents led Palmerston to draft a severe response that could have led to war. Albert interceded to tone down the language, and a compromise was achieved.

It was Albert's last diplomatic act. In 1859 he turned forty, but looked more like a man of sixty. His hair had receded, he was overweight and unfit, and he suffered from chills, exacerbated perhaps by the frigid conditions that the Queen maintained in her residences. As well as chronic stomach problems, he suffered from sore gums and was often weak, but he would not give in to his frailties; making light of his condition, he drove himself all the harder. Victoria, too, ignored the signs, but towards the end of 1861, his condition worsened, and she became increasingly concerned. The doctors diagnosed typhoid fever[2], but he did not rally, and by Saturday 14 December, it was clear the end was near. Surrounded by his family, Victoria bent over him and asked for 'einen Kuss'. He raised his lips and then fell into a doze. Albert died at ten to eleven in the evening, and Victoria fell upon the still and cold body, crying out every fond name she had used over their twenty-two years together.

At midnight, the great bell of St Paul's began to toll, and throughout Sunday, the bells of London rang out the solemn slow beat of mourning. A wave of public sympathy replaced the antipathy to his nationality, and Albert was praised by the press as a great statesman and consort. Victoria was in shock and inconsolable. She went meekly along with the arrangements, but wrote to her uncle, the King of the Belgians, that she was now an 'utterly broken and crushed widow of forty-two! My life as a happy one is ended! The world is gone for me!' For years afterwards she slept with Albert's nightshirt in her arms, and she wore black mourning for the rest of her life.

* * *

During the next three years, Victoria suffered violent grief: paroxysms of despair, yearning for her lost love, and longing for her own death so she could rejoin him. With Albert's influence gone and the Queen preoccupied by grief, the monarchy's involvement in affairs of state declined; a situation that the government was happy to accept, at least to begin with.

Eventually, in 1864, the Queen at last took a renewed interest in government, stirred by the threat of war with Germany. As Prussia opened hostilities with Denmark over the

Schleswig-Holstein question[3], she persuaded Palmerston not to intervene on Denmark's behalf and kept the country neutral. Although her son, Bertie, had married a Danish princess, her sympathies continued to be with Germany, the opposite of national sentiment. Such conflicts of interest with her children were bound to arise as she married them off to the princes and princesses of Europe. Two years later, during the seven-week Austro-Prussian war, she watched as her daughters Victoria and Alice worried about their husbands from opposite sides of the conflict.

Victoria remained reclusive, and the British public became impatient with her continued withdrawal. Her guiding principle in politics was 'what would Albert have done?' and she continued to encourage every form of memorial. She gave a knighthood to the mayor of Wolverhampton, the first town to unveil a statue, which encouraged many others. The impressive Albert Memorial was built in Hyde Park, scene of his biggest achievement, the Great Exhibition, and in 1867, she laid the foundation stone for the Albert Hall, just to the south of the monument.

During this time Victoria found solace and friendship in an unlikely commoner. She had first met her Scottish ghillie[4], John Brown, when Albert was still alive. A devoted, forceful, and plain-speaking Highlander, he always seemed to emerge from the shadows when needed. Twice he was there to save her from serious injury, when he stopped a runaway horse and, in 1863, when the Queen's coachman drove into a ditch in the darkness. Seven years her junior, Brown cut a fine figure in a kilt, liked his whisky, and was given to outspoken and sensible observations that ignored rank. He was brought down to Windsor in 1865, and encouraged Victoria to begin riding and going for drives again. The therapy slowly worked and, in February 1866, she opened Parliament for the first time since Albert's death.

After a succession of lacklustre governments, Benjamin Disraeli took over as the Tory Prime Minister in 1868. Victoria found him strange but charming, full of 'poetry, romance and chivalry'. She began to look forward to reading his letters and receiving him. But he was in power for less than a year, and the Queen had to deal instead with Gladstone and the Liberals, as the successors to the Whigs were now called. William Gladstone was fiercely religious and a more austere character, although he was much involved in rescuing prostitutes, reputedly doing the job personally at night and writing their names down in a little book. His persuasive skills with the electorate failed to charm Victoria, and she agreed with the Honourable Emily Eden, an author, who wrote that if Gladstone 'were soaked in boiling water and rinsed until he were twisted into rope, I do not suppose a drop of fun would ooze out'. Victoria again withdrew from the business of government and declined many proposed functions on the grounds of her poor health. This, however, did not seem to affect the things that she wanted to do.

By this time, Brown had become Victoria's personal outdoor servant and took orders from her alone. She became increasingly fond of him and he could do no wrong. As her confidant, jealousies arose in the court and amongst Victoria's children, and she started to be slanderously referred to as 'Mrs Brown'. She used him as her emissary to carry orders to those of much higher station, which often invoked their fury, and nobody was allowed to cross him. Referring to the way that the Queen only seemed to be happy with her favourite servant, the scandal sheet *Tomahawk* published a cartoon of the Queen on horseback being led by the Highlander with the caption, 'All is black that is not Brown'.

While the Queen remained reclusive and respect for her declined, fears were also growing for her safety. In early 1867, there was an unsuccessful uprising by Irish Nationalists in Dublin and the south-west of Ireland, supported by the Fenian Brotherhood of America. In Chester, supporters attempted to raid the castle to steal arms prior to an attack on Dublin, and later in the year, the Fenians started a dynamite campaign in England. While the Queen was in Scotland, the government uncovered a plot to seize or murder the sovereign. Victoria said it would be 'too foolish' to ring Balmoral with troops, although she later reluctantly consented to the presence of a company of the 93rd Highlanders. However, she would have no escort when driven around by John Brown, and the Home Secretary had to be content with two men following at a distance, armed with revolvers. Later, when she was in Osborne, he deployed extra police and ships to patrol the coast.

Remembering the previous attacks, she dwelt most on the blow to her head, where the mark had remained for ten years. Guns she had not minded, 'as if they missed there was nothing to trouble you & a moving carriage prevented a good aim'. A few months later, she was forced to recognise the danger of firearms. At the end of October 1867, her second son Prince Alfred became the first member of the royal family to tour Australia, spending nearly six months in the colony and visiting all of the states. But many inhabitants of the country had Irish origins, and on 12 March 1868, while enjoying a picnic on the beach at Clontarf, Sydney, he was shot in the back. The bullet missed the spine, and after spending two weeks in hospital under the care of Florence Nightingale-trained nurses, the prince made a full recovery. The assailant, Henry James O'Farrell, was hanged.

Republicanism was also gaining more support. Following the Franco-Prussian war in 1870, Napoleon was defeated and a republic was proclaimed in Paris. In England, the Queen was still practically invisible, the Prince of Wales was not respected because of his philandering and louche lifestyle, and there was heavy criticism of the expensive Privy Purse needed to support the whole extended family. The radical *Reynold's Newspaper* exemplified the mood of the more extreme when it announced a royal birth by saying, 'We have much satisfaction that the newly-born child of the Prince and Princess of Wales died shortly after birth, thus relieving the working classes of England from having to support hereafter another addition to the long roll of State beggars they at present maintain.'

As well as these threats to the future of the monarchy, Victoria suffered from more personal woes. In the summer of 1871, safely hidden away from pubic gaze in Balmoral, she fell seriously ill. The cause was undiagnosed, but it involved severe throat inflammation and an underarm abscess, and kept her in bed for the best part of three months. After the abscess was lanced, the Queen reappeared, carried downstairs by the faithful John Brown, thinner, paler, and 2 stone lighter. While the first symptoms were relieved, rheumatic gout appeared in swollen hands and feet, and kept her debilitated through the early autumn.

In November, her health at last began to return, just as her son contracted typhoid fever. The Queen hurried to Sandringham, the Prince of Wales's residence. Distressingly, the height of the illness was predicted to occur on the tenth anniversary of Albert's demise, supposedly from the same condition. The newspapers milked the drama, and now sympathy for the royal family grew, while the tide of republicanism suffered a setback as news reached England of the French republic's bloody crushing of the Paris Commune. The crisis passed and her son survived, to widespread jubilation.

The chances of another attack on the Queen should now have diminished, but instead, one was just a few days away. On Tuesday 27 February 1872, the recovery of the Prince of Wales was celebrated by a great thanksgiving service at St Paul's Cathedral, and a rare royal spectacle was provided by the procession of eight carriages from Buckingham Palace. Victoria sat with her son in an open landau – to her the February cold was hardly worse than a Balmoral summer – and the huge crowds were enthusiastic, making her wonder about all the talk of republicanism. At Temple Bar, she took hold of her son's hand and raised it in the air, before bringing it down and kissing it. The crowd went wild.

Victoria found the service overlong, but rejoiced in the enthusiastic reception she received. She returned pleased at the rapturous assertion of loyalty amongst her subjects. Two days later, in the afternoon, the Queen held a court at Buckingham Palace, with the royal children, the Maharajah Duleep Singh, Prince Hassan of Egypt, the Nawab Nazim of Benghal, Prince Suleiman Kudr Vahid Ali Bahadoor, and several hundred ambassadors, aristocrats, ministers, and other dignitaries. Afterwards, she took a drive in an open carriage with the Princes Arthur and Leopold, and with Lady Jane Churchill, lady-in-waiting, who sat beside her. They were escorted on each side by the two equerries, Major-General the Honourable Arthur Hardinge and Lord Charles Fitzroy. Two outriders rode in front and two grooms behind.

They drove around Regent's Park and Hyde Park, and then returned to Buckingham Palace along Constitution Hill. Safely past that dangerous thoroughfare, the cortège went through the enclosure and the garden gate into the inner courtyard. Held back by police, a large crowd stood in front of the palace, cheering. Occupied with the throng, the police failed to notice a young man standing about fifty paces from the entrance, at the point where the garden wall abutted a corner of the palace. Seeing he was unobserved, the man took off his coat and eyed the ten-foot-high iron railings. He checked the gun in his pocket and climbed over.

* * *

The young man's name was Arthur O'Connor. He was born in Limehouse, East London, eighteen years earlier, to respectable but poor parents. His father, George O'Connor, had worked for many years as a ticket collector for the Iron Steamboat Company. Like thousands of others, he had emigrated from County Cork during the lean years, and married Catherine O'Bryan in London in 1851. Arthur was their eldest son, with four younger brothers and two sisters aged from two to fifteen. Although they lived in reduced circumstances, some of their antecedents were wealthy and famous.

Among Arthur's ancestors were adventurers, rogues, revolutionaries, and the aristocracy, and some had a direct bearing on the events about to unfold. Arthur's grandmother, who was still alive and lived with the family, was the great-niece of Lord Longueville of Castle Mary, County Cork. Arthur's paternal line could be traced back to Roger Connor, born in 1728 in Ireland to wealthy English merchant parents. Roger Connor, Arthur's great-grandfather, had three sons: Robert, Roger, and Arthur. The eldest styled himself Robert Longfield Connor (after his mother's maiden name), and became a pillar of the establishment, with his residence at Fort Robert, County Cork.

Roger and Arthur, however, became Irish patriots, and changed their surnames to O'Connor, after the ancient line of Irish kings. Arthur was a leader in the United Irish movement, suffered several years' imprisonment, and narrowly escaped the hangman. He spent most of his life in exile in France, becoming one of Napoleon's generals. While Arthur prospered across the channel, Roger embezzled his brother's Irish estate, torched his own property for the insurance money, and in 1817 held up the Galway mail coach. Unwaveringly loyal to the Crown, their brother Robert repeatedly called for the execution of Roger and Arthur for their treasonable and criminal activities, an attitude that shocked even the Irish authorities.

Roger O'Connor had four sons. The eldest, Roderic, emigrated with his two illegitimate sons to Van Diemen's Land, becoming one of the colony's largest land owners, and was described by the wife of the Lieutenant Governor as 'a man of blasted reputation, of exceedingly immoral conduct, and of viperous tongue and pen'. His brother, Francis Burlett O'Connor, travelled in the opposite direction, to South America, where he became a general in Simon Bolivar's army of liberation and also his Minister of War. Arthur, the grandfather of the Queen's assailant, greatly upset his father when he married across the family divide, to his first cousin Mary, the daughter of Robert Longfield Connor.

But the most famous of Roger's sons was Feargus O'Connor. He became MP for County Cork in 1832 and later for Nottingham in England, and was both the most popular and reviled of the Chartist leaders. A great orator, he toured the country whipping up support and published his views through the *Northern Star*, a Leeds-based newspaper which he founded. He served eighteen months in prison for seditious libel, and was the leader of the last great Chartist demonstration in 1848.[5]

In the 1850s, Feargus's activities became more and more irrational, characterised by memory loss, emotionalism, and delusion. In 1852, after several offensive and bizarre acts in the House of Commons, he was examined by Dr John Connolly, the consulting physician to the Hanwell Lunatic Asylum. He was committed to the care of Dr Thomas Harrington Tuke, Connolly's son-in-law, who ran a private lunatic asylum in Chiswick.[6]

Feargus had been living with his sister Harriet in London, who was dependent on him for financial support. She asked for a part of his property to be assigned to her, and when that failed, petitioned for his release back into her care or transfer to another asylum, claiming that the treatment was deficient and that Tuke had appropriated Feargus's money. But her real aim was to gain control of his estate. She was fiercely opposed by Feargus's nephew, who saw that he was receiving the best available care, and arranged that he and his estate be placed under the protection of the Lord Chancellor.

This nephew was George O'Connor, Arthur's father. The young Arthur O'Connor was just one year old when Feargus died in August 1855, but the tales of the O'Connor family were a common topic in the household as he grew up, and later in life, he often talked of going to Ireland to see the origins of his famous ancestors.

As the firstborn, Arthur had to adjust at the age of three to having siblings, when his brother John was born. Soon after, there was a sister and then three more brothers, providing baby playmates for the growing child. But at the age of six, Arthur became ill and subsequently suffered from a lot of sickness, including typhoid fever. However, he survived, and was educated at the church school of St Dunstan's in the East, Fleet Street, where he excelled and showed himself to be an intelligent child. He left school at the age of eleven and was apprenticed to a law stationer's, aiming to become a clerk, a step up from his father's unskilled position.

Arthur seemed be doing well, but his promise was sabotaged by accident and disease. In 1868, he was making his way down Chancery Lane, when he was knocked down by a cab. He was rendered unconscious and taken to hospital, where the wound and lacerations were treated. He remained unconscious for some time and eventually underwent an operation, which left a permanent scar on his left temple. Soon after this, he started to suffer a scrofulous condition of the system[7], which later showed in the symptoms of consumption.

He was forced to give up his apprenticeship through ill health when he was sixteen, and took a job as a clerk to Mr Marshall, a publisher. He left home and went into lodgings at 125 Fleet Street, living with five other young men, all of whom worked as newsagent clerks. But again he had to go into hospital, this time to treat a diseased bone in the toe. He had four operations under the care of Dr Henry Smith of King's College Hospital, but finally his big toe had to be amputated. After that, he was unemployed for three months and returned to the family home.

When he was well, Arthur enjoyed reading, writing, and drawing, and had read extensively amongst the works of Dickens, Thackeray, Bulwer Lytton, Victor Hugo, Dumas, Cooper, and Samuel Lover. He had a humorous nature which he used to amuse his brothers and sisters by telling them stories, and was generally mild and gentle. But his outlook first changed after the accident, when he became more irritable. Puberty arrived much later than normal, and while he was unemployed, he became discontented with his position in life, and fell out with his parents. He complained of headaches, insomnia, and suffered terribly from indigestion, with pains in his jaw bone, dizziness, and a feeling of fullness in the head.

On 1 January 1872, he was taken on as a clerk in the wholesale warehouse of Livett Frank & Son, oil and colour warehousemen[8], in the Borough. He was paid 12s a week each Friday, which he normally handed over to his mother for housekeeping. Arthur often thought of his ancestors and was angry at the way the people of Ireland had been unjustly treated. He strongly believed that the Fenian prisoners should be released and wondered what he could do to help. It was Sunday 18 February, on his favourite walk by the Serpentine in Hyde Park, that the idea of shooting the Queen first entered his head. He thought about it all day, but abandoned the idea, as he believed that Prince Albert would succeed her, which would not help the Irish prisoners. Instead he decided to draw up an order for their release and force Her Majesty to sign it at gunpoint as she walked through St Paul's Cathedral for the upcoming thanksgiving service. In Arthur's mind, everyone else froze in immobility as he carried out the deed, but after she had signed, he would probably be bayoneted.

The following Friday, Arthur refused to hand over all of his wages to his mother, retaining 7s for a reason he refused to disclose. The following afternoon, he bought a pistol from Arthur Layman's shop at 102 High Street, Borough. He paid 4s and asked how it was loaded and where he could get a flint. On the Sunday evening, he attempted to fire the pistol, but broke the lock in the process. He decided that he could still attain his aims just by showing the pistol, but he also purloined a knife from his father, which he intended to use to intimidate the Queen if necessary. That evening he burnt a lot of his papers, much to his parents' surprise, as he had previously talked of getting them printed.

He absented himself from work on Monday, claiming to be ill, because, after all, he would not need his job back. Late that evening, he went out, taking the pistol and knife, and arrived at St Paul's around 11 p.m. Preparations for the thanksgiving service the next day were already largely complete, and the policeman on duty turned him away, but he managed to sneak in and hide under a bench. His hiding place was found by the verger on account of the mud left by his boots on the carpet, and he was turned out. He hid in an outer porch, but was again discovered by a policeman with a bull's-eye lamp. Despondently, he walked the streets until 5.30 a.m., and then went home.

He hid the pistol, knife, and order of release under his pillow, but went out again at eight o'clock. He tried to find a place where he could intercept the Queen on her way to the Cathedral, but could not get close enough because of the vast crowds. He returned home at seven in the evening and slept through the night. The next morning he went to Buckingham Palace, but there was no sign of the Queen. That evening, he took his little nine-year-old brother, Roderick, to see the illuminations along Fleet Street, between Charing Cross and Bank, and around St Pauls; a blaze of colour provided by gas lamp and limelight.

On the morning of Saturday 29th, Arthur felt weary and jaded, and complained of having had no rest because of the pains in his head. He was also suffering from chills. He returned to the palace in the afternoon and saw the Queen's carriage departing along Constitution Hill. A helpful policeman said she would soon return. He waited until the carriage was going through the gates of Buckingham Palace, and then climbed over the railings.

Nobody took any notice as he ran across the yard. He also managed to pass unseen through the garden gate, while the porter was occupied keeping the entrance clear for the cortège. The carriage stopped close to the private entrance to the palace, with the left side towards the door. On that side sat Lady Churchill with Prince Leopold facing her; the Queen was next to her and Prince Arthur opposite. John Brown was in the rumble. He got down to open the door and the two equerries dismounted.

Arthur mistakenly ran to the left side and stopped about a yard from the nearside carriage door. The entourage at first thought that he was one of the gardeners or men employed in the grounds. Arthur tried to attract the attention of Lady Churchill, mistaking her for the Queen, but was pushed away by Brown. Lord Fitzroy turned towards him and told him to go away. Realising his mistake, Arthur then ran round the back of the vehicle to address Victoria, putting his left hand onto the carriage. At first, the Queen thought it was a footman, but then realised it was an unknown man peering over the door. His right arm was raised and he was trying to say something to her in a strange voice. Prince Leopold was horrified to see that he held a pistol.

Arthur moved forward to try to take hold of the Queen. Victoria threw herself over Jane Churchill crying, 'Save me!' But Brown had followed the man and grabbed him by the neck, while Prince Arthur lunged forward, knocking the gun from his grasp. One of the outriders, Charles Tomkins, jumped down and caught the attacker by the wrists. He was thrown to the ground.

* * *

General Hardinge and Lord Fitzroy came up and said they had seen something fall from Arthur's grasp. Then they spotted the pistol lying on the ground, and many of the assembly who hadn't realised the threat turned white. Lady Churchill was almost crying, while Prince Leopold looked as if he might faint. Arthur was lifted from the ground and taken into custody. A servant picked up the gun and gave it to General Hardinge, who examined it. The pistol was an old-fashioned weapon, with a flint and steel lock, which appeared to be broken. In the barrel was a piece of greasy rag. Arthur was asked by General Hardinge whether the pistol was loaded, and he answered, 'You can see that it is not.'

He was searched and a document taken from his trouser pocket. The parchment was in the form of a royal decree ordering the release of Fenian prisoners. As he was led away by police Sergeant Jackson, who had been on duty at the garden gate, Arthur said several times, 'I wish to God I had succeeded; then they could have done with me as they pleased.'

The Queen was escorted into the hall in Buckingham Palace, and General Hardinge showed her the extraordinary document, while Sir Thomas Biddulph, Master of the Household, came running, greatly horrified. The Princess of Wales, who was due to take tea with the Queen, met her in her dressing room. According to Victoria's journal, 'Dear Alix [...] was so horrified and distressed and said she was glad she had not been in the carriage, and it was no pleasure being a Queen, to which I most readily agreed.' The Queen thanked God 'for His great mercy, and for preserving me once again'. General Hardinge was sent to inform Gladstone of the events; Sir Thomas Biddulph was dispatched to the Home Office and Lord Charles Fitzroy to the police station.

The Queen gave all the credit for her rescue to Brown. In a letter to her eldest daughter she wrote, 'It is entirely owing to good Brown's great presence of mind and quickness that he was seized before he could touch me.' She had been about to institute a medal as a reward for long and faithful service among her domestics, and gave a gold medal and an annuity of twenty-five pounds to John Brown for his alertness and devotion on this occasion. It was engraved round the edge 'Victoria Devoted Service Medal'; the Queen never found occasion to give another.

Meanwhile, Arthur O'Connor was taken to the police station at King Street, where he was interviewed by Superintendent Mott. He was seen to be just a youth, 5 feet 6 inches tall but very thin, poorly dressed, and wearing a black felt hat. Later he was visited by Dr Bond, the medical officer. During the course of the evening, several members of Parliament called at the police station in order to see the prisoner, but times had changed and their requests were refused. The pistol was taken to the House of Commons, where Gladstone had asked to examine it to ensure that it really was unloaded.

The following morning, Arthur was visited by Dr Sutherland and Dr Bond, who were tasked with examining his mental condition. He denied suffering from any illusion or mental aberration, and was much amused by the term 'insanity' being used with reference to himself. Arthur liked to talk and was pleased to have the opportunity to vent his political opinions. He denied seeking notoriety and said his actions were simply for the good of his country. The doctors saw him as an enthusiastic, fanatical boy, perhaps spurred on to carry out the deed by the excitement of the thanksgiving ceremonies. They concluded that there was nothing to suggest an unsound mind.

The Document Taken from Arthur O'Connor

I, Victoria, Queen by the grace of God, do make the following declaration:-

Whereas there are at the present moment confined in various prisons throughout the United Kingdom a number of men, Irish by birth, who are known and celebrated as 'Fenian prisoners'; and whereas the said prisoners have been in prison and kept in durance by order of my Government, and with my sanction, for the crime of high treason, the said Fenians having rebelled and conspired against my Crown, endeavouring by various unlawful means to weaken and destroy my power and authority over the Irish nation; and whereas, it is a well known fact that the sympathizers of the Fenian prisoners and the nation have at various times humbly petitioned for their pardon and release – notwithstanding which they are still deprived of liberty.

Now I, the said Victoria, Queen of Great Britain, Ireland, and the Colonies, do hereby, with the consent of my Parliament, grant a free pardon to each and every one of the said men known and celebrated as the Fenian prisoners, who are now suffering imprisonment for the crime of treason against my Crown. And I, the said Queen of Great Britain, Ireland, and the Colonies, do solemnly pledge my royal word, and swear to keep and see carried out the following five clauses:-

Clause 1. That all the men known and celebrated as the said Fenian prisoners shall be restored to liberty without any delay whatever.

Clause 2. That all the said Fenians shall be allowed free and entire liberty for the remainder of their lives.

Clause 3. That for the remainder of their lives the said Fenians shall be as free from the police supervision and restraint with the rest of my subjects.

Clause 4. That the said Fenians shall be allowed to return to their native country, town, or place where they may choose to visit, without any interference whatever from my Government.

Clause 5. That, notwithstanding the fact of my agreeing to the above conditions only through fear of my life, I will not attempt to depart from any of them on that account, nor upon any other reason, cause, or pretext whatever will I depart, or attempt to depart, from any of them; neither will I listen to any advice which my Ministers may wish to give towards causing me to depart from my word, or towards the violation of anything above stated, but shall adhere strictly to everything.

So help me God.

Signed this 27th day of February, in the Year of Grace 1872.

Witnessed by

Whereas, a person named Arthur O'Connor, residing at 4 Church Row, Hounsditch, in the City of London, having committed an outrage against my Royal person, has surrendered himself into my hands, he, the said Arthur O'Connor, being perfectly willing to suffer for such offence – Now I, the said Victoria, Queen of Great Britain and Ireland, do solemnly pledge my Royal word to the effect that if the said Arthur O'Connor be found guilty of death by my judges, after a just and fair trial, he the said Arthur O'Connor shall not be strangled like a common felon, but shall receive that death which is due to him as a Christian, a Republican, and as one who has never harmed a human being – that is to say, he shall be shot, and after death his body shall be delivered to his friends to be buried wherever they may choose.

Signed this twenty-seventh day of February in the year of grace one thousand eight hundred and seventy-two

By me

Witnessed by

Large crowds had gathered at Bow Street magistrates' court at ten o'clock, when it was said that the prisoner would appear, but nothing happened. Arthur was actually first taken to the Home Office, and did not appear before the magistrates until after two in the afternoon. The courtroom was full, and when the attacker was brought to the bar, he was hissed. Arthur leaned on the rail and surveyed the court coolly. The prosecutor was Mr Poland, instructed by the Treasury solicitors, while the defendant had no legal representation. The lead magistrate was Sir Thomas Henry. Part-way through the hearing, His Royal Highness Prince Leopold arrived, to be greeted by cheering and clapping. Also present as witnesses were Lord Charles Fitzroy, General Hardinge, Colonel Henderson, and several other gentlemen. Prince Leopold gave his evidence in a loud, clear voice, but when John Brown was called, he spoke in a Scottish lilt that was scarcely audible 6 feet away.

Arthur was charged with pointing a pistol at Her Majesty under the Peel act of 1842. The facts of the case were explained by Mr Poland, who said that it was probably lucky for the prisoner that he had not managed to carry out the deed, as the crowds would probably have seen to it that he did not live to face the charges. This statement was greeted by loud applause from the gallery, and the magistrates repeatedly had to call for order.

After John Brown had described what happened, Arthur was asked by the magistrate whether he had any questions for the witness. He answered rather gruffly, 'No, I have no questions to ask. I should like to make a statement.' He was told that he would have the opportunity later, but in fact contented himself at the end with just correcting some of the details mentioned by the witnesses.

Arthur was committed for trial at the Central Criminal Court, and taken away in a Black Maria van to the hissing and hooting of the assembled crowd. He was conveyed to Newgate gaol, where he spent over a month on remand. While in prison, he was often visited by his parents, but he would not say why he had committed the deed. Instead he complained about the prison food, saying that he particularly disliked the gruel and that the meat was hard. Arthur told his mother that, if he could get off the charge, he would change his name and leave London. He again expressed a desire to go to Ireland and see the place where the O'Connors were once so powerful.

The week after his remand, Arthur's father called on Dr Harrington Tuke, who he had not seen since the doctor cared for his uncle Feargus, seventeen years earlier. George O'Connor asked for Tuke's aid, saying that he felt his son's brain was affected, and he begged the doctor to visit him to give his medical opinion. Grateful for George's help during the earlier litigation, Dr Tuke agreed to provide his services at no charge. He first visited the prisoner on 12 March, when Dr Gibson, the surgeon of the gaol, was also present.

Tuke thought Arthur was of a weak and feminine appearance, with his head irregularly shaped and smaller than it should be, and his palate highly arched, but otherwise found him shrewd and intelligent. His eyes glistened and the pupils were widely dilated, symptoms of disease. His right lung was dull on percussion, he occasionally spat blood, and his pulse was excessively weak. The doctor talked to the prisoner for an hour and a half, listening to his life story and his reasons for the attack, which he recounted in a calm and collected manner. The doctor concluded that only insanity, caused by genetic inheritance and the accident with the cab, could have brought on the action in such an inoffensive youth.

Dr Tuke visited Arthur again ten days later, taking with him Dr Maudsley, and confirmed his diagnosis. He also read some of Arthur's papers that had escaped the fire, consisting of seventeen pages of foolscap sewn together. The contents were an incoherent mix of quotations from Byron, nursery rhymes, prayers, and law papers, with some passages underlined in red ink, such as, 'Woe to the hand that shed this costly blood; and it did.' Arthur's mother confirmed that she had heard all these ravings before, and had complained to her son that he was wasting paper and ink. He had replied, 'You know nothing about it, mother; it is very valuable, and some day will be printed and published.' At Dr Tuke's instigation, three other doctors visited Arthur: Dr Tweedie (who had attended Feargus); Dr Sabben, the proprietor of Northumberland House Lunatic Asylum in Stoke Newington; and Mr Henry Smith of King's College, who had amputated the boy's toe. They all confirmed his opinion.

* * *

The Grand Jury sat to consider the case against Arthur O'Connor on 9 April 1872. Prince Leopold and Mr John Brown, newly returned from accompanying the Queen abroad, gave witness to the events. Later in the day, Arthur was brought to the bar to plead, charged with presenting a pistol at Her Majesty with intent to alarm her. Much to everyone's surprise, in a bold and confident manner, he pleaded guilty. He later said that he had no desire to compound his folly by uttering an untruth.

The full hearing was held two days later before Baron Cleasby. The Attorney General, Sir John Coleridge, with Mr Poland and Mr Archibald, led the prosecution. At the request of some of Arthur's relatives, Mr Hume Williams appeared for the defence, instructed by Messrs Dickson & Lucas of Bedford Road. It was expected that the judge would just pass sentence, but Mr Williams said that the prisoner was unfit to plead, and therefore the plea of guilty should be withdrawn. The judge asked whether the Treasury solicitor had been informed of this intention, and was most annoyed when it became clear that he had not. In the end, the decision was taken to try the matter of whether the prisoner was fit to plead before a jury.

Mr Williams said that he would show that the prisoner was mad before he committed the act, at the time, and now, while the judge kept emphasising that the issue at present was just his fitness to plead. The defence barrister described the strong disposition to insanity in the family, citing not only his great-uncle Feargus, but his grandfather and aunt, who had also been in lunatic asylums at one time or another.

The first witness was Arthur's father, who was clearly in two minds as to whether defending his son on the grounds of insanity was the right course of action. It was emphasised by the prosecutors that insanity would mean confinement to a lunatic asylum for life, ignoring the fact that it was at Her Majesty's pleasure, while a custodial sentence would be of limited duration. Arthur's father had been unaware of the plea of guilty until he read about it in the paper, but he then wrote to the Treasury solicitor asking for leniency in return. He said that it was not at his instigation that the plea was challenged, but of some other gentlemen friends, who wanted to get the boy off. In the witness box, he said that he did not think his son was insane at that moment, but it was up to the medical men to pronounce.

Arthur's mother appeared next, telling the court about how her son had instructed her to burn some of his papers, which he did not want seen. Counsel then read extracts from the document which had survived, to illustrate a confused mind. However, when questioned specifically, his mother said that she did not think her son was mad.

Dr Thomas Harrington Tuke was then called, introduced as an expert on the study of insanity for the last twenty-four years. He described his visits to see the prisoner and what he had found. He concluded that he was a delicate, weakly boy, in both body and mind, and that he suffered from hereditary insanity, exacerbated by the blow to the head, which had produced a paroxysm around the time of the attack. He thought it would be dangerous to leave him at large, because, although he may be now much better and sorry for what he had done, there could be a recurrence.

Dr James Thompson Sabben thought the prisoner was of low bodily type with a weak intellect and inferior development. Dr Henry Smith deposed that his bodily constitution was rather that of a girl, but he was very intelligent and his conversation was perfectly rational, except with regard to this affair. The Newgate surgeon also gave evidence, but then the foreman of the jury interposed to say that they had reached the conclusion that the accused was perfectly sane, both when he pleaded and now. Baron Cleasby said that he was of the same opinion.

The plea of guilty was therefore accepted, and the judge, after conferring with Alderman Sir David Salomons, moved to pass judgement. He considered that there were aggravating circumstances: the occasion on which the crime was committed and the manner, the contrivance, and the cunning with which it was done; but there were also extenuating points, such as the prisoner's age and the absurdity of the attack. The judge also emphasised the need for deterrence. He concluded that 'the sentence that I feel it my duty to pass upon you is that you be imprisoned and kept at hard labour for one year, and that during that time you be once whipped – that is, that you receive twenty strokes with an instrument called a birch rod.' When the latter was pronounced, there was a loud shriek from Arthur's mother. The prisoner, who showed no emotion, was removed from the bar.

There followed a furious debate in the pages of *The Lancet* over the medical evidence and the verdict. Dr Bond and Dr Sutherland, who had first examined the boy when he was taken into custody, had already described in the journal their conclusion that the prisoner was sane. After the trial, Dr Edgar Sheppard, Medical Superintendent at the Colney Hatch Lunatic Asylum, wrote that he was astounded that 'his friend Dr Harrington Tuke should, by a flimsy and insubstantial plea, seek to widen the breach already existing between the two professions of law and medicine in reference to criminal insanity'. He had also visited the prisoner twice and found him perfectly sane, just suffering from 'hysterical excitement, simulating that form of neurosis appertaining chiefly to what in earlier days was termed the weaker sex'.

Dr Sheppard went on to say that it was the accused's leanings towards Fenianism and the reading of sensational fiction that had led him 'to mistake crime for heroism'. The document written by the prisoner that was read out in court was:

a wild rhapsodico-hysterical shriek of Victor-Hugoism [...] It bore no more internal evidence of insanity than some of Hugo's screaming nonsense written to his countrymen during the German occupation of France. I would label 'poison' upon the works of this author and Dumas, and place them out of the reach of British youth.

The leader writer in the same issue joined in the scathing attack on Dr Tuke, regretting his decision to advance the plea of insanity, saying he had been humiliated by the sarcastic cross-examination of the prosecution, and stressing that the lay press was now jubilant over the latest snubbing of the 'mad doctors'. Tuke was forced to respond, and a long defence of his position appeared in the following week's issue. He reiterated the reasons for his conclusions, again saying that the attack took place when the prisoner's 'reason and judgement were temporarily weakened, as they may be again'.

The Queen was also less than pleased by the verdict, but for different reasons. She wrote to Gladstone, expressing her:

surprise and annoyance at the extreme leniency of O'Connor's sentence, especially as regards the length of imprisonment [...] To let this deluded youth out again, in a year, when he has himself only the *other day avowed*, that he would *not have minded if he had been torn to pieces*, if he had *obtained* the release of the Prisoners, is *most dangerous*.

She railed that she was more unprotected in some ways than her subjects, and the constant danger would make it almost impossible for her to go about in public, or at all in London, if she had no security from such miscreants.

Gladstone wisely wrote back that he too was surprised and annoyed by the light sentence. He felt that much mischief resulted from the gratuitous intervention of Dr Tuke, but that the judge had also wholly mistaken his duty. Gladstone consulted the Home Secretary and the Attorney General, who concurred that the conduct of the judge was to be regretted and condemned. But the sentence could not be changed.

* * *

On Monday 15 April, Arthur was moved from Newgate to Coldbath Fields in Clerkenwell[9] to serve his sentence. The prison was one of London's oldest, dating from the early seventeenth century, but was rebuilt in 1794 and extended in 1850. It was here that he would be flogged. The rod consisted of a bunch of fifty to seventy leafless twigs from the birch tree about 3 feet long, bound together at one end and usually soaked in brine to increase their flexibility and strength. The victim was laid face down on a 'birching donkey', bare-backed down to the buttocks. Earlier, the Queen had expressed satisfaction at the terror invoked by the prospect of a birching, which she hoped would deter others by the thought of the degradation. But the punishment was put on hold in a letter to the Governor from the Home Secretary, who perhaps thought it might be useful as a bargaining counter to prevent the prisoner remaining in London after the end of his short sentence.

Arthur was, however, also sentenced to hard labour, and many in the prison were put to the ordeal of the treadmill. This was like an elongated mill wheel, with twenty-four steps, each 8 inches high, making the circumference 16 feet. The wheel revolved twice per minute, and every thirty revolutions a bell sounded to end a spell of work. Prisoners worked fifteen fifteen-minute sessions per day, the equivalent of climbing Ben Nevis twice. Convicts were separated from each other by wooden partitions, and, with no way to stop the device, the weak or inexperienced could scrape their flesh or fall off, occasionally into the machine, leading to mutilation or death.

Arthur was probably not judged healthy enough to be put on the wheel, but he would have been assigned to pick oakum. Convicts sat in rows on eleven benches in a huge shed, 90 feet long. They were packed so close together that, as they worked, their heads moving from side to side, they resembled a corn field waving in the wind. Each prisoner had an individual pile of rope, weighing from two pounds for normal sentences up to six for those doing hard labour, which had to be turned into tufts of flax suitable for waterproofing the wooden hulls of ships. They could only leave their task when their whole allocation was done. The ropes could be white and sodden, or hard and black with tar, and they had to be untwisted into strands and then unravelled into individual fibres. A fine dust rose from the flax and covered the heads and shoulders of the workers.

The Queen had expressed a desire that the man should not return to the streets, and she wrote to her Prime Minister saying that it should be within 'the power of the law to have such a man sent out of the country and not allowed to return except under surveillance'. Gladstone responded that perhaps under the current circumstances it might be possible 'by commutation and voluntary inducement to get him out of the country for good'. In November, Arthur was approached and agreed that he was 'willing and desirous to depart from England to a distant country provided only it be one favourable to my health'. Apart from the Queen's safety, this stratagem also avoided a planned demonstration at the end of his sentence, when some Fenian sympathisers had proposed the formation of a large procession.

On 30 November, Arthur sent a petition through the Governor to the Home Secretary. He proclaimed his innocence from any intention to harm the Queen and begged for the threat of the flogging to be removed, to avoid 'the intolerable shame and lifelong reproach'. Because of his consumption, he wanted to escape another English winter, and said that he was willing to leave for some warmer colony. The Home Secretary agreed, but said that the pardon would be conditional on his never returning to England.

With the interest taken by the highest levels of government and successive meetings with the Governor, Arthur began to realise the power he wielded. Like his Irish ancestors before him, he recognised an opportunity when he saw it. He rejected the Home Secretary's offer, saying he would 'never agree to permanent exile', never seeing his friends and relations again, and perhaps dying from consumption far away. Instead, he asked for a term to be put on it, suggesting five years. The authorities wanted something from him, and he behaved less and less like a submissive prisoner. He became more and more obdurate, saying, at the end of December, that he would accept no conditions to any pardon. His father was brought into the discussion, and Arthur finally consented to leave the country after the government agreed to pay his passage, provide for outfitting, and allow him two days at home.

Arthur received his pardon on 27 January, and in the end, perhaps through incompetence, no conditions were written into the document. He also spent longer with his family, as a suitable berth on a ship could not be found. Cheekily, his father asked the government for £10 to cover the expense of looking after him for a fortnight. The Home Secretary wrote angrily on the letter that £50 16s had already been spent and the man was 'not entitled to a shilling'.

On 14 February 1873, Arthur quietly left London aboard the *Lodore*, a sailing ship of 850 tons; his release and departure unknown to the press. The ship was a cargo vessel carrying mixed goods, including a large consignment of tobacco, and the government had procured for Arthur a second-class cabin. On his first sea voyage, Arthur was at first struck by the boundless ocean as they sailed down the channel in fine weather. On the twenty-fourth a storm blew up, and Arthur suffered greatly from seasickness. Further south, the warm weather of the tropics, the strange fish, the 'gorgeously beautiful sunsets' and the 'superb moonlights' all pleased him greatly.

But Arthur was very bored. There were only two other passengers, both in steerage class, so he had no one to talk to. Captain Sully, who knew his origins, berated him throughout the voyage and refused permission for him to talk to the sailors. Once he had read all the books he had brought with him, he found little to amuse himself, and his health was also often poor. After passing the Cape of Good Hope, the weather turned cold, and they were pursued by storms and towering seas for the rest of the voyage. The ship was damaged and leaked dangerously, so Arthur was much relieved when land was sighted off Melbourne. He disembarked in Sydney on 20 May.

* * *

The Earl of Kimberley, the Secretary of State for the Colonies, sent a confidential letter to the Governor of New South Wales, asking that the police should monitor the movements of O'Connor without trying to control them. He authorised the colony to pay sums for his maintenance for a limited period until he found suitable employment. Arthur was told of the arrangement, but railed against any kind of supervision, which he felt was incompatible with being a free man.

When Arthur arrived, however, he did as he was told and reported to the Colonial Secretary, taking the assumed name of 'George Morton'. In his first weeks in Sydney, he behaved with propriety, but expressed disappointment with the dullness of the town, with few outlets for expressing his literary talents. However, he liked the landscape, the climate, and especially the people, who were not given to London airs and graces. The colonial government spent £16 on his maintenance during the first three weeks, until he found employment on a six-month contract with a butcher named Geary out at Morpeth, a small town on the Hunter River, 160 miles north of Sydney. For a weekly wage of 10s plus board and lodging, his job was to keep the shop book and ride out for orders. Back in England, he had expressed a desire to work in the open air rather than to labour all day at a desk. Morpeth was a day's journey away by steamer, and he left Sydney on 11 June.

Whilst in Sydney, Arthur had written a letter to the Queen, and the Governor, Sir Hercules Robinson, forwarded the letter to the Home Office, as well as providing details of his movements. The seven-page missive was written as if Arthur was talking to his mother, describing the voyage and his arrival. In it he said he would only stay in the colony until his health had recovered, and dismissed the idea of working in business in favour of achieving literary fame. He asked the Queen humbly to make him Poet Laureate when the current incumbent passed on. The letter was intercepted in London and Victoria never saw the plea.

If Arthur had found Sydney dull and devoid of literary outlets, a frontier town in the outback was many times rougher and more uncivilised. Less than two weeks after he had left, Arthur returned to Sydney, saying that the situation was altogether unsuitable. He looked for alternative employment, but concealing his true identity and without references, the task was difficult. The Governor felt that helping him openly or finding a government situation would be too risky, because of the scandal which would result if his true identity was revealed. Instead, the Governor resumed the subsistence payments.

But a couple of months later, a quiet word was had with a member of the assembly, and by September Arthur was working as a copying clerk for a firm of solicitors, Messrs Holdsworth & Brown, in Pitt Street. The Governor hoped that the man would take advantage of the chance he now had. After a month, Arthur expressed satisfaction with his job, but, recognising the power of his position, he audaciously added that he was finding it difficult to live on the salary of 15s a week. The Governor authorised a regular supplement from government funds of a pound.

The news that Arthur was now settled in a situation reached the Home Office early in 1874, but a month or so later, a ciphered telegram arrived with the shocking news that George Morton had embarked for London. Having seen an advertisement from someone wishing to sell his boat ticket to England, Arthur had managed to persuade the man to give him the ticket, saying that he would pay for it in England (he never did). On 21 February, the Governor had received a surprise visit from Arthur, who said that he was quitting the colony. The chief of police was unavailable to consult, being out of town, and the Governor found himself unable to come up with any legal means of preventing Arthur's departure. He advised against it, and his employers, being well satisfied with his work, even offered him a raise to 25s a week, but he would not be dissuaded.

Still under the name of George Morton, Arthur left Sydney on 25 February aboard the *Hydaspes*, an iron sailing ship of 2,000 tons, bound for London via China, India, and the Suez Canal. The Governor tried to reassure London, saying that Arthur was now well behaved, and that he felt that he could believe the man's assurances that he would cause no trouble to the authorities in England.

Arthur arrived back in London in the middle of June and returned to live with his parents at 8 Vine Street, near Aldgate. On 7 July, he was visited by Inspector George Clarke and Sergeant Williamson. They found him out of employment, but quiet and with no signs of insanity, and devoting his time to reading and writing 'what he calls poetry'. His parents were supporting him with great difficulty, as his father only earned 25s a week to provide for the whole family. His mother saw no chance of her son obtaining employment because of the loss of his character.

Over the winter the family moved around the corner to 5 Bull Inn Yard in Aldgate High Street. The authorities hoped that Arthur would cause no more trouble, but by April the Home Secretary's concerns had increased. He feared that O'Connor might try again to present a petition to the Queen, and the Secretary of State wrote to Dr Tuke asking him 'to use every means […] to ascertain whether O'Connor is insane'. Dr Tuke took him to Sir William Gull and Dr Tweedie, FRS, while the police were asked to increase their surveillance.

On 5 May, Arthur was followed from his lodgings by Detective Sergeant Daniel Davey to St James's Park. On the appearance of the Guard's Band, Arthur became very excited, pushed his way to the front and generally started behaving oddly. He was close to Buckingham Palace, and Victoria was in residence as it was the day of the Queen's Drawing Room. Arthur O'Connor was arrested, and admitted as he was taken to Scotland Yard that, 'I had no right to be here'. Whilst in custody he wrote a deposition of his own symptoms of physical and mental ill-health:

Back like ice.

Wind after eating.

Want of ability to swallow food.

Sinking in stomach.

Blood spitting at times.

Sexual excitement and continual nocturnal emissions.

In cold weather one moment deadly chilled, the next burning hot as fire.

Pains in the head.

Completely stupefied by cold weather.

Want of rest.

Thought continually revolving upon religion.

Visions at night of angels hurling men down precipices to die for ever because they had not given up all they loved to go and sell Bibles to the unconverted.

Sense that unless I gave up the drama, witty and happy society, and the world generally I should be everlastingly damned.

In a word, one unceasing mania concerning Jesus Christ; the intellect warring with mania yet unable to crush it.

Sense of utter want of constitution and energy, a feeling as if I was half dead.

He continued:

Naturally I am poetical loving the Dramatic writers and poet of nature and desirous of imitating them – at one time of my life, that is before I became utterly debilitated and subject to the above symptoms, I was quite insusceptible to the present mania, which leaves me no rest day or night. Naturally I am devoured by energy, running in my walk and in everything else, but when stupefied by dyspepsia scarcely able to drag a foot. Of late my brain agony has terribly increased. I awoke the other night raging to commit suicide; the idea presented itself as a very delightful one, but just as I was about to leap from my bed, I recovered my senses and fell back trembling, and utterly horrified. Since then my feelings have risen to absolute madness continually, and I know I think so at least, that unless I

recover from my bodily disease, sooner or later delirium will come upon me. My home is
very wretched, it is in fact a hell to me.

He was seen by Dr Tuke, who diagnosed another attack of insanity, and Dr Tweedie, who
concurred. Arthur O'Connor was brought before Bow Street magistrates the day after his
arrest, and the evidence and medical opinions heard. He was committed to Hanwell Lunatic
Asylum. On the admittance papers, his mental disorder was classified as imbecility[10],
caused by hereditary factors and masturbation. He was diagnosed as being both suicidal
and homicidal. The Home Secretary was extremely grateful for what Dr Tuke had done,
and paid his expenses out of 'Secret Service money'.

Dr Tuke chose the pages of the *British Medical Journal* to triumphantly declare that he
had been right all along. He criticised the Attorney General's 'unfortunate advocacy' at
the original trial when 'the apparently unanswerable evidence of the insanity of O'Connor
[...] was demolished by [...] his cross-examination, mildly described in *The Times* as
"occasionally caustic".' He accused him of imperilling the life of the sovereign by his stance,
but magnanimously forgave him for the personal attack on himself.

Dr Sheppard responded in the next issue. Prefacing his comments with the words, 'I do
not pretend to say that Dr Tuke is not infallible, although I call to mind many cases in
which he has not succeeded in establishing his infallibility in a court of law', he went on to
attack his arguments. The important issue was whether O'Connor was insane at the time of
his attack, and many learned medical men had said that he was not. He snidely concluded
that he thought the Attorney General would appreciate Dr Tuke's graceful forgiveness of
him. The acrimony spread to the next issue, when Dr Tuke responded to the accusations
and was supported by letters from Dr Sabben and a doctor from the West Riding Asylum,
both of whom said Dr Tuke deserved his triumph.

On admittance to Hanwell, Arthur was described as of wild appearance, excitable, very
haughty, but intellectual. He conversed freely, but in a pompous, bombastic manner, using
extravagant far-fetched expressions. Since his return from Australia, he said that he had
been very miserable, unable to cope with the world and life in general. He thought that the
government ought to give him a good situation with little to do, as then he might cultivate
his talents. The doctor noted that he spoke in a very consequential manner, making use of a
great deal of grandeur of language and eloquence. He denied ever having had any desire to
injure Her Majesty.

During Arthur's stay in Hanwell, he generally gave no trouble and was usually in fair
health. He walked in the grounds and, after a few weeks, started to help the gardener in his
work. He grew more cheerful and happy, but then towards the end of October he suffered a
relapse. He became very restless and unsettled in mind, chafed considerably at his detention,
and started to talk in his old bombastic strain. He insisted that he should leave and support
his parents by his intellect, refusing for several days to do any work in the garden.

He wrote a letter to Dr Rayner[11], the Medical Superintendent:

Sir
    Your determination to keep me confined some time longer has generally disgusted me. I
hated the place from the first, the system is an outrage upon humanity. Leaving all that out

however I must tell you without any affectation that my patience is exhausted. I felt from the first that confining a person quite intelligent suffering simply from over worry of life, in the midst of lunatic idiots in a word in a mad house, I repeat I felt such a thing was bad. I saw that from the newspapers others had their ideas on the subject. It is worse than bad; it is cruelty, you suffer horribly, and I repeat my patience is exhausted; I am sick, sick, sick for want of change, it is not weakness, it is the natural pall upon the mind I will not hear it. You can be drunk from drink, drunk from insanity, and drunk from something more painful, ennui.

If I do not have a change, if something is not done, I shall kick up such a devil of a row that you will have no peace day or night from me. Why not give some repose to my troubled life let me out on a month's trial. Young blood cannot always act philosophers patience. I have done so half a year but I am sick and weary of the den. And if you do drive me to be noisy it will not be any uncontrollable excitement on my part but my steadfast determination to keep kicking against the pricks until I hear something from you.

Most respectfully yours,
Arthur O'Connor

The authorities ignored his demands, and his outlook again improved. The following March, the doctor noted that 'in bodily condition he continues to improve, he is quiet & orderly, has lost a great deal of his former impulsiveness [...] & works regularly in the garden: manifests still a certain amount of imbecility'. By May, he was still seen as wayward and emotional, but beyond that, exhibiting no trace of insanity. By the end of August, the doctor was able to write that he 'continues quiet, well-behaved & rational in conversation, he works daily out of doors with the Gardener, & appears to be convalescing'. On 16 November 1876, after eighteen months in the asylum, and probably unknown to higher authority, he was classified as cured and released.

After his discharge, Arthur found work as a copying clerk and spent some time in the Patent Office, at last able to help his parents with funds. But after two years, he again had to stop because of ill health, and while unemployed became in a much reduced state. In the summer of 1879, his father died of bronchitis, aged fifty-six, and his mother took to drink and was often violent when intoxicated. A year or so later, on 28 December, still unemployed and tired of his mother's nagging and aggression, he went to Scotland Yard. He spoke to Chief Superintendent Williamson and boldly asked to be returned to Australia, where he could again earn a living. The Home Office, happy to have another chance to get rid of him, agreed to the expense, including the same arrangements in New South Wales for his initial support, and Arthur expressed his gratitude.

Arthur O'Connor sailed quietly out of London once more on 4 January 1881, aboard the *Helenslea* bound for Sydney, travelling again in the name of George Morton. A cipher telegram and a confidential dispatch were sent to the Governor, telling him to expect the return of his former guest.

* * *

The *Helenslea* docked in Sydney on Easter Monday, 18 April, without mishap.[12] The authorities were ready for the disembarkation of George Morton and kept a close watch on him, but found him very different from seven years earlier. He took accommodation in Macquarie Street and secured work in a solicitors' office again, but started drinking heavily. Sir Henry Parkes, the Colonial Secretary and Prime Minister of the state government, wrote that 'on his first visit he was a thoughtless youth, he has now become an unmitigated ruffian'. The Inspector General of Police, Mr Fosbery, reported that there was no doubt that he was insane. When Arthur was frustrated, he would become extremely violent, and in July, he inflicted serious injury on a policeman.

On 11 July, he was committed to the Callan Park lunatic asylum, about 3 miles west of Sydney harbour. The committal papers declared that he was 'in a very excitable state and irritable, and suffers from melancholia', and that he says that 'he cannot answer for himself, that he might commit suicide, or do some injury to others'. The surgeon also noted that he was subject to fits of masturbation, which led him to drink and rendered him uncontrollable. Dr Frederic Norton Manning, the Inspector General of the Insane, reported to the Governor that he needed to be kept under observation, while Mr Fosbery noted that his health had suffered considerably from his 'habits of self-indulgence'.

On his admission, Arthur complained of intestinal injury, which he said led him to a desire for drink that he could not control. The superintendant, however, found him to be healthy, although Arthur's confession that he had contracted syphilis at one time was borne out by the scars of buboes in the groin. He described Arthur as a stern young man, with dark hair and complexion, good features and a normal expression, who weighed 9 stone 4 pounds, which was quite emaciated for his 5 feet 9 inches height. He was put in number two ward under restraint.

Callan Park had only been open three years when Arthur was admitted. It was a progressive institution set up following extensive research by Dr Manning. In the 1860s, he had been Medical Superintendent at Gladesville lunatic asylum, where he had been appalled by the overcrowded conditions. After petitioning the Colonial Secretary, he was sent on a research tour of the United Kingdom, Europe, and the United States. He visited hundreds of institutions and authorities, and after his return, wrote a 300-page report on best practice in everything from architecture to water supply.

In 1873, the Colonial Secretary purchased 104 acres of land at Callan Park, and not long after, Dr Manning was appointed as Inspector of the Insane with responsibility for all the asylums. He was noted for his humanitarianism, and in Callan Park, he specifically did not want to create another 'cemetery for deceased intellects'. The building was based on the design of Chatham Asylum, with larger windows, high ceilings, wide verandas, and covered walkways. Patients had views of Sydney and the Blue Mountains, and the use of ha-ha style steep banks before the perimeter wall reduced the feeling of incarceration. A 'pleasure garden' was created for the inmates, and in the 1880s, the surrounding 11 acres were landscaped by Charles Moore, curator of the Sydney Botanic Gardens.

Arthur's first days in Callan Park were quiet and orderly, although he continued to complain about his health, which the authorities put down to hypochondria. He was allowed to enter into the life of the asylum. But on 12 November, while supposedly going to bed, Arthur managed to escape from the grounds. He was retaken by the police and returned two days later. Because of his stated intention of trying again, he was then kept under strict surveillance.

Meanwhile, back in England, Arthur's brother William received a letter from him in December complaining that he had not heard from his family. William asked the Home Office to forward a letter to him, and the authorities sent it to Australia with the proviso that it should only be given if it would cause no mischief. In February 1882, Dr Manning reported that Arthur was still suffering from 'considerable mental visitation which is fostered by his debased habits'. He was described as extremely discontented, with a most exaggerated idea of his own importance and capabilities, and given to sudden attacks of excitement. But a month later, Arthur's irritability had eased, and he was tried at work, but he would have none of it.

At the end of April, news arrived of another attempt on the life of the sovereign, and Arthur related a vivid dream in which he saw his younger brother pointing a pistol at the Queen. On 3 May, he tried again several times to escape and made an attempt at strangling himself with his neckerchief, complaining that he was lost in body and soul. The night attendant was forced to apply muffs.[13] Arthur complained of voices that told him to blaspheme and curse God Almighty and, by way of prevention, he spent long periods muttering prayers. The doctor prescribed a sedative in rum, which was continued for some considerable time.

But Arthur believed that he was the guardian of his mother and brothers and chafed at being unable to go to them. Voices told him that he must stand in the yard and pray incessantly, that he must not eat or drink; else he would drown the Virgin Mary who lived inside him. He was restless by night and low-spirited by day. By 31 October, Arthur's weight had fallen to 8 stone 10 pounds.

As the Antipodean spring advanced, Arthur seemed to improve, and he began to work outside. On 8 December, being now more trusted, he was taken to the cricket paddock with some other patients, but he escaped once more, and was again recaptured by the police the following day. His behaviour continued to be erratic, once breaking two mugs by hurling them against a wall. In January 1883, he secreted a knife in his trousers at dinner, with the aim of stabbing the medical superintendent. He wrote incoherent letters to his mother, but then a few months later his behaviour became more normal and his letters lucid.

This set the pattern for the next twenty or so years, with further escapes, stolen knives, and well-behaved intervals, when he worked in the mess rooms or garden. In 1884, Arthur's brother John wrote to the Earl of Derby, the Colonial Secretary, asking for assistance to send his brother Roderick to Australia. Arthur had repeatedly said that he felt the lack of any relation or friend in the colony, and John thought that, with Roderick there to watch over and protect him after his release, he would 'reside quietly with his brother and no more disturb the government'. The government did not see the point, and no funds were advanced.

By 1900, Arthur was trusted enough to go with the outside carter into Sydney and to help take the pigs to the butcher, although more than once he returned the worse for drink. He frequently complained of a lack of amusements, but one time at a mixed social event, when he asked a female inmate for a dance, she said, 'Oh dear', and promptly fainted.

On 15 October 1908, he was transferred to Rydalmere Hospital for the Insane, situated in the western suburbs of Sydney. His admission notes describe him as intelligent and a good worker, but also restless, querulous, and a hypochondriac. In September 1909, he made an attempt to escape, but was found in the neighbouring convent grounds. In April 1910, he was moved with nineteen others to Morisset Hospital, situated on the coast about 60 miles north of Sydney. Later that year, he quarrelled with another patient early one morning and received a black eye. He returned to Rydalmere in April 1912.

Throughout the 1910s he exhibited the same symptoms, working well in the ward and the grounds, but continually writing letters to men of importance asking for his release. He was often depressed, saying that if he could not be free, then he would rather be dead. By 1921, when he made his last attempt at escape, he was a grey-haired old man, peering through his monocle and continually muttering to himself.

Arthur O'Connor spent forty-four years in the lunatic asylums of Sydney, and it would appear that he was never granted his wish to see his relations again. Despite her excessive drinking, his mother lived on until 1901, supported by her children, and died at the age of sixty-nine. Coincidentally, Arthur, still known only as George Morton in Australia, lived to the same age. He died on 6 December 1925. The post-mortem revealed that the cause of death was *tuberculous peritonitis*, a rare condition where the lining of the abdominal cavity becomes infected with the TB bacterium, causing stomach pain, tummy upsets, fever, and weight loss. These were symptoms that Arthur had complained of for the last forty-four years to a succession of unbelieving medical superintendents.

Both the medical establishment and the courts got it wrong this time. Arthur O'Connor was sick in body and mind, and was treated on both counts either too late or not at all. But, unlike previous assailants, he did not meekly comply with what he was told. He was intelligent enough to take advantage of the opportunities that arose from his comparatively light sentence. After he realised their fear that he might reoffend, he led the authorities a merry dance for a while, a preoccupation of the highest in the land.

Another lesson learned, the government would make sure that this did not happen again.

7

The Disaffected Artist, 1882

By Thursday 16 February 1882, Roderick Maclean had been in Southsea for a week. As usual, he felt hungry, depressed, and angry. He had just received a letter from his sister, which included the expected postal order, but she had also said that she could not carry on with the payments beyond the current month. She wrote that he should not trust to the charity of friends, but rather should take a broom and sweep a crossing.[1] It was a cynical put-down. He had been brought up as a gentleman and was practised as an artist; he could not be expected to do the work of ragamuffin boys.

His sister Annie owned a house valued at £1,500, and all of his brothers were wealthy, yet they thought he could exist on just 6s a week. Now his sister was saying that the house had not been rented for nearly a year, and she could not afford to continue with the weekly payments. In another letter, his brother had written that Roderick was of weak intellect and should be placed under restraint. He was being disowned.

He talked about the situation with his landlord and landlady, Mr and Mrs Sorrell, a couple about seventy years of age, and another lodger, Edward Hucker, who also inhabited the small house in Cecil Grove, a cul-de-sac in a pedestrian passage close to the sea behind the Pier Hotel. They agreed that it was unfair that after his family had supported him for eight years they should just cut him off like that. Of course he told Mrs Sorrell that he received 15s; he didn't want her thinking that he was a pauper. One of his brothers was related by marriage to Augustus Harris, the proprietor of the Drury Lane Theatre, and he wrote back to Annie saying that he would walk to London and ask the man for a job.

During the day, Roderick wandered around Southsea and neighbouring Portsmouth, while in the evening he read and played his old concertina. He liked to talk and he would air his radical views with his landlady and Edward Hucker. He particularly denounced the treatment that Charles Bradlaugh had received in the House of Commons. The elected member for Nottingham, an atheist, republican, and fiery orator, had been refused admittance because he would not take the oath of allegiance by swearing on the Bible. His seat fell vacant as a result, but he had been elected again by the people of Nottingham, and the standoff continued.[2]

Although he too was a republican, Roderick asked Mrs Sorrell about Osborne House and whether he would be allowed to enter the grounds. He wondered, if the Queen saw him sketching, whether she would acknowledge and speak to him. He was surprised to learn that she often passed through Portsmouth on her way to the Isle of Wight. On being told that she was not currently there, he asked after her whereabouts. Mrs Sorrell said that she would be at Windsor Castle in April, for the wedding of the Duke of Albany, Prince Leopold.

Close by his lodgings was Southsea Common, where there were views out across the sound. On his walks, Roderick frequently passed a gunsmith's shop by the common, and on that particular Thursday, he went in and asked for a cheap revolver, saying that he was going abroad. The model he was shown cost 13s, which Roderick said was too dear. Instead, he walked the mile into town and went into a pawnbroker's in Queen Street, Portsea, asking to look at a revolver on display in the window. Giving his name as Campbell, he claimed to be off to join the Cape Mounted Rifles. The assistant would not budge from the listed price of 5s 9d, so Roderick left a deposit of 2s to secure the item.

He returned to the gunsmith and asked for bullets. The shopkeeper offered a box for half a crown, but in the end Roderick settled for eighteen loose rounds at the cost of a shilling. The following Wednesday, he received another postal order from his sister, with a letter begging him to stay in his lodgings for the present. He went back to the pawnbroker's to pay off the balance of 3s 9d, and he also raised another florin by selling his concertina and scarf.

At seven o'clock on Thursday 23 February, he left his lodgings, heading north. The weather was mild, and he did not miss his scarf too much as he walked the highways and byways. However, in the village of Newton Valence, he suffered a fainting attack. The Revd Archibald Maclachlan saw him staggering and fall, and thought him half-starved and deadly pale. The clergyman gave him tea and bread and butter, and was struck by his restless eyes and his ability only to talk in a whisper. After he had recovered, the Reverend sent his gardener to help Roderick obtain lodgings back in Petersfield. The next day, Roderick hiked the 25 miles to Guildford and on Saturday, another 18 miles to Windsor. He walked into town at three o'clock in the afternoon, with a little money still in his pocket and the gun nestling in his carpetbag. The royal standard was flying over the castle, indicating that the Queen was in residence.

Roderick found lodgings later that afternoon in the house of Mr Knight, a baker, at 84 Victoria Cottages. A week's rent was 2s 6d, but Roderick said that he was currently short of money, and was allowed to stay for just 1s in advance. He claimed to have a situation in view in Eton, and in any case, he said he was expecting another order in the post. For the next three days, he left the house after breakfast, returning for tea, ostensibly spending the day looking for employment. His landlord was struck by the fact that he never took off his overcoat, even in his room when it was quite hot. He kept smoothing down the front, as if to conceal any bumps in the fabric.

On the third day, Tuesday 28th, the Queen drove out of the castle, heading for the station, where she boarded a train for London, bound for Buckingham Palace. Roderick went to see her, but missed her departure. He found out that the Queen would return on Thursday. On Wednesday, Roderick complained of toothache, and his landlady let him remain in the house all day, and to eat dinner in the afternoon.

After her arrival in London, Victoria met with the French ambassador, and the following day visited the Empress Eugénie. On Thursday 2 March, she took dinner with several of her family and Princess Helen of Waldeck-Pyrmont, Leopold's fiancée, who was returning to the Continent that day. Later in the afternoon, the Queen set out for the return journey to Windsor, accompanied by Princess Beatrice, the Dowager Duchess of Roxburghe, General Viscount Bridport, and Colonel Sir John Carstairs McNeill. The party was escorted to Paddington by a detachment of the Second Life Guards. Resplendent in their plumed helmets and shining breastplates, they were a bodyguard belonging to another age.

Six months earlier, Victoria had learned of the assassination of the American President, James Garfield, and sent a message of sympathy to his wife, as she had done to Mrs Lincoln, sixteen years earlier. American assassins seemed to have a better aim, or maybe it was their use of the modern revolver, rather than ancient flintlock weapons.

The Queen's special train left Paddington at ten minutes before five o'clock. At exactly the same time, the stationmaster at Windsor, Mr Smythe, came across an ill-dressed man in the first class waiting room. Little believing his claim that he was waiting for the train, he asked him to leave. Roderick went to join the crowds in the yard, the revolver hidden in the right-hand pocket of his coat. The Queen's train drew in punctually at 5.25 p.m. The platform was carpeted and railed off on each side to hold back the waiting assembly. After a few moments, the Queen descended from the train, walked across the platform, and through the waiting room.

She passed into the station yard where, the weather being very cold, a closed carriage stood waiting. Victoria, accompanied by Princess Beatrice and the Duchess of Roxburghe, took their seats. The onlookers from the platform joined those crowded in the yard to cheer as the outriders set off. The Queen was clearly visible through the open window of the carriage.

The yard was full of Eton schoolboys, who, as usual, had occupied the best positions. Roderick was close to the yard entrance, but could not find a spot with a clear view of the royal cortège. As the horses pulled away, pressure from the scholars squeezed the onlookers ever closer together. Roderick managed to force his way to the front, but then had difficulty removing his hand from his pocket. When the carriage was about halfway towards him, he finally broke free. He stepped away from the crowd and pulled out the revolver. He levelled the gun, his arm straight out from the shoulder. As the carriage approached, Roderick fired.

The report was loud and broke through the cheering. Heads turned in Roderick's direction. Chief Superintendent Hayes of the Borough Police was near the wicket gate of the yard, facing the roadway. At the sound of the gunshot, he quickly turned and saw the man with the pistol in his raised arm. He bounded across the three yards that separated them and seized the man by the collar. A photographer, James Burnside, grabbed Roderick's wrist and forced him to drop the pistol. Inspector Fraser of the Royal Household Police and some bystanders joined in the affray, and the attacker was pushed back against the railings.

An Eton schoolboy, George Chesney Wilson[3], grabbed his arm and hit him on the head with an umbrella. His friend, Leslie Murray Robertson, followed suit. Roderick spoke up, 'Don't hurt me; I will go quietly.' The Queen looked on at the commotion as the carriage swept out of the yard, making for Windsor Castle.

* * *

Eight years earlier, much to Victoria's relief, Gladstone lost a general election and Disraeli returned to power. By then he was seventy, and, despite his dyed black hair, he looked it, but to Victoria he was charming, with his courtly manners and flashing eyes, and she openly warmed in his presence. He called her the Faery Queen, ignoring the fact that she was now seriously overweight and hardly fair of face. By unspoken agreement, Disraeli made no objections to royal appointments, while Victoria let him have his way with home affairs. Reform followed, with many moves to protect the citizen, including a Public Health Act, a Factory Act, and a Sale of Foods and Drugs Act.

The Queen agreed to open Parliament in 1876, because, as on all previous occasions since Albert's death, she wanted something. Two of her daughters might one day accede to the title 'Empress', which was of higher rank than mere 'Queen'. The Prince of Wales was enjoying a successful tour of India; a good time, thought Victoria, to add 'Empress of India' to her other titles. Disraeli did not think it an opportune moment, but after an acrimonious debate in the Commons, Victoria got her way.

Disraeli's health was failing; he was suffering from gout, chronic bronchitis, and the effects of heavy smoking. Victoria would not hear of his offers to resign and instead gave him a peerage so that he could carry on from the House of Lords and avoid the taxing work in the Commons. One critical foreign policy issue at the time was the Balkans, where atrocities against Christians had enraged public opinion against the Turks. But Victoria knew that dismembering the Ottoman Empire would expose the weak Balkan states to the control of the Russians and their German and Austrian allies, upsetting the balance of power. In April 1877, Russian troops crossed the Turkish border. The government did not want to get involved, but Victoria feared that the Russian forces would not stop before they had taken Constantinople and threatened British interests.

Key to any military action was the navy, but the First Lord of the Admiralty died in July 1877. With Victoria's reluctant approval, Disraeli appointed a replacement from the middle classes, William Henry Smith, the bookstall proprietor. Two years later, he became the inspiration behind the 'Ruler of the Queen's Navee' in Gilbert and Sullivan's *HMS Pinafore*. Initially the Ottomans held the Russian advance, but in December they crumbled. After a year of cabinet indecision, Disraeli at last put the military on a war footing. Public opinion was also swinging against the old foe, with the music hall song:

> We don't want to fight, but, by Jingo, if we do,
> We've got the ships, we've got the men, we've got the money too …

A fleet of battleships was sent to intimidate the Russians and stop their advance. Once assurances that Russia would not try to take Constantinople were received, the British fleet withdrew from the Dardanelles, and the Ottomans were forced to sue for peace. They were left with just a sliver of land in Europe and 50 miles less of the Black Sea coast, while an enlarged Bulgaria stretched across to the Aegean Sea, a Russian satellite state. The Queen was outraged. Disraeli struggled to the peace conference in Berlin and faced off Bismarck to reach a satisfactory deal. As part of the settlement, Britain acquired Cyprus and pledged to defend Turkey from any more expansionism.

In the spring of 1880, despite a gallant fight, Disraeli lost the general election campaign to a Liberal landslide. He died a year later, charming the Queen to the very end. Victoria was forced to welcome back Gladstone, who now also had several radical republicans in his party. He was, by then, seventy and growing deaf, but he used his deafness strategically to ignore many of the Queen's opinions. During Disraeli's ministry, Victoria had often appeared more energetic in the defence of her country than the ailing Prime Minister, and Gladstone was very unhappy with the sovereign's prominence in public affairs. For her part, Victoria was worried that Gladstone's popularity was turning him into a demagogue.

Gladstone was again more concerned with domestic matters and balanced his budget by placing a tax on beer, uninterested in Victoria's view that a charge on wine would affect those better able to pay. Abroad, he shied away from hostilities. Withdrawal from Kandahar on the north-west frontier in Afghanistan was proposed, and the first Anglo-Boer war, over the collection of taxes in the annexed Transvaal, was not pursued energetically. Victoria worried what would happen if Britain was seen to be weak. In August 1881, the Transvaal was given limited independence, thereby avoiding serious conflict. But this merely sowed the seeds of a much bigger confrontation twenty years later.

Six months after, Victoria was more concerned with the approaching marriage of her son, Prince Leopold. She met his fiancée in London, and it was on her return to Windsor that the would-be assassin struck. As the carriage pulled out of the station, Victoria heard a sound that she thought was an explosion from an engine. Princess Beatrice, who was sitting beside her, actually saw the man take aim and fire directly at the carriage, but, seeing the Queen unperturbed, she said nothing. At the castle, John Brown and others informed her of the details of what had happened. She confided to her journal that she did not feel shaken or frightened, 'so different to O'Connor's attempt [when she had been terribly alarmed], though [this] was infinitely more dangerous'. The next day, she walked down to the mausoleum with Beatrice and, she wrote, 'knelt by my beloved one's tomb and offered up prayers of thanksgiving for my preservation to God our Heavenly Father'. She realised that it was almost exactly a decade since the previous attack.

* * *

Roderick Edward Maclean's upbringing was initially comfortable, if unconventional. He was born on 10 February 1854, at 144a Oxford Street, London. His father, Charles[4], was a carver and gilder, who turned out thousands of picture frames, and ran a thriving business called the Commercial Plate Glass Company, dealing in looking glasses and plate glass. Apart from the premises in Oxford Street, the company also had workshops at 58–60 Fleet Street. In 1852, Charles gained fame by fitting his shopfront with plate-glass panes sized 10 feet by 16 feet, believed then to be the largest in the world. *The Sun* newspaper said that it was 'the most magnificent thing of its kind in London', a 'perilous undertaking' and speculated that 'the cost must have been immense'.

Charles appears to have been something of a maverick. He does not seem to have registered the birth of many of his children, and baptised the first four all together when they were aged nought to six. In 1861, he became the proprietor of a new weekly magazine called *Fun*, a rival to *Punch*. He gave over No. 60 Fleet Street to the operation, and the first edition was published on 21 September. It was twelve pages and cost one penny, as opposed to *Punch's* threepence, and thus became known as 'the poor man's Punch'. The first editor of *Fun* was Henry J. Byron, who used to call the proprietor 'Maclean teeth', because of his expansive smile and shining teeth.[5] The magazine featured Mr Fun, the jester, and his cat, to be compared with Mr Punch and his dog Toby. The magazine had a young upstart liveliness, which by then Punch had lost, and was well received, reaching a circulation of 20,000 by 1865.[6]

As well as the unconventional exploits of his father, Roderick no doubt heard about the antics of his father's brother, Edward, who caused a scandal some time before Roderick's birth. In 1845, he was assaulted at his premises in the Strand, where he was a picture dealer, by his brother-in-law, John Mayer. Edward made a complaint, and at the magistrate's court it emerged that the reason for the assault was that Edward had made Mayer's daughter, his own niece, pregnant. She was then living with Edward, while his wife was in the country during her own lying-in period. The magistrate would not grant bail to Mayer, despite the provocation, but an application for *habeas corpus* before a judge was successful, the charge was dropped, and the magistrate reprimanded. Roderick's infamous uncle Edward died just a few months before Roderick was born.

The first years of Roderick's life were happy, and he was sent to a school in Harley Street, Cavendish Square; an establishment for 'delicate young gentlemen requiring maternal care'. The family moved to accommodation separate from the glass business at 8 Gloucester Road in West London. But *Fun* was not proving a financial success, and his father gave up ownership of the magazine in May 1865. Twelve months later, he also suffered badly with the collapse of the Overend, Gurney & Company bank[7], which took much of his accumulated capital.

That same year Roderick suffered the accident that would change his life. One day in March 1866, his father asked him to run across the road to get change for a florin. On returning, he slipped and fell as he entered the house, cutting his head severely. He was treated by Dr Towers Smith of Kensington over the next six weeks, but he never felt the same thereafter. Pulling the hair even gently over the place where the cut was, caused a curious sensation down the side of his face, like pins and needles or a slight electric shock. He complained of pains in the head, and said that 'worry, trouble and anxiety always seem to fly to it'.

As a youth, he travelled abroad and learnt to speak French and German quite well, but his behaviour was becoming more erratic. He expressed a desire to go to sea and embarked on a ship bound for America. But he insisted on being put ashore at Gravesend, as he thought some of the sailors were intent on murdering him. His father booked a berth on a larger ship, but Roderick refused to join the vessel, as he thought his father had arranged with the captain to have him thrown overboard.

Like two of his sisters, he listed his occupation as 'artist', but he never had a proper job. He was very fond of amusement and regularly attended the theatre. When he was seventeen, he committed some sort of forgery, for which he later said he was never forgiven. That same year, 1871, Roderick went to stay with an artist friend, Samuel Stanesby, in Sutherland Gardens, Paddington. His friend reported that he often displayed overweening vanity and thought himself a great actor, and as well, showed clear signs of insanity.

When he was eighteen, on the advice of a medical man, his father found him a situation with a farmer in Margate. It was thought that work in the open air might strengthen his mind. His father accompanied him to the farm, but they had to pass through a churchyard to gain access, and Roderick refused to take the job, as he said it was all set up so that he could easily be interred.

The Commercial Plate Glass Company was also now in difficulties, and Charles Maclean sold up and opened a stationer's in Maddox Street, near Regent Street. Roderick liked to help, but his behaviour continued to be a problem. In 1873, he refused to work and started hiding himself about the house, in corners of the rooms and passageways, secreting knives on his person and saying that he would kill his father one day. Whenever Roderick passed someone in the street dressed for mourning, he felt that he himself would die before the next morning. He often imagined he would die on a certain date, but that if he survived beyond that, he would live forever. In early 1874, he tried to gain admittance to St George's Hospital, but nothing was found to be wrong with him.

In June 1874, his father approached Henry Essex, the receiving officer for Kensington guardian's office. In the company of a Justice of the Peace (JP) and Dr Godrich, Mr Essex visited Roderick, but the doctor was not sufficiently convinced to issue a certificate under the lunacy acts. Dr Godrich advised Charles to send him away from home, if possible to an institution fitted for such cases.

But his father could not afford to pay for a private clinic, so instead sent him to work for another farmer, Stephen Dale, at Waters End near Dover. Again it was not to Roderick's liking, and he left in disgust in August. On his way back, he wandered onto a bridge spanning the London, Chatham & Dover railway at Ewell, close to the farm. Seeing some children playing, he gave one of the boys a halfpenny to place a ball of chalk on the line for the fun of seeing the train smash it. He then offered sixpence to them to put a wooden sleeper on the line. Luckily they couldn't move it, and some women in an adjacent garden asked the boys who had sent them onto the line. Subsequently, the company took out a summons against him.

On Roderick's return to the family home, now at 112 Earl's Court Road, his father called on Dr Henry Maudsley to assess his son's mental health. On 18 September, the doctor issued a certificate stating that Roderick Maclean was not of perfectly sound mind, and recommended placing him under supervision, as there was every reason to believe that he would someday perpetrate some mischief. In October, Dr Alfred Godrich looked at the boy again and was of the same opinion. But Roderick was not committed, and in December, he was tried at Maidstone Assizes before Baron Bramwell for having aided and abetted a boy named Cheeseman in placing an obstruction on the railway at Ewell. The charge involved a threat to safety, and luckily for Roderick, was dismissed as the boy was incapable of lifting the sleeper.

Two years later, when Roderick was twenty-two, his father died. His mother lasted another couple of years, but the family gradually dispersed, and Roderick was left to his own devices. Little money had been left by his father, although all of his siblings were becoming quite wealthy. His two surviving sisters, Caroline and Annie, both spinsters and then thirty-eight and twenty-four years old, had private means. Caroline died not long after, leaving an estate worth £1,510 to her sister, a considerable sum. Annie went to live in Addington, near Croydon, where she owned a house said to be worth a similar amount.

Of his three brothers, Charles was an artist fourteen years older than Roderick, who reputedly managed a picture gallery and was related by marriage to Augustus Harris, the theatre impresario, from whom Roderick later hoped to obtain employment. Hector Maclean, just two years older than Roderick, gave up his work as a picture editor after he married the rich widow of an engineer. His brother Donald, two years younger than Roderick, is believed to have emigrated to Australia, where he worked as a lawyer.

So the whole family was well off, with Roderick the one exception. With his frequent demands and strange behaviour, he must have been a trial to his siblings. When they each moved, they did not give him their new address, and left his maintenance to Annie. Roderick, with all his mental problems, was allowed to drift, existing on some meagre handouts channelled through his sister. He first moved north, spending several months in County Durham, but then returned in 1877 to lodge in Guildford for two months with a widow, Mrs Jeffery. While he was there, he made his first contact with Queen Victoria, sending her a poem on a half sheet of notepaper, which read (verbatim):

On your thrown you set and rule us al',
By justice you make known
All your power, and the people like
To cheer the Queen they call their own.
When your lamented husband left us,
And went were troubles find no share,
How we felt for you and tried too lessen
The sting of bad fate you had to bare,
But God knows whats for our best
Sent you comfort in your most trying hour,
And made you bare your troubles as a nobly woman should,
And the people showed their love, and liked your power,
When History tells, of your good reign,
They will think of you and say,
Its the Queen who made her people happy,
By affection and justice thats how she rule the sway.

But Mrs Jeffery was not keen on her lodger, especially after he showed her the dagger that he carried with him to the local fair, allegedly for protection. She showed him the door, so Roderick never saw the abrupt reply that came from a lady-in-waiting at Buckingham Palace:

Lady Biddulph is obliged to return Mr Maclean his verses. The Queen never accepts manuscript poetry.

Roderick roamed across the South of England, increasingly resembling a tramp. Much of his time was spent on the South Coast, in towns such as Ramsgate, Margate, Brighton, Worthing, and Shoreham, never stopping in one place for more than a few weeks or months. At one point, he ventured across the Channel and lived in Boulogne for a while. But he soon returned, and in early 1880, he ended up in the Bedminster Union workhouse in Somerset, where he said he was an out-of-work artist. After six weeks, he moved on to Clevedon on the Severn Estuary and, in May, to lodgings in Weston-Super-Mare. Whilst living in the seaside town, he wrote two letters to his sister Caroline talking of murder. His ravings attracted attention, and at the beginning of June he was seen by Dr Charles Vernon Hitchins and a JP, who issued a certificate committing him to the Bath & Somerset Lunatic Asylum at Wells.

His insanity was diagnosed as homicidal mania, as he thought that all the people in England were against him and he must do harm to someone. He also suffered partly from melancholia. But he remained in the asylum for only just over a year, and on 21 July 1881, after a period of probation, he was diagnosed as cured and released. He resumed his wanderings across the country, often staying in the wards of workhouses. From Wells he went to Axbridge, Shepton Mallet, London, Brighton, and Eastbourne. He called in at Windsor and visited the castle, telling a sentry that he wanted to see the Queen and asking which rooms she occupied. Existing on the pittance of 7s 6d a week (later reduced to 6s) sent by his sister, and feeling almost starved, he tried to obtain employment, but was unsuccessful because of his shabby appearance. He raged against the miserliness of his wealthy siblings.

Later, he spent five or six weeks in the Eastbourne workhouse. He tried to get into the infirmary, but was said to be shamming and instead was set to work digging potatoes. The guardians were not satisfied with his performance and found him eccentric and a liar. He spent a lot of time writing letters. One day, having had no dinner and little breakfast, he set off for the top of Beachy Head intending to commit suicide. But he passed through a beautiful landscape, where children were picking blackberries, so he did the same and forgot about his intentions.

He moved on to the Brighton & Steyning Union Workhouse at Shoreham for a month, and then, at the beginning of February 1882, he set out to walk to Portsmouth. From there he moved on to Windsor.

* * *

At half-past ten on the Monday following the attack on the Queen, the scholars of Eton College formed up outside the walls of the school. Smartly dressed in black tailcoats with top hats and canes, they marched across the bridge, through the town, and up Castle Hill, 900 strong and four abreast. They entered the quadrangle of Windsor Castle and moved into lines, the school captains to the fore. The Queen came out, surrounded by her entourage, to greet them, and listened attentively to their prepared congratulatory address on her escape. She then read her own reply, thanking them for their kind and hearty congratulations, and hoping that they would forever uphold 'the honour and glory of this ancient kingdom'.

When Wilson and Robertson had returned to the school after the dastardly attack, news of their actions in striking the villain over the head with their umbrellas had gone before them. They were treated to a rousing ovation, and the story of their exploits grew with each retelling. By Sunday, *Reynold's Newspaper* reported that it was thanks to the quick wittedness of the scholars that the would-be assassin's revolver had been spotted and the alarm raised. According to this fanciful account, the scoundrel was then overpowered by three of the larger boys, forcing the shot to miss the carriage and ricochet harmlessly off the cobbles. Victoria did not show that she knew otherwise and shook the hands of the two heroes.

Chief Superintendent Hayes certainly knew how the attacker had been disarmed, but after he had arrested the villain, his main thought was to save the man from the mob. With the help of Inspector Fraser, they hustled Roderick up Station Hill, followed by the hooting crowd. In the High Street, they found a cab, and managed to get him away to Windsor police station. Roderick was quiet on the journey, just saying, 'I am starving, otherwise I should not have done this.'

Once safely in the police station, Hayes had an opportunity to look at the weapon, which had been given to him by the man who had picked it up, James Burnside. It was a medium-sized, six-chamber revolver of Belgian manufacture, and of the six chambers, two were empty, two contained the shells of discharged rounds, and two – the next to be fired – held live cartridges. Roderick was searched, and the following articles taken from him: fourteen further cartridges, an old pocket book, two old clay smoking pipes, a metal box, an old knife, a necktie, a brass scarf ring, two buttons, a latchkey, two pieces of metal chain, a piece of cord, two combs, a pocket looking glass, two rather dirty handkerchiefs, a purse, 1¾d in copper coins, a daily newspaper, two envelopes, two pieces of pencil, and a sheet of paper. The latter seemed to be a draft for a letter:

> I should not have done this crime had you, as you should have done, paid the 10s per week instead of offering me the insulting sum of 6s per week, and expecting me to live on it. So you perceive the great good a little money would have done, had you not treated me as a fool, and set me more than ever against those bloated aristocrats, led by that old lady Mrs Vic., who is an accursed robber in all senses.
> Roderick Maclean
> March 2, 1882
> Waiting room, Great Western Railway.

No doubt the intended recipient was his sister Annie, a cry for help in the face of the injustice of his treatment by his siblings and the world. The pocket book held no evidence related to the attack, containing many other notes, including what appeared to be an idea for a book: '*The Fourth Path*, a novel by Roderick Maclean. Four drops of sweet nitre[8] and half a tumbler of water.' His lodgings were searched, and his carpet bag impounded. It contained two dictionaries; two pairs of very old shoes; a bundle of rags rolled up; some dirty pocket handkerchiefs; and some old newspapers. Mr Simpson, a Justice of the Peace, arrived at the police station and Roderick Maclean was formally charged with shooting at Her Majesty the Queen with intent to do her grievous bodily harm. He gave his address as 84 Victoria Cottages, Windsor. He was taken to the cells.

The following morning, a search of the station yard was made by the Great Western Railway police. Close to some trucks, and 15 yards from the Queen's waiting room, they discovered a bullet embedded in the ground. It was of the same type used in the confiscated revolver. A mark was found on a truck that could have been caused by a bullet ricochet. At about 5 feet 5 inches above the ground, there was a mark on the last '7' of truck number 21377, and a small amount of white paint was found on the bullet. Knowing where the attacker had stood and where the bullet was found, an attempt was made to reconstruct its trajectory. The Queen's carriage would have passed through the line.

Roderick told a different story, and wrote out the following statement:

Police Office, Windsor, March 3, 1882

I am not guilty of the charge of shooting with the intention of causing actual bodily harm. My object was by frightening the Queen to alarm the public, with the result of having my grievances respected – viz., such as the pecuniary straits in which I have been situated. All the circumstances tend to prove this statement. Firstly had I desired to injure the Queen I should have fired at her when she was quitting the railway carriage. Quite on the contrary, I pointed the pistol on a level with the wheels: but as I felt a slight kick, doubtless the contents may have lodged in one of the doors.

If Her Majesty will accept this explanation, and allow the words, 'with intent to intimidate her', instead of 'with intent to cause grievous bodily harm', to be inserted in that count, I will offer all the assistance in my power to bring the charge herein specified to a speedy issue.

I hope Her Majesty will accept the only consolation I can offer – namely, I had no intention whatever of causing her any injury.

Roderick Maclean

At half past one, Roderick was taken in an open fly[9] across town to Windsor Town Hall, where he was brought before the Windsor magistrates. Thanks to a thorough wash in the cells and the help of a constable in tidying up his appearance and lending him some boots, he presented a slightly better aspect to the court. He nevertheless wore a pair of shabby, light trousers, a well-worn long brown overcoat, and an exceedingly dilapidated round hat. Handcuffed to a plain-clothes officer, Roderick was charged with having fired a pistol at Her Majesty with intent to kill her. The prosecution was handled by Mr Stephenson, solicitor to the Treasury.

After Superintendent Hayes gave evidence as to what had happened, Roderick cross-questioned him in detail about exactly what he saw. The jury joined in a debate as to whether or not the gun was pointed at the centre of the carriage. Joseph Turner, an inspector in the Engineer's Department of the Great Western Railway, next gave evidence as to his discovery of the bullet, followed by James Burnside, the man who had, together with Hayes, first reached the prisoner. Roderick cross-examined both men and, despite stuttering badly, the newspapers later wrote that his questions were astute and those of a well-educated man.

Roderick was remanded in custody for a week, and was put in a closed cab for the return journey to the police station, surrounded by a large body of police to prevent the gathered throng from getting too close. They would have been better to have adopted the diversionary tactics used by the Metropolitan Police to move suspects. As Roderick left, the large crowd in the street hooted, and outside the town hall the mob were so excited that they tried to overturn the carriage that was taking him back to the cells. There, he was photographed by the London Stereoscopic & Photographic Company to help with further enquiries. Having learnt their lesson, the next day the police transferred the prisoner to Reading gaol with great secrecy, so as to avoid further public attacks. A closed fly drove up to the police station at eight o'clock, and he was taken through the streets of the town and across to Slough station, where it was felt he would attract less attention. But the prisoner was spotted, a crowd gathered, and he had to be taken into the booking office. Roderick was hustled onto the 8.20 a.m. train while eating a biscuit, apparently unconcerned by the attention.

On Friday 10th, he again appeared before the magistrates at Windsor Town Hall. Extensive evidence was given by a dozen or so witnesses for the prosecution, but Roderick reserved his defence. Several people claimed that the gun was indeed pointed at the carriage, and that if he had not been apprehended, he would have fired again. He was remanded to the next Berkshire Assizes on a charge of high treason.

Although Roderick was not represented during the hearing, the solicitor of Roderick's brothers, Mr Haynes, was present, together with Edmund Thomas of Hare Court, Temple, their counsel. Mr Haynes subsequently wrote to the Treasury Secretary asking for financial help to pay the fees of two doctors, Dr Maudsley and Dr Hitchins, who would examine the mental state of the prisoner. The brothers, he wrote shamefacedly, had 'exhausted their pecuniary means' and it appears that the request was acceded to, at least in part.

* * *

By half-past ten on Wednesday 19 April, the courtroom of Reading Assizes was densely packed. The four windows, shaped like a cross in the flat roof, illuminated the grey walls and yellowing varnished oak of the benches, whilst a loud buzz of conversation filled the room as the audience waited expectantly for the forthcoming spectacle. The gallery to the left was packed with the Grand Jurymen, whilst opposite sat the magistrates and their wives, mostly dressed in sombre hues, but with flashes of colour from the spring primroses pinned to the women's costumes. The gallery facing the bench was full of the friends of the High Sheriff, whilst down below the space reserved for the general public was packed tight with onlookers. The only spaces unoccupied were the bench, the seats for counsel, and the dock. The county constabulary checked the tickets of the attendees and tried to prevent people from straying from their allotted place into some other forbidden fold.

As the half hour chimed forth from a neighbouring steeple, the curtains behind the bench were swept aside and the two judges entered the room. The Lord Chief Justice of England, Lord Coleridge, and Mr Baron Huddleston, lead judge for the Oxford circuit, were resplendent in their scarlet coats fringed with ermine, their heads covered in full-bottom wigs. They were joined on the bench by the High Sheriff and several other dignitaries.

The prosecution team consisted of the Attorney General and three others, while Mr Montagu Williams and Mr Arthur Yates appeared for the defence. The Attorney General read out the charge, which still held that it was the prisoner's intention to kill the Queen, and he was prosecuted under the law of high treason established by Edward III in 1352 and modified by the statute of George III. The Grand Jury were asked to consider the charge and, after half an hour's deliberation, they found a true bill against Roderick Maclean for high treason.

The prisoner was brought into the dock. Roderick had spent over a month in Reading gaol, and the time had not improved his constitution. He looked weaker, both physically and mentally, as he gazed at the hundreds of people staring at him, the lamentable centre of attention. His complexion was unhealthy and sallow, stubble covering his cheeks and chin, and a badly cut crop of black hair fell down low over his wrinkled forehead. With no sign of linen, his thin neck emerged from a dingy overcoat of indeterminate colour, which time and dirt had rendered a muddy greenish grey. A small figure in the vast expanse of a dock designed to hold many, his face twitched before the might of the scarlet-clad judges, the aristocrats, court officials, and the dozens of other dignitaries assembled to try him.

The indictment was read, that the prisoner did 'traitorously and maliciously compass the death of Her Majesty'. In reply, Roderick managed to whisper, 'Not guilty, my Lord.' The names of the jury were called, a mixture of tradesmen and farmers, and they took their seats in the jury box. The Attorney General, the same gentleman who had led the successful prosecution of Arthur O'Connor, opened the case for the Crown by outlining the basic facts. Perhaps aware of the unfortunate outcome of the previous case, he emphasised that the Crown would not hold back any evidence related to the sanity of the prisoner. Evidence was then called for from Superintendent Hayes, James Burnside, and three other witnesses to the events: Francis Orchard, a royal servant; Roger Errington, a cattle spice manufacturer from Sunderland; and one of the Eton students.

Thomas Davidson, the borough surveyor, produced a plan of Windsor Station and yard. Joseph Turner gave evidence on the finding of the bullet. The stationmaster described how he had earlier turned Roderick away. The gunsmith and pawnbroker from Portsmouth gave their evidence. During all this time, there had been no cross-questioning from the defence, and the Attorney General decided not to call any further witnesses, as the facts of the case did not seem to be under question.

In a subdued tone, Mr Montagu Williams opened the case for the defence by extolling the virtues of the monarch and saying it was impossible to imagine any sane person wishing to do her harm. Evidence was then given by Dr Towers Smith on the prisoner's original head injury, and by numerous medical men on his possible insanity. Roderick's friend Samuel Stanesby and the Revd Maclachlan (who had helped Roderick in Newton Valence and, by a curious coincidence, was also present at the shooting) also spoke about the prisoner's behaviour and demeanour. The defence did not call Roderick's sister or brothers, as it allegedly 'would be extremely painful' for them.

Dr Maudsley quoted from the report he had written after visiting Roderick in gaol. Roderick had spoken of the great pains in his head near to the injury and that he had attempted suicide through poison once, but had not succeeded. He said he suffered from fainting attacks, which the doctor thought were probably epileptic seizures. He also admitted that 'he had been greatly addicted to the vice of masturbation'.

Dr Manning, the medical superintendent of Laverstock Asylum in Salisbury, had visited Roderick twice in gaol and read from his report. He held that the prisoner suffered from three delusions:

That there was a determination on the part of the people of England to keep him in debased circumstances and to starve him;

That persons were in the habit of dressing in blue to mock and insult him, he being a notable person and in the habit of wearing blue;

And that he had been endowed with extraordinary supernatural power from on high, and that this power was expressed in the numerals 4, 14, 44, 440, and so on.

Two letters from Roderick to his sister Annie, written in 1880 from Weston-super-Mare, were read out in court. He wrote that, 'millions of people are trying to injure, annoy, and vex me on every opportunity' and 'if they don't cease wearing blue, I will commit murder'.

The next to speak was Dr Sheppard, the medical superintendent at Colney Hatch Lunatic Asylum, who had also visited Roderick twice in Reading gaol. He said that the scar on the right side of his head from the accident was still much in evidence, 2 inches long and very tender under pressure. Roderick had revealed many of the same delusions reported by others, and claimed that he had a perfect right to do what he did as he had a great and secret power over mankind. He also said that he was as related to the royal family as George IV had been, and that the Crown would have torn him to pieces but for Jesus Christ.

Dr William Orange, the medical superintendent at Broadmoor Criminal Lunatic Asylum, saw him three times in Reading gaol, and supported Dr Sheppard's assertion that he was of unsound mind. Dr Oliver Maurice, the surgeon at Reading gaol, concurred.

The case clearly revolved around whether the prisoner was insane or not, and both counsels summed up to that effect. The judge said that the jury needed to decide whether it had been proved that the prisoner 'did not know the nature and quality of the act which he was doing, or, if he did know its nature and quality, that he did not know that he was doing wrong'. After retiring for just five minutes to consider their verdict, the jury returned. The foreman stood and said, in a nervous voice, 'Not guilty, on the grounds of insanity.' Lord Coleridge ordered the prisoner to be detained in custody during Her Majesty's pleasure.

Roderick appeared uninterested in the verdict, and seemed to be unaware that the trial was over until an officer took him by the arm and led him away.

* * *

Victoria, however, was extremely interested and upset by the verdict. She reputedly said, 'Insane he may have been, but not guilty he most certainly was not.' She wrote, 'The bullet found, and yet he is only to be shut up. It is Oxford's case over again.' The government felt that the result of the trial was as they intended, but Gladstone replied tactfully that he agreed that the verdict was not in a satisfactory form. After a lot of debate, the wording was changed in 1883 in the British Trial of Lunatics Act to 'guilty but insane'. The law and medical professions were scornful, and the *Medical Times and Gazette* commented that it saw no reason 'to put in place the cumbrous machinery of legislation and to pass an Act of Parliament, for the sole purpose of altering one form of words for another form of words having virtually the same meaning and exactly the same practical effect'.[10] The events in Windsor also inspired publication of an ode by William Topaz McGonagall, considered by some to be the worst poet in the English language.

The Attempted Assassination of the Queen

God prosper long our noble Queen,
And long may she reign!
Maclean he tried to shoot her,
But it was all in vain.

For God He turned the ball aside
Maclean aimed at her head;
And he felt very angry
Because he didn't shoot her dead.

There's a divinity that hedges a king,
And so it does seem,
And my opinion is, it has hedged
Our most gracious Queen.

Maclean must be a madman,
Which is obvious to be seen,
Or else he wouldn't have tried to shoot
Our most beloved Queen.

Victoria is a good Queen,
Which all her subjects know,
And for that God has protected her
From all her deadly foes.

She is noble and generous,
Her subjects must confess;
There hasn't been her equal
Since the days of good Queen Bess.

Long may she be spared to roam
Among the bonnie Highland floral,
And spend many a happy day
In the palace of Balmoral.

Because she is very kind
To the old women there,
And allows them bread, tea, and sugar,
And each one to get a share.

And when they know of her coming,
Their hearts feel overjoy'd,
Because, in general, she finds work
For men that's unemploy'd.

And she also gives the gipsies money
While at Balmoral, I've been told,
And, mind ye, seldom silver,
But very often gold.

> I hope God will protect her
> By night and by day,
> At home and abroad,
> When she's far away.

> May He be as a hedge around her,
> As he's been all along,
> And let her live and die in peace
> Is the end of my song.

On 8 May, Roderick was moved from Reading gaol to Broadmoor Criminal Lunatic Asylum. Roderick was taken to his single cell, which measured 12 feet by 8 feet. The asylum was divided into six 'wards', separating the violent criminals from those of lower risk. Roderick was probably placed in the latter category, and trusted to organise his own day. He was woken at six o'clock, had to be up by seven, and in bed by eight in the evening. His linen was changed twice a week, and he was expected to have a bath once a week. It was very cold in the asylum during the wintertime, but two years after Roderick was admitted, heating was installed for the first time.

The asylum was situated on a high ridge among pine woods less than a mile from the village of Crowthorne in Berkshire. The view from the terrace extended over 20 miles of Hampshire and Surrey, and was deemed a healthy site for curing the insane. Boundary walls 16 feet high encircled two separate enclosures containing the men's blocks (14 acres) and the women's (3½ acres). In between was the medical superintendent's house. Inside the walls was a large kitchen garden, and outside, a 170-acre farm.

Roderick was expected to work, either on the farm or in the workshops, which comprised a tinsmith, carpenter, upholsterer, and shoemaker. The output contributed to the running costs of the asylum[11], but Roderick was also paid one-eighth of the value of what he produced to spend on small luxuries. During leisure time he could enjoy the dayrooms for meals and socialising, with newspapers, games, billiard tables, pianos, and a small library. He was encouraged to attend a religious service every day, which was one of the few times that men and women met. A teacher was employed for the illiterate, of little use to Roderick, but he also gave music lessons. He taught the patients to sing in the choir and also supervised the staff brass band.

But life in the asylum, with so many disturbed and occasionally violent inmates, was not without danger. Dr Orange, who was the medical superintendent during Roderick's first four years in the institution, was one of those who suffered. A month after Roderick's incarceration, the superintendent survived an attack by an inmate, the Revd Dodwell. The man struck him on the head with a stone swung in a handkerchief, the weapon of choice for attacks on staff. The clergyman had been committed for firing a pistol at the Master of the Rolls, and was still trying to garner publicity for his supposed wrongs.

Hopefully, Roderick escaped most of the violence and he probably prospered physically, but he railed against the curtailment of his freedom. In February 1884, he wrote a petition to the Home Secretary asking for his release, or alternatively for transfer to the county asylum. In June 1885, he wrote again, requesting that he be restored to society, if necessary conditional on leaving England for Australia or one of the other colonies. Further petitions followed in 1886 and 1887, and again in 1905, but all were refused, and Roderick was destined to spend the rest of his life in Broadmoor.

Immediately after Roderick's trial, the Queen had arranged for £5 to be gifted to Chief Superintendent Hayes. James Burnside, the man who had also helped disarm the attacker, also looked for recognition and a reward, but was rebuffed. His father carried on the campaign for many long years, until, in 1895, he finally lost patience with the Home Office. He wrote from his home in the Channel Islands to the *Guernsey Times*, which published a series of articles in which he claimed the police had unfairly exaggerated the role of the superintendent and taken the glory for disarming the assailant from his son.

Even less deserving of recognition were the Eton schoolboys. In 1900, the journal *Mainly About People* published an article under the heading 'The Boy Who Saved the Queen', which read, 'Few people are aware that Major Gordon Wilson, who is now shut up in Mafeking, [...] was the plucky Eton boy who so promptly "downed" the lunatic who made a mad attempt to assassinate the Queen, at Windsor Railway Station, many years ago.' James Burnside was almost as incensed by this claim as he was by the Home Office's attitude, and he wrote to *The Times*, but his letter was never published.

Roderick, shut away from society, may have seen these articles, but did not respond. However, he continued to write letters to both officialdom and his relations. In one petition, he asked if he could live on Mull, 'the isle of my ancestors'. In another, he threatened to kill his cousin, whom he considered to be associated with the female voices that were tormenting him. He also tried to get some poems published and attempted to open a correspondence with the Queen, all to no avail. In 1917, then aged sixty-three, he wrote about his declining health and some sexual hallucinations. Finally, after thirty-nine years in Broadmoor, he died of apoplexy[12] on 9 June 1921, aged sixty-seven. The inquest, two days later, returned a verdict of death by natural causes.

For once, the law had correctly found the accused insane. This time, the authorities had also not bent to any humanitarian instinct, and kept the perpetrator locked up for the duration of his life. But the next threat to the sovereign would be different again. After a long line of lone youths and madmen, a terrorist organisation was targeting the Queen.

8

The Jubilee Plot, 1887

On 1 June 1887, *The Times* published some startling revelations about the activities of Irish militants in America. The Fenian Brotherhood Council had announced the resumption of active operations, including a 'pyrotechnic display in honour of the Queen's Jubilee'. With the pinnacle of the celebrations for the fiftieth anniversary of Victoria's reign set for twenty-one days' time, a dynamite atrocity was expected. The suspected target was Westminster Abbey, where the Queen and her ministers would all be assembled.

For many years, politics had been dominated by the 'Irish question': how to respond to the growing demands for Irish independence. Two organisations, both supposedly committed to non-violence, led the campaign for the nationalists. The powerful leader of both movements was the same man: Charles Stewart Parnell.

Parnell was born on 27 June 1846 in County Wicklow, the third son of a wealthy Protestant landowner and his American wife. He never became a Catholic, but grew to be one of Irish nationalism's most fervent supporters. He went up to Cambridge University in 1865, but due to a drunken scuffle one night and the demands of the Wicklow estate that he inherited from his father, he never completed his degree. He became High Sheriff of Wicklow in 1874, and was elected to Parliament as a Home Rule League candidate in 1875.

The Home Rule League was founded by Isaac Butt in 1873, with fairly modest demands for an Irish parliament. But Parnell became one of the organisation's most extreme supporters, obstructing the business of the Commons using technical procedures and filibusters to force greater consideration of Irish issues. In 1880, he became the president of the Home Rule League.

The Irish Land League was founded in 1879 by Michael Davitt, who had earlier spent seven years in Dartmoor for gun running. Parnell was elected president of the new organisation. Their demands on behalf of all tenants were for a fair rent, security of tenure, and the ability to sell their interest in the holding, free from interference by the landlord. The official policy was to campaign through rent strikes, but some resorted to the maiming of cattle, intimidation, and murder. But the landlords continued to hold sway, and in 1880 alone over 10,000 people were evicted from their farms in Ireland.

Parnell had made secret contact with prominent Fenian leaders abroad in Paris and elsewhere. At the end of 1879, he went on a famine relief fund-raising trip of America, where he visited the President of United States, spoke to the House of Representatives, and gave speeches in sixty-two cities. He was so well received in Toronto that he was dubbed 'the uncrowned King of Ireland'.

In the general election of April 1880, which returned the Liberals to power, sixty-three Irish nationalists were elected to the House of Commons, including twenty-seven 'Parnellites'. Charles Parnell became the leader of the Irish Party in Parliament. Gladstone tried to appease the rebels through a bill which would provide compensation for evicted tenants. The bill was defeated in the House of Lords, but the following year he managed to get the Second Irish Land Act onto the statute books, thanks to help from the Queen. It provided most of what the Land League had demanded, but they put little effort into making it work, and the concession just made the campaigners move on to what they really wanted – home rule.

Gladstone was disgusted by their lack of support for the Land Act, and in October 1881, he had Parnell and four of his radical lieutenants imprisoned in Dublin for incitement, using the new Coercion Act, which suspended *habeas corpus*. Six months later, the two leaders reached a compromise, and Parnell was released. Gladstone felt that this would be a gesture of goodwill to the Irish, as well as securing more support for the Liberals in Parliament. However, he did not tell Victoria in advance, and she felt that the ensuing violence was down to his lax and lenient policies.

Four days after Parnell's release on 6 May 1882, Lord Frederick Cavendish and Thomas Burke, the new Chief Secretary for Ireland and his undersecretary, were stabbed and killed by Fenians in Phoenix Park, Dublin. A group called the 'Invincibles' claimed responsibility. That very day, Victoria had opened Epping Forest as a London park and had threaded her way through enormous crowds, where an attack would have been very easy. Gladstone invoked further emergency powers and arrested the Invincibles' members and, following their trials, five were hanged.

On the mainland, rumours circulated of an impending terrorist campaign. In March of the previous year, Tsar Alexander II had been killed by a bomb whilst out driving in his carriage in St Petersburg. Dynamite, invented by Alfred Nobel in 1867, was starting to reach the hands of revolutionaries. One report in England warned that dynamite would be used to blow up Windsor Castle, with the charge hidden in the coffins in the chapel and ignited by electric battery.

On 20 January 1883, dynamite rumours turned to reality. A large gas holder in Glasgow exploded in a sheet of flame, quickly followed by an explosion at Buchanan Street Station in the city. In March, at the back of *The Times'* offices, a device in a lady's hatbox misfired and emitted a cloud of black smoke. Shortly afterwards, a bomb exploded outside the Home Office premises in Charles Street, the noise penetrating even into the House of Commons.

Security raced up the government's agenda; armed detectives were assigned to protect ministers, and troops were readied to protect government establishments. It was time to take the war into the enemy's territory. The Special (Irish) Branch was set up at Scotland Yard, replacing the previous loose arrangement between Dublin, the Home Office, and the police 'Fenian Office'. The head of the new organisation, Chief Inspector Williamson, reported directly to the Home Secretary. Sometime later, the 'Irish' modifier was dropped.

Two of the key men in the fight against the terrorists were Edward Jenkinson, undersecretary for the police in Dublin and then at the Home Office, and Robert Anderson of the Secret Service, who also moved to the Home Office, and finally became Assistant Commissioner of the Metropolitan Police. These two 'spymasters' built up an impressive network of informers amongst the Fenians. But there was a lack of cooperation and the infighting between government departments and individuals did not stop with the formation of the Special Branch. Nevertheless, it marked a step-up in clandestine operations.

But the terrorist campaign continued. On 30 October 1883, a bomb exploded on a Metropolitan train at Paddington, seriously injuring seventy-two passengers. Eleven minutes later, a device detonated in a tunnel near Westminster Bridge, enveloping a District Line train in dust. On 12 January, dynamite was found in the Primrose Hill tunnel, and the following month the contents of a handbag exploded in the left luggage office at Victoria Station. Clandestine operations started to pay off when an Irish American was arrested in April at Birkenhead with several parcels containing nitroglycerine. But then, at the end of May, bombs exploded outside the Carlton Club, in front of a politician's house in St James's Square, and in a public urinal beneath Scotland Yard.[1]

In December, three men were killed by their own device as they tried to set a bomb under London Bridge, and in January, there was an explosion in the Metropolitan railway tunnel between King's Cross and Gower Street stations. On Saturday 24 January 1885, a bomb exploded at the Tower of London, a device burst into flames in the medieval crypt of Westminster Hall, and moments later, a third bomb exploded close to the Treasury Bench in the Commons Chamber itself, mercifully empty for the weekend. The papers called it 'Dynamite Saturday'.

While the terrorists fought on the streets, the home rulers battled in Parliament. The Liberals were still in charge, but Gladstone was trying to recover from lost popularity following events in North Africa. Britain effectively controlled Egypt and the Sudan after the defeat of Orabi Pasha at Tel el-Kebir in 1882. Early in 1884, Gladstone advised the Khedive of Egypt, a sympathiser installed by the British, to give up the lands south of Aswan to the followers of Mohammed Ahmed, the 'Mahdi', but agreed to one final intervention to evacuate the garrison at Khartoum. General Gordon was sent, but he had ideas of his own to defeat the warrior. He lost and was killed when Khartoum fell after a long siege in early 1885. A relief force arrived too late, and the Queen and many in the country blamed Gladstone for his tardy response to the situation.

While the Liberals lost popularity because of foreign affairs, the leader of the opposition, Lord Salisbury, made secret overtures to the Irish Party. In June 1885, Parnell decided that he would get no more from the Liberals, and switched allegiance to the Conservatives, leading to the defeat of the government budget and Gladstone's resignation. Lord Salisbury tried, with difficulty, to form a minority government supported by the Irish nationalists, and the Queen reluctantly returned from Balmoral to deal with the crisis. The Tories held power for little more than six months.

At the general election of January 1886, the Conservatives (and their allies) gained eighty-four fewer seats than the Liberals. Nevertheless, Victoria tried hard to prevent the re-emergence of Gladstone and encouraged Salisbury to form a government with the eighty-six Irish home rulers. She even agreed to open Parliament in January 1886, although she handed her speech to the Lord Chancellor to read. It was her last parliamentary appearance, and it only delayed the appointment of a Liberal government by a week or so.

Although the Conservatives had repealed the Coercion Acts in the new Parliament, Lord Salisbury introduced a bill to ban the National League (for Home Rule). He was playing a devious game. Naturally, Parnell switched allegiances again and Gladstone, seventy-seven years old, somewhat deaf, and with a chronic hoarseness that made public speaking most difficult, was again in power.

The 'Grand Old Man', as he was sometimes known, was determined to tackle the Irish question above all domestic matters. He first tried to get multiparty support, but Salisbury would have nothing to do with it. In April 1886, he introduced a Home Rule Bill in the Commons, which would establish a separate parliament in Dublin with control over all internal affairs. It split his party and, in June, the bill was defeated. In July, he gave way, and an appeal to the electorate only led to a loss of seats. In August, a government of the Conservatives and Liberal Unionists was formed, led by Lord Salisbury. The devious plan to split the Liberals had worked, and the new grouping had an overall majority of 117 seats.

The new government was firmly opposed to any concessions on Irish home rule, so a resumption and increase in the terrorist campaign seemed likely. The following year would pose additional problems for security with the Golden Jubilee of the Queen's accession, when Victoria would be involved in many public engagements. An occasion that the Fenians were planning to mark in their own particular way.

※ ※ ※

On 10 April 1887, General Francis Frederick Millen boarded the SS *Gascogne* in New York harbour for the eight-day crossing to Le Havre. He had won his military rank in wars in Guatemala and Mexico, but he came from Tyrone and was a key member of the Fenian Brotherhood, organising the failed uprising of 1865. Recognising that it was Jubilee Year, the American Fenians had decided to finance 'the celebration of Mrs Brown's health'. General Millen, chairman of the Military Council of Clan na Gael, was commissioned to arrange the 'celebrations'.

The money and material for the dynamite campaign of the previous few years had come from the United States, and most of the terrorists were Irish Americans. But the organisation of the nationalists in America suffered from even more rivalry and infighting than amongst the Government anti-terrorist groups in London. The Fenian Brotherhood was established in 1858 with the primary aim of financing the Irish Republican Brotherhood (IRB), founded in Dublin in the same year. After the American Civil War, many of the 190,000 soldiers of Irish origin flocked to join the Fenian Brotherhood, which then split, with one faction organising an invasion of Canada in 1866 and again in 1870. Both invasions were easily defeated.

The IRB chose not to support either faction, but rather switched support to another organisation, Clan na Gael. In 1876, the Clan financed and manned an expedition to Western Australia aboard an old whaling barque, where they freed six Fenian convicts held in Fremantle gaol. The success led to them becoming the leading American nationalist force. The Clan worked with the Irish Land League and Home Rule League across the Atlantic, but in 1882, a new hard-line leadership took control of the organisation. They ignored the Revolutionary Council set up to coordinate with the IRB, and started organising a secret bombing campaign of their own in England. They were behind the atrocities that had rocked the country, using dynamite stolen from American construction sites by Irish navvies.

While the nationalists were planning to use violence to achieve their ends in Jubilee year, reactionary forces were attacking with the pen. In March, *The Times* published a sensational article entitled 'Parnellism and Crime', linking the Irish Party to renewed farm rent strikes, criminal damage, and murder. The editor, George Buckle, had obtained apparently genuine letters from Parnell and others that he held back as documentary evidence. As well as the Irish leader, *The Times* was also attacking the Liberals, accusing Gladstone of 'deliberately allying with the paid agents of an organisation whose ultimate sanction is murder'. In April, Buckle went further, publishing a document that linked Parnell specifically to the Phoenix Park murders.

The pressure on the Irish Party continued to build in May, when a series of articles started to appear under the heading 'Behind the Scenes in America', describing in detail the activities of the US Fenians, including their role in the funding of Parnellite MPs. Anti-Irish opinion was also fostered by news stories about an impending bombing campaign. On 4 May, the *New York Times* wrote, 'Extreme nationalists in this country are preparing for another series of dynamite outrages in England, and many signs point to the Queen's Jubilee as the time fixed upon for the beginning of the reign of terror.' At the end of the month, an exclusive interview with a Fenian exiled in Paris, Michael Flannery, appeared in the *Morning Advertiser* in London, in which he said that a new dynamite movement had mobilised against English national power. When specifically asked if there would be explosions on Jubilee day, he refused to answer.

After his boat docked, General Millen took the train from Le Havre to Paris, where he made contact with other Fenians intent on resuming the bombing campaign. Some time later, a case containing twenty-four tins of explosives allegedly arrived in the capital addressed to him. On 12 May, Millen left Paris for Boulogne, where he intended to base his operations. He summoned his wife from Dublin, thus enhancing his cover story of a little holiday. They stayed in the seaside resort for more than a month and became friendly with a Mr and Mrs Thomson from England.

Mr Thomson was, in fact, recently retired Superintendent Thomson of Scotland Yard, assigned to keep an eye on General Millen. Even if the American did not suspect his friend, he would have realised that he was under surveillance when Chief Superintendent Williamson arrived to interview him. He was trying to find out what Millen was up to, but Williamson left not knowing whether Millen had already dispatched a dynamite gang to England.

Victoria was, of course, aware of all the rumours of atrocities and had braved herself to face the many public engagements that were expected of her. This was a change because, over the last five years, she had again been largely a recluse, following another terrible bereavement. John Brown had worn himself out in her service, being on hand seven days a week despite several chills and a fever. In March 1883, he suffered an erysipelas infection[2] to his face, which led to a high fever and, after just four days, coma and death.

In a personal letter to Brown's sister-in-law, Victoria wrote:

Weep with me for we all have lost the best, the truest heart that ever beat. My grief is unbounded, dreadful, & I know not how to bear it, or how to believe it possible [...] Dear, dear John – my dearest best friend to whom I could say everything & who always protected me so kindly and who thought of everything – was well and strong and hearty not 3 or 4 days before.

Victoria had seen Brown every day for eighteen and a half years; now she would see him no more. Already invalided by a knee injury following a fall, the Queen again withdrew from public and court view. She ordered that Brown's room should be left unchanged, and a flower placed on his pillow every day. Because she never countermanded the order, the practice continued daily for nearly twenty years.

Victoria started to re-emerge from seclusion three years later. In May 1886, she made one of her first public outings on a visit to the Colonial and Indian Exhibition in Kensington. Designed 'to stimulate commerce and strengthen the bonds of union now existing in every portion of Her Majesty's Empire', it included a sumptuous Indian hall, an exotic facsimile bazaar, and other fascinating exhibits from Australia, Africa, and other British colonies around the world. The Queen walked the entire length of the exhibition with just the aid of a walking stick. Although Victoria was much fatigued by the day, she wrote about 'how pleased my darling husband would have been at the whole thing' – the highest of praise. Other events followed, with wheelchairs employed whenever the Queen was out of public view.

But the big upcoming event was the extravaganza prepared for 21 June 1887. The man in charge of security was James Monro, assistant commissioner of the Metropolitan Police, head of the CID, and undeclared head of the 'Secret Department'. He was a serious Scot, with a reputation for integrity and honest police work, and had been in post for three years. Previously, he was Inspector-General of Police in Bengal, where he had enjoyed steady success against militant Muslim secret societies. Monro had the daunting task of protecting Queen and country during the Jubilee celebrations, when hundreds of thousands would be thronging the streets.

On 15 June, the sensationalist *Central News Agency* in London put out a report emanating from an 'official source at Scotland Yard' that there was now no doubt that 'dynamiters have arranged to commit an outrage in Jubilee week'. As the great day approached, the ancient crypt of Westminster Abbey was thoroughly searched. The water closets in the Palace of Westminster were closely inspected after it was realised that Irish labourers had recently overhauled the plumbing. Elsewhere a scandal erupted when it was discovered that some dignitaries had sold their tickets to the ceremony for large sums, possibly facilitating the entry of an unknown assassin.

Jubilee Day on 21 June was a beautiful summer's day, and everywhere there was a festive mood, with both police and onlookers smiling and joking. At eleven o'clock precisely, a fanfare of trumpets echoed around the royal parks, announcing the departure of the procession from Buckingham Palace. First to leave were a squadron of the 1st Life Guards, followed by equerries, *aides-de-camp*, and the carriages of visiting royalty, whose jewellery sparkled in the sunshine. An escort of the 2nd Life Guards broke ranks to accompany the Persian and Siamese guests, and the Queen of Hawaii. Then, with another fanfare and the excited roll of kettledrums, the open carriages of the royal family came into sight, escorted by Indian cavalry. The appearance of the Queen, dressed in black, as always, but in a sumptuously gilded landau, pulled by six large, cream-coloured horses, evoked a wave of rapturous cheering across the ocean of faces, with hats thrown in the air and handkerchiefs waved, as if her subjects were drowning in their joyous excitement.

The procession took a circuitous route along Constitution Hill, Piccadilly, Regent Street, Pall Mall, Trafalgar Square, Northumberland Avenue, and Victoria Embankment, to Parliament Square and Westminster Abbey. Everywhere was richly decorated, with spectacular floral displays created by an army of florists overnight. More than a million people lined the route; many having paid large sums to sit on the terraced benches beside the roadway constructed using 10 miles of scaffolding. Ranks of soldiers marched past between the royal personages, their colourful uniforms and polished swords shimmering in the sun.

At Trafalgar Square, Victoria was particularly taken by the crescendo of approval from her more lowly citizens. The wide space was literally black with spectators, mostly of the poorer classes, who from benches and boxes, from costermongers' barrows, from the backs of the famous lions, and from one another's shoulders, generated a continuous roar of excitement. Everywhere there was enthusiasm, and everywhere perfect order, so that nothing marred the occasion.

As the Queen approached Westminster Abbey, Assistant Commissioner Monro was not so sure. Despite the work of his agents, the thoroughness of his preparations, and the hundreds of plain-clothes police who mingled with the crowds, he instructed his family not to take their allotted seats in the Abbey. He had received an anonymous letter that day saying there was dynamite in the vaults, and it was too late to carry out further searches.

The Queen progressed through the Abbey and sat in the coronation chair that had once held Edward the Confessor, Her Majesty a tiny black figure surrounded by the elite of the realm. Monro wondered whether he should raise the alarm and order an evacuation. Instead, he took his own seat, and started to pray to God for deliverance. The Jubilee thanksgiving service began and ran its course. Finally, Victoria processed back down the nave and took the return journey to Buckingham Palace. The Jubilee Plot had seemingly been averted.

*** *** ***

On 11 June, three Irish Americans boarded the SS *City of Chester* in New York, bound for Liverpool. Secreted in their trunks were three Smith & Wesson revolvers. Sewn into their clothing were over 100 pounds of full-strength dynamite. The bookings for the task force had been bungled, and they had been unable to catch an earlier boat as all the berths were taken. They would now only arrive in England on 21 June, Jubilee Day itself. They consoled themselves with the thought that, after all, it was meant to be Jubilee Year, and they could still wreak havoc against what they considered to be an evil empire.

During May, the leader of Clan na Gael, Alexander Sullivan, received reports of the activities of his military council chairman, General Millan, and felt a lack of confidence. He decided to dispatch a second mission. After their arrival in England, the 'dynamitards' went to ground and considered what to do. On an open day in Windsor Castle, one of them reconnoitred the state apartments and timed how long it would take to get from there to the railway station. Other options were considered.

On Thursday 4 August, Joseph Melville, the assumed name of the leader of the hit squad, presented his card at the stranger's entrance to the Palace of Westminster. With one of his colleagues, they asked for Mr Nolan MP, an Irish Parnellite, who met them in the lobby. But the watchful constable on duty noted the name Melville, which was on a list of Fenian suspects, and called an inspector. Melville was shadowed around London and traced to a modest boarding house at 7 Gladstone Street.[3] He was followed into Baring's Bank, where he was seen to convert a draft into Bank of England £5 notes. The policeman afterwards conferred with the cashier and took a note of the numbers.

Assistant Commissioner Monro instructed an inspector to interview Melville, who said he was an agent for the Pennsylvania & Reading Railroad. But when Monro cabled Pinkerton's Detective Agency, his American credentials did not check out. A few days later, Melville left for Paris, before returning to London where he was interviewed again. The police continued to watch him as he left for a trip to Killarney, and then, on 9 September, when he embarked for Paris again. He was followed around the French capital, where he was seen to make contact with another suspect, General Millen. A week later, perhaps realising that he was being closely monitored, rather than return to England, he took ship for New York.

During the surveillance of Melville, Monro came to realise that the suspect had at least two accomplices in England, but he had no idea of their true names or whereabouts. He ordered a watch to be kept for suspicious Irish Americans. On 19 October, a woman in Lambeth Road reported to police that she had found one of her lodgers, a Mr Cohen, dead in his room. He had died from advanced consumption, but he had received at least two suspicious American visitors. By chance, on the same day, one of the visitors, known as Mr Brown, was interviewed at his lodgings in Islington. He was already being followed by police of the Secret Department, who had been alerted by the local constabulary to suspicious activity. Smith & Wesson revolvers were discovered at both addresses, and a letter found on Mr Brown was addressed to one of the contacts in America used by Melville. But there was no sign of any dynamite.

A week later, the inquest was held into Cohen's death. The proceedings had barely started when Assistant Commissioner Monro announced his presence and went on to hijack the enquiry. He interviewed Cohen's landlady and then Mr Brown, revealing in the process that Cohen was an agent of Clan na Gael, that the head of the organisation in Europe was General Millen, and that his operative in London was a man calling himself Joseph Melville. Monro said that their objective was to commit dynamite outrages and also revealed the link with Joseph Nolan MP. Monro's objective was to flush out more information and locate further suspects, and the newspapers in both Britain and America duly obliged by making a splash with the revelations about a Jubilee plot.

The day after the inquest, Mrs Bright of 24 Baxter Road, Islington, discovered she had a blocked toilet. Her American lodger admitted that he had ill-advisedly flushed away some spoiled tea samples to do with his trade. Next door, the following day, little Charlie Johns was playing in his garden when he discovered some strange white stuff by the garden wall. He put it in his mother's range to dry out. Fifteen minutes later, there was a blinding flash, and the kitchen filled with acrid smelling smoke.

On 18 November, a telegram arrived in Monro's office from the Bank of England. One of the notes drawn by Melville had been cashed, and the man was being followed by City of London police. It was Mrs Bright's lodger, and when the house in Baxter Road was turned over, almost thirty pounds of water-logged dynamite was retrieved from the dustbin. The detonators were only found several years later in Finsbury Park lake.

The lodger confessed his real name, Thomas Callan, and an incriminating letter was discovered in his possession. Traces of dynamite were also found in the cases belonging to the dead man, Cohen, and Mr Brown, whose real name was Michael Harkins. Callan and Harkins were charged with unlawfully and feloniously conspiring to cause explosions. The press announced that the Jubilee plotters had been apprehended, and crowds gathered to see them conveyed to Holloway Prison in Black Maria vans, guarded by armed officers and an escort of mounted police with cutlasses drawn.

The trial took place at the Central Criminal Court on 1 February 1888. Callan and Harkins were indicted on two counts: firstly, 'for feloniously conspiring with other persons to cause an explosion in the United Kingdom of a nature likely to endanger life and cause serious injury to property', and secondly, possession of an explosive substance intended for an unlawful object. The facts of the case were detailed and the evidence presented. Harkins and Callan were identified as two of the men who had arrived on the SS *City of Chester* in June; the third was Melville, while Cohen was already in England. The connection with the Irish MP was made. General Millen was not mentioned, but in any case he was still out of the court's jurisdiction, having returned from France to the United States in October. The jury only needed a few minutes to find the defendants guilty. They were sentenced to fifteen years' imprisonment, and taken to Chatham gaol.

The operation had been a great success for Monro. No explosions had disturbed the Jubilee Year and a high profile conviction had been achieved. For his masters, the Home Secretary and the Prime Minister, Parnell had also been implicated in terrorist activities, seriously undermining the home rule campaign.

* * *

Parliament decided that the connection between dynamitards and members of Parliament warranted investigation. In March 1888, a select committee was appointed, and the following month, evidence was heard from Monro. General Millen, it was revealed, had sent a letter to Nolan introducing Melville as an old friend. Nolan denied receiving any such letter, or knowingly consorting with terrorists. The enquiry found nothing specifically incriminating to pursue.

In another public airing, an action against *The Times* by an Irish MP, Frank Hugh O'Donnell, came to trial on 2 July, alleging libel in the articles published the previous year. More, apparently genuine, letters were produced linking Parnell to the Phoenix Park murders, and the jury found for *The Times*. Parnell demanded that a parliamentary committee should examine these letters, but Lord Salisbury had other ideas. He introduced a bill setting up a Special Commission, which would not only look at the letters, but also the involvement of the Parnellites in the dynamite outrages and a decade's worth of crime in Ireland. After a stormy passage, the bill became law in August.

Because the authenticity of the letters was at the heart of the proceedings, the 'prosecution' was conducted by *The Times*, and the government even got the newspaper to pay the legal costs. The Parnellite 'defendants' were accused of 'conspiracy to bring about the absolute independence of Ireland'. Over the next eighteen months, three judges oversaw 128 sittings with 450 witnesses and several tons of written evidence in a political opera that by turns fascinated and bored the country. A rival distraction erupted the same month the enquiry began, when 'Jack the Ripper' struck for the first time.

A sensation happened the following February, when Major Henri Le Caron, a supposedly Anglophobic Frenchman, gave evidence to the commission. He revealed that his baptismal name was, in fact, Thomas Beach, and that he had been a British informer at the heart of the Fenian Brotherhood and Clan na Gael since their foundation. The government had risked bringing the spy 'in from the cold' to testify to links between Parnell and the terrorists. But the effect on the enquiry was dwarfed later that month, when Richard Pigott, the man who had supplied the incriminating letters to *The Times*, was called. After two days of questioning, he crumbled and admitted, outside the courtroom, that the letters were forgeries, before escaping to Paris and then Madrid. When the Spanish police knocked at his door with an extradition warrant, he blew his brains out.

A year later, in February 1890, the judges announced their findings, which cleared Parnell of the charges, but implicated his party in the rent strikes, and said that the links to terrorists were 'not proven', rather than disproved. Although they claimed a victory, due to the judges' support on the subsidiary charges, *The Times* lost financially and were forced to pay costs of around £250,000, as well as £5,000 to Parnell in a separate out-of-court libel settlement.

But Parnell's downfall was not far off. Later that year, he was cited as co-respondent in a divorce case for adultery, which he did not defend. Parnell had been having an affair with the wife of a fellow MP for ten years. Gladstone and the Catholic bishops deserted him, and the Irish Party split. But he upheld his principles to the end, saying in his last speech that 'we fight not for faction, but for freedom'. Parnell died the following year, aged forty-five.

In 1890, Monro, who was by then Commissioner of the Metropolitan Police, mysteriously resigned, fêted as a hero in the eyes of the Queen and the public. The following year, he founded the Abode of Mercy medical mission in Ranaghat, Bengal. After fourteen years of helping the sick and destitute, he retired to Chiswick and died in 1920. The two convicted bombers did not complete their sentences. Michael Harkins was released in 1891, terminally ill, and died in Philadelphia the following year. Thomas Callan was quietly released two years later by the outgoing Tory Home Secretary. He died the following year after falling from a garbage cart in Lowell, Massachusetts.

But the most sensational discoveries did not occur until over a hundred years later, when various secret files were declassified.[4] The British had more than one spy at the heart of Clan na Gael, who relayed detailed American Fenian plans, and several informers elsewhere in the United States, Ireland, and France. What's more, General Millen, the exposed leader of the Jubilee plot, had actually been in the pay of the British for over twenty years. He was designated by his controller, Edward Jenkinson, as Agent X. The government would have used him again in the special commission, but he died in mysterious circumstances in New York before he could embark to give evidence.

Throughout much of the 1880s, Parnell had dominated Parliament by exploiting the balance of power held by the Irish party. Lord Salisbury believed that if the union between Ireland and Great Britain was sundered, then it would presage an end to the Empire. He was determined to smash the Parnellites and home rulers. Locking Parnell up hadn't worked; Gladstone's appeasement had failed; Salisbury fixed on a third way: to discredit him by linking him to explosion and murder.

Salisbury authorised the use of Millen to fuel the plot to kill the Queen and to link it to the Irish Party. The charade in Boulogne with the general had featured a Scotland Yard chief superintendent interviewing a deep-cover spy who had become friends with a Secret Service agent. At the time, General Millen was being paid for his holiday by Clan na Gael, the Home Office, and also by his professed employer, the *New York Herald*.

In addition, the articles linking Parnellism to crime in *The Times* were actually written by the Home Office spymaster Robert Anderson, and the Prime Minister was the driving force behind the Special Commission. At the behest of their masters, the Secret Service had played a dangerous game in apparently fostering treason. But in the end, Parnell was not brought down by government machinations, but by a sex scandal.

Employing very dubious methods, the Conservative government had used the activities of the Fenians for political advantage over the Liberals and the Irish Party. No doubt they were exceedingly relieved that the details of their plotting remained secret for so long.

Epilogue

As the Special Commission dragged on in London, Victoria reached her seventieth birthday. Passing into old age, she relished the regularity of her daily routine and stays at Balmoral and Osborne, with an annual spring holiday in the south of France or Italy. The public saw more of her after the Jubilee than for a long time, and she continued to read the contents of the red boxes and give her views to the government.

Like the proverbial bad penny, Gladstone returned to power in 1892, a decade after he himself had said that he was no longer well enough for office. He was eighty-three, but with his sight failing, he did not last long, and resigned in 1894 after sixty-one years in Parliament. The Grand Old Man died five years later. In government, he was replaced by the Earl of Rosebery, a favourite of Victoria's amongst the Liberals, although she did not like some of his policies. Increases in death duties and an attempt to limit the power of the House of Lords, she felt, would alter the natural order and the supremacy of the aristocracy. Much to her pleasure, Lord Salisbury returned to power in 1895, and the Conservatives remained in charge for the rest of Victoria's life.

Her son and heir was a continuing worry for the Queen, with his disreputable lifestyle and adulterous affairs the talk of scandal sheets. She also continued to be concerned about the lives of her other offspring and was heavily involved in the marriage arrangements for many of her dozens of grandchildren. In 1894, her first great-grandchild was born, the future Edward VIII.

Amongst her staff, Victoria had another unusual favourite, Hafiz[1] Abdul Karim, better known as 'the Munshi'.[2] He had been brought over from India as a servant for the Golden Jubilee, and initially worked as a waiter at Windsor. A young man in his twenties, with a black beard and dark eyes, resplendent in a white turban, he gradually grew in the Queen's affections and began teaching her Urdu. She elevated him to the position of her secretary for all matters associated with India, and he began to accompany her everywhere. Like John Brown before him, his anomalous position in the establishment caused anger amongst many in the royal household.

In 1895, Victoria was saved from another madman, this time while she was in the fastness of Balmoral. A young slater, Benjamin Mitchell, was walking along the road in his home town of Balater, not much more than 5 miles from the castle, when he was disturbed by the noise of a gun being fired. He accosted the culprit, Thomas Dron, a farmer's son, but the gunman became aggressive and pointed the revolver at him. They grappled and, with the help of another passer-by, the two men disarmed Dron, and took him to the police station. On his person were found fifty rounds of ammunition, a letter to Mr Vanderbilt expressing the desire to marry the American millionaire's daughter, a letter to Gladstone in which he mentioned that he was about to become King, and a paper headed 'To the Queen'. He was declared insane.

Celebrations in 1897 marked the Diamond Jubilee of the Queen's accession. She had reigned longer than any other English monarch, but she now found reading government papers difficult, since her sight was failing and spectacles were useless as cataracts gradually spread across both eyes. The veneration on Diamond Jubilee day, 20 June, was, if anything, even more rapturous than the event a decade earlier. The population of London tripled to four million, and the route for the procession was unimaginably crowded. Most watching had known no other sovereign, and she had become more myth than monarch.

The Conservative government was committed to regaining the territories given up by Gladstone's administrations. In 1898, Khartoum was retaken, and the Queen honoured Sir Herbert Kitchener with a peerage. Around the time of her eightieth birthday the following year, she received a petition from 20,000 British subjects in the Transvaal asking for her help in relieving Boer oppression. The Boer actions were in direct contravention of the agreement of 1880, made when Gladstone had ceded government of the colony. President Kruger rejected the Queen's suzerainty and demanded that British reinforcements landed at the Cape should be withdrawn.

War broke out in October 1899, and became the largest overseas conflict ever. Around half a million men from Britain and the Empire fought, and the Queen was exceptionally active in support, inspecting troops, visiting hospitals, and sending wishes of good fortune. For Christmas, Victoria arranged that every soldier was sent a tin box of chocolate embossed with her head, and this gift was so revered that many refused the offer of two months' pay to sell it.

Ineffective leadership and blundering led to early defeats, but gradually the weight of numbers told. The much smaller force of Boers adopted guerrilla tactics, and Britain had the dubious distinction of being the first to set up concentration camps, designed to hold those who might otherwise succour the enemy. Towards the end of 1900, military successes meant that many of the soldiers could return home, although a final peace was not signed until the middle of 1901.

Victoria welcomed home some of the troops, but she did not leave her carriage. Her health was deteriorating. She suffered from insomnia, yet would nod off during the day, and attacks of aphasia[3] became commonplace. At the beginning of January 1901, she seemed to improve. But the reprieve was brief, and after showing symptoms of a stroke, Victoria Regina died on Tuesday 22 January.

The following day the newspapers were edged in black, and the funeral was held eleven days later, on Saturday 2 February. The Queen died at Osborne House on the Isle of Wight, and the funeral party left by barque from Cowes on the Friday, passing down a line of thirty-eight British warships on a placid blue sea, to the thunder of cannon in unending royal salute. From Gosport, the coffin and cortège were conveyed to London. The following day, a great procession set off across the city, through the grieving multitude to Paddington Station, and thence to Windsor and St George's Chapel. The funeral ended with a moving service that included the prayer 'God Save the King', the first time it had been heard for more than sixty years.

So Queen Victoria finally died in her bed and not at the hands of an assassin. But why was she the target for so many assailants? In some ways, the number of the attacks was not abnormal for the time – there were four serious attempts on the life of George III during his sixty-year reign: three with knives and one with a gun.

Perhaps the question should rather be: why have there been so few attacks on our current Queen? Two similar incidents have occurred, both perpetrated by seventeen-year-olds. In 1981, Marcus Sargeant fired blanks at the Queen during the trooping of the colours, and in 1986, Christopher John Lewis fired a .22 rifle during the monarch's visit to New Zealand, but was unable to get a clear shot at the Queen. So why only two attempts during such a long reign? Certainly the Metropolitan Police and the Royalty Protection squad are better organised and have the benefit of modern-day communications and intelligence. Following the firearms act of 1920 and later legislation, it is also much harder than in Victorian times for a youth or mentally ill person to get hold of a gun. More important, however, for those who are promoting some cause, is the way that we view the sovereign. Although the monarch has had little real power since the civil war of the seventeenth century, Victoria was still seen as the head of the country, whereas today's Queen is acknowledged as the figurehead that she really is.

Examining the condition and motives of the assailants is also revealing. The British courts managed to get the Victorian trial verdicts right in only five out of the eight cases. John Francis, John Bean, William Hamilton, and the Jubilee conspirators were treated as sane, and probably largely were, while the verdict that Roderick Maclean was insane was also correct. But Edward Oxford was almost certainly not mentally ill, although he did suffer from youthful delusions, while Robert Pate and Arthur O'Connor were, at least temporarily, insane. Of those that were sane, four were primarily seeking notoriety, and only one case, the Jubilee conspirators, were plotters truly driven by a cause.

Dr David James and colleagues have completed a wider analysis of attacks on the royal family between 1778 and 2008, and come to the conclusion that few are rooted in terrorism. Most are rather caused by the mentally ill and those seeking notoriety. In 2007, the Fixated Threat Assessment Centre (FTAC) was set up, with Dr James as the clinical director. Working closely with the Home Office and the NHS, the unit is staffed by psychiatrists, psychologists, and police, and analyses some 10,000 strange, worrying, or threatening communications received by the Royal household each year, in an effort to prevent future attacks.

Victoria lived through times when technology and psychological understanding were primitive by comparison. We can only be thankful that advances in weaponry also came later, so the chances of an attacker succeeding in their attempt were also low. Otherwise, British history would have been very different, and we might now be referring to the nineteenth century as the extravagant Ernestian era (after Victoria's uncle, who was initially next in line), or the great Edwardian age.

But she did escape unscathed and lived until she was eighty-one. Queen Victoria reigned longer than any other British monarch, gave her name to an age that spanned the best part of a century, witnessed the greatest transformation of her country in history, and survived eight attacks and attempts on her life. All these are superlatives that have yet to be equalled.

Money, Inflation & Imperial Units

Before decimalisation in 1971, a British pound (£) was made up of twenty shillings (s) and a shilling of twelve pence (d). Shillings and pence could be written as, for example, 3s 6d, 3/6d or 3/6, although in this book only the first form is used. During Queen Victoria's reign, there were gold coins for £1 (a sovereign) and 10s (a half sovereign); silver coins for 2s 6d (half a crown), 2s (a florin), 1s (a bob), 6d (a tanner), 4d (a groat or a joey), and 3d (thru'penny bit); and bronze coins (known as coppers) for 1d (penny), ½d (ha'penny), and ¼d (a farthing).

A guinea was not a coin but a commonly used term referring to the sum of £1 1s. The name stems from the country of origin of the gold used in the first machine-struck coin for £1 of 1663. A rise in the value of gold meant that it was worth 21s during the reign of Charles II.

Comparing the buying power of Victorian currency with present-day money is fraught with difficulty, as it all depends what items make up the 'basket' of products and services being compared. However, very roughly, a Victorian £1 was worth, on average, around £100 in 2011, 1s worth £5, and a penny worth 40p. There was overall inflation of around 10 per cent between 1837 and 1901, but this gradual rise is dwarfed by periods of rising and falling prices in different decades.

The units of length used then were feet and inches, where 12 inches make up 1 foot, 1 foot is 0.3048 metres and 1 inch is 25.4 mm. The units of weight were stones, pounds, and ounces. A stone is made up of 14 pounds (lb), and 1 pound of 16 ounces (oz); 1 pound is 0.454 kg.

Sources

Sources for Several Chapters

Arthur Christopher Benson and Viscount Esher (eds), *The Letters of Queen Victoria*, John Murray, London, 1908

George Earle Buckle (ed.), *The Letters of Queen Victoria: Second Series 1862–1885*, J. Murray, 1926–28

Christopher Hibbert, *Queen Victoria: A Personal History*, Harper Collins, London, 2000

Lee Jackson, *www.victorianlondon.org*

Dr Kurt Jagow (ed.), *Letters of the Prince Consort 1831–1861*, J. Murray, London, 1938

James, D.; Kerrigan, T.; Forfar, R.; Farnham, F.; Preston, L., 'The Fixated Threat Assessment Centre: Preventing Harm and Facilitating Care', *Journal of Forensic Psychiatry & Psychology* 21 (4): 1, 2010

Norman Lowe, *Mastering Modern British History*, Third Edition, Palgrave, Basingstoke, 1998

Helen Rappaport, *Queen Victoria: A Biographical Companion*, ABC-CLIO, Oxford, 2001

Lytton Strachey, *Queen Victoria*, Chatto & Windus, 1921

Stanley Weintraub, *Victoria: Biography of a Queen*, Unwin Hyman, London, 1987

Censuses of England 1841–1911, The National Archives

London and National Newspapers, especially *The Era, The Morning Chronicle, The Morning Post, The Observer, The Standard and The Times*

The General Register of Births, Marriages and Deaths, General Register Office

The International Genealogical Index, www.familysearch.org

The Proceedings of the Old Bailey, www.oldbaileyonline.org

The Treasury Solicitor's Transcript of the Trials of Edward Oxford, John Francis, John William Bean and Roderick Maclean, The National Archives TS36/25, 1840–82

1 Edward Oxford

Patricia H. Allderidge, *Proceedings of the Royal Society of Medicine: Criminal Insanity: Bethlem to Broadmoor*, 1974 67(9), 897–904

Jonathan Andrews et al., *The History of Bethlem*, Routledge, London, 1997

The Convict Probation System: Van Diemen's Land, 1839–1854, Ian Brand, Blubberhead Press, Hobart, 1990

J. J. Colledge, *Ships of the Royal Navy*, Greenhill, London, 1987

John Freeman, *Lights and Shadows of Melbourne Life*, Simpson Low, London, 1888

Vere Langford Oliver, *The History of the Island of Antigua, one of the Leeward Caribbees in the West Indies, from the First Settlement in 1635 to the Present Time*, Mitchell & Hughes, London, 1894

Henry Rollin, *Forensic Psychology in England, 150 Years of British Psychiatry vol. 2: The Aftermath*, edited by Hugh Freeman and German Berrios, p. 247, Athlone, London, 1996

F. B. Smith, *Lights and Shadows in the Life of John Freeman*, Victorian Studies vol. 30 no. 4 pp. 459–73, 1987

Broadmoor Revealed: Some Patient Stories – Edward Oxford, Berkshire Record Office, 2009

Edward Oxford Bethlem Hospital Medical Record, Bethlem Royal Hospital Archives

Edward Oxford Broadmoor Hospital Case File, Berkshire Record Office D/H14/D2/1/96
Greenwich Hospital Admission Registers, The National Archives ADM 73/58, ADM 73/67
Hertfordshire Burial Index 1801-50, Hertfordshire Archives
Home Secretary's Papers Relating to Edward Oxford, The National Archives HO44/36, 1840
HMS Medusa Muster Book, The National Archives ADM 36/15155 and 16779, 1801 and
    1804–05
Index to Unassisted Inward Passenger Lists to Victoria, Victoria PRO, 1868
James Bowen Death Certificate, General Register Office of Victoria, Australia, 1874
James Gordon of Moor Hall, The House of Commons volume 1 p. 36, 1790–1820
John McKinley and James Bowen Death Register Index Entry, Registry of Births, Marriages
    and Deaths, Western Australia
John Freeman Marriage and Death Certificate, General Register Office of Victoria, Australia,
    1881 and 1900
Melbourne Citizen List, Victoria Public Record Office, 1877/78
Metropolitan Police File on Edward Oxford, The National Archives MEPO3/17
'Moor Hall', *Country Life*, 3 September 2009
Much Hadham List of Men available for the Militia, Hertfordshire Archives, 1758–86
Much Hadham Parish Rate Book, Hertfordshire Archives D/P44/4/4, 1755–61
Much Hadham Parish Register, Hertfordshire Archives
Papers of John Freeman 1862–1889, Australian National Library MS 243, 1889
Lloyd's List and Register of Shipping, Guildhall Library, 1867–68
Requests for Rewards Related to the Edward Oxford Case, The National Archives
    HO144/290/B974, 1879–1907
South Melbourne Rate Books, Victoria Public Record Office, 1881–99
Stanford's Library Map of London and Its Suburbs, London, 1862
The Age, Melbourne, 1874–1900
Victorian Electoral Roll for the Federal Referendum, State Library of Victoria, 1899
Will of John Oxford, The National Archives, 1804

2 John Francis

Charles Bateson, *The Convict Ships 1787–1868*, Reed, New South Wales, 1983
Ian Brand, *The Convict Probation System: Van Diemen's Land 1839–54*, Blubber Head Press,
    Hobart, 1990
Alan Brooke and David Brandon, *Bound for Botany Bay: British Convict Voyages to
    Australia*, The National Archives, Kew, 2005
Clifford Carig (ed.), *The First Hundred Years, 1863–1963, of the Launceston General
    Hospital*, Board of Management, Hobart, 1963
David T. Hawkings, *Bound for Australia*, Phillimore, Chichester, 1987
Robert Hughes, *The Fatal Shore: A History of Transportation of Convicts to Australia, 1787–
    1868*, Vintage, London, 1987
Adrienne Phillips, great-great-great-granddaughter of John and Maria Clarke of Launceston,
    Personal Communication, New Zealand, 2010
Christopher Sweeney, *Transported: In Place of Death*, Macmillan, Australia, 1981
Walter Thornbury, *Old and New London volume 3*, Cassell, London, 1878
Edward Walford, *Old and New London volume 4*, Cassell, London, 1878
A Brief Guide to St Andrew's Launceston, St John's Street, Launceston, Tasmania, 2011
Assessment & Valuation Rolls for Launceston, Launceston Library and Archives Office of
    Tasmania, 1853–1868
Australian Birth, Marriage and Death Index, ancestry.co.uk
Citizen Lists for Melbourne, Victoria Public Records Office, 1871–1891
Convict Conduct Register, Archives Office of Tasmania, CON33/1/29
Convict Transportation Registers Database, State Library of Queensland

Description List of Male Convicts, Archives Office of Tasmania, CON18/1/33
Idents of Male Convicts, Archives Office of Tasmania, CON14/1/16
Hampshire Advertiser & Salisbury Guardian, July 1842
Insolvency Papers for John Francis, Victoria Public Record Office VPRS759 Po Unit 198 Case 12042, 1869
John Francis Death Certificates, General Register Office of Victoria, Australia, 1885
Lloyd's List and Register of Shipping, Guildhall Library, 1842–43
Martha Francis Death Certificate, General Register Office of Victoria, Australia, 1872
Metropolitan Police File on John Francis, The National Archives MEPO3/18
Petitions to the Queen and the Home Office on behalf of Robert Pate and John Francis, The National Archives, HO45/3079
Pioneer's Index and General Register of Births, Marriages and Deaths for Tasmania, Launceston Library, Tasmania
Port Arthur: Visitor Guide, Information and Commentary, Tasmania, 2011
Proceedings of the Inquest on Henry Burdett Francis, Victoria Public Record Office VPRS24/ Po Unit 495 Desc 1886/370, 1886
Sands & McDougall Melbourne Directory, 1868–85
Ship Agreements and Crew Lists for the Marquis of Hastings, 1837–45, The National Archives BT98/374
South Melbourne Rate Books, Victoria Public Record Office, 1867–73
Surgeon's Log from Marquis of Hastings, The National Archives ADM101/50/6, 1842
Tasmanian Marriage and Birth Registers, 1848–63
The Age, Melbourne, 1867–85
The Law List for 1843, ancestry.co.uk

3 John William Bean

Metropolitan Police File on John William Bean, The National Archives MEPO3/19
South London Chronicle, July 1882
South London Observer, Camberwell and Peckham Times, July 1882
South London Press, July 1882

4 William Hamilton

Charles Campbell, *The Intolerable Hulks – British Shipboard Confinement 1776–1857*, Heritage Books, Maryland, 1994
Gale E. Christianson, *Secret Societies and Agrarian Violence in Ireland 1790–1840*, Agricultural History vol. 46, no. 3, pp. 369–384, Agricultural History Society, Florida USA, 1972
S. J. Connolly, *The Oxford Companion to Irish History*, Oxford University Press, 2007
Rica Erickson (ed.), *Dictionary of Western Australians vol. 2*, University of Western Australia Press, 1981
Rica Erikson (ed.), *The Bicentennial Dictionary of Western Australians pre 1829–1888*, volume II, 1988
Rica Erikson, *The Bride Ships*, Hesperium Press, WA, 1992
Darren Fa, Clive Finlayson and Adam Hook, *The Fortifications of Gibraltar 1068–1945*, Osprey, Oxford, 2006
R. F. Foster, *Modern Ireland 1600–1972*, Penguin Books, London, 2002
Audrey Holland, *Personal Communication*, Western Australia Genealogical Society, 2010
Sir William G. F. Jackson, *The Rock of the Gibraltarians*, Gibraltar Books, Northants, 1993
Tom Stannage (ed.), *A New History of Western Australia*, University of Western Australia Press, 1981

Index to Death Register, Register General, Western Australia

Metropolitan Police File on William Hamilton, The National Archives MEPO3/19B

Prison Quarterly Returns for the Hulks Owen Glendower and Euralyus, The National Archives HO8/102-120, 1849–54

Prison Register for Pentonville, The National Archives PCOM2/63, 1849

Prison Register for the Hulk Europa, The National Archives PCOM2/137, 1849–54

Ship's Log for HMS Hercules, The National Archives ADM53/3587, 1849

Surgeon's Log for the Ramillies, The National Archives ADM101/253/1B, 1854

The Cork Constitution, 1849

The Limerick Chronicle, 1850

Transportation Register, The National Archives HO11/16, 1849

5 Robert Pate

Valentine Bolam, *Wisbech Desperado*, Wisbech Society 59th Annual Report p. 7, 1998

Valentine Bolam, *Robert Pate – Neither Drunk nor Mad*, Wisbech Society 60th Annual Report p. 9, 1998

Valentine Bolam, *Research Archive and Personal Communication*, 2010

Michael Brander, *The 10th Royal Hussars*, Leo Cooper, London, 1969

Frederic John Gardiner, *A History of Wisbech and Neighbourhood During the Last Fifty Years*, Gardiner & Co., London, 1898

Robert Hughes, *The Fatal Shore: A History of Transportation of Convicts to Australia, 1787–1868*, Vintage, London, 1987

A History of the County of Cambridge and the Isle of Ely volume 4, Victorian County History, 2002

Alumni Oxonienses

Assessment & Valuation Rolls for Hobart, Archives Office of Tasmania, 1847–67

Chancery Affidavit of Mary Elizabeth Pate, The National Archives C31/2044, 14 February 1866

Chancery Cause Book for Case S264, The National Archives C32/304, 1856

Chancery Court Orders and Decrees for Startin v Peckover S264, The National Archives C33 and J15 series, 1856–78

Chancery Pleadings for Startin v Peckover, The National Archives C15/339/S264, 1856

Convict Conduct Register, Archives Office of Tasmania CON33/1/98

Convict Transportation Registers Database, State Library of Queensland

Description List of Male Convicts, Archives Office of Tasmania CON18/1/52

Diary of John Campbell, Surgeon on the William Jardine, National Library of Australia AJCP M385, 1850

Hobart Town Directory, Archives Office of Tasmania, 1859

Idents of Male Convicts, Archives Office of Tasmania, CON14/1/42

Kelly's Directory for Cambridgeshire, 1847

Land Tax Assessment for the Hundred of Wisbech, Cambridgeshire Archives 283/09, 1798–1803

Lloyd's Register of Shipping, 1850

Millbank Prison Register, The National Archives, HO24/5, 1850

Notebooks of Mr Justice Talfourd, Bershire Record Office, D/EX 1410/1/3/2

Pigot's Directory for Cambridgeshire, 1823–40

Petitions to the Queen and the Home Office on behalf of Robert Pate and John Francis, The National Archives, HO45/3079

Poll Book for Wisbech, Wisbech and Fenland Museum, 1831

Probate Calendars, Probate Registry, 1865–1900

Regimental Service Record for Robert Pate, The National Archives WO76/540, 1841–46

Request for Information on Robert Pate, The National Archives HO45/9750/A58430, 1896

Slater's Directory for Cambridgeshire, 1850
The Army List, 1842–56
The Bury and Norfolk Post, 1821–78
The Cambridge Chronicle, 1818–21
The Colonial Times, Hobart, 1833–56
The Courier, Hobart, 1835–65
The Launceston Examiner, Launceston, Tasmania, 1850–65
The Mercury, Hobart, Tasmania, 1860–79
The Norwich Mercury, 1830
The Will of Mary Ann Pate, The National Archives PROB 11/2207, 1852
The Will of Robert Francis Pate, The National Archives PROB 11/2240, 1856
The Zoist, vol. 8 p. 303, 1850
Wills and Probate for Robert Pate and Mary Elizabeth Pate, Probate Registry, 1895 and 1901

6 Arthur O'Connor

Roger Fulford (ed.), *Darling Child: Private Correspondence of Queen Victoria and the Crown Princess of Prussia,* 1871–78, Evans Bros, London, 1976
Laurence M. Geary, *O'Connorite Bedlam: Feargus and His Grand-Nephew, Arthur,* Medical History vol. 34, 1990
Philip Guedalla, *The Queen and Mr Gladstone,* Hodder & Stoughton, London, 1933
Frederick Norton Manning, *Report on Lunatic Asylums,* Sydney, 1868
D. M. Potts and W. T. W. Potts, *Queen Victoria's Gene: Haemophilia and the Royal Family,* Sutton Publishing, Stroud, 1999
Neil R. Storey, *Prisons & Prisoners in Victorian Britain,* The History Press, Stroud, 2010
A Brief History of the Rozelle Hospital, The Open Day Committee, Mitchell Library, Sydney, 1990
British Medical Journal, pp. 672–73, 729, 756–58, 1875
Callan Park Admission File for George Morton, NSW State Records 3/3317 no. 196, 1881
Callan Park Case Book for George Morton, NSW State Records 3/4652A pp. 100–103 and 3/4653 p. 1, 1881–1908
Darlinghurst Reception House Register of Admissions & Discharges, NSW State Records Series 5014 item 5/8, 1881
Hanwell Lunatic Asylum Register of Admissions, London Metropolitan Archives H11/HLL/B/05/009, 1875
Hanwell Lunatic Asylum Register of Male Admissions, London Metropolitan Archives H11/HLL/B/04/004, 1875
Hanwell Lunatic Asylum Case Book, London Metropolitan Archives H11/HLL/B/20/013A, 1875–76
Hanwell Lunatic Asylum Certificates of Discharge, London Metropolitan Archives H11/HLL/B/09/010, 1876
Home Office File on Arthur O'Connor, The National Archives HO144/3/10963, 1872–85
Index to Unassisted Inward Passenger Lists to Victoria, Victoria PRO, 1873
Rydelmere Mental Hospital Medical File for George Morton, NSW State Records 19/11587, 1912–25
Rydelmere Mental Hospital Legal File for George Morton, NSW State Records 19/113731, 1912–25
Rydelmere Mental Hospital Admission & Record of Visitors Card for George Morton, NSW State Records 19/15836B, 1912–25
The Lancet, pp. 341–42, 515, 535–36, 546–47, 571–72, 1872
The Melbourne Argus, 1873

7 Roderick Maclean

Ralph Partridge, *Broadmoor: A History of Criminal Lunacy and Its Problems*, Chatto & Windus, London, 1953
M. H. Spielmann, *The History of Punch*, Cassell, London, 1895
Alan Sullivan (ed.), *British Literary Magazines 1837–1913*, Greenwood Press, London, 1984
Stephen White, *What Queen Victoria Saw: Roderick Maclean and the Trial of Lunatics Act 1883*, Barry Rose Law Publishers, Chichester, 2000
Assize Courts Oxford Circuit: Criminal Depositions and Case Papers, The National Archives ASSI6/18, 1882
Assize Courts Oxford Circuit: Crown Minute Books, The National Archives ASSI2/43, 1882
Assize Courts Oxford Circuit: Indictment Files, The National Archives ASSI5/192/1, 1882
Broadmoor Hospital Case File for Roderick Maclean (Extracts), Berkshire Record Office D/H14/D2/2/1/1095, 1882–1921
Directory of British Picture Framemakers, National Portrait Gallery, www.npg.org.uk
Fun, volume 1, 1861–62
Home Office File on James Burnside, The National Archives HO144/467/V19056, 1892–1900
Home Office File on Roderick Maclean, The National Archives HO 144/95/A14281, 1882–1921
Probate Calendars, Probate Registry, 1881
Reading Mercury, 1882
Surrey Advertiser, 1882
Windsor & Eton Express, 1882

8 The Fenian Plot

George Earle Buckle (ed.), *The Letters of Queen Victoria: Third Series 1886–1901*, J. Murray, London, 1930
Christy Campbell, *Fenian Fire: The British Government Plot to Assassinate Queen Victoria*, Harper Collins, London, 2002
Fenian Fire, Television Documentary on RTÉ One, 2008

Epilogue

Dr David V. James et al., 'Attacks on the British Royal Family: The Role of Psychotic Illness', *Journal of the American Academy of Psychiatry and the Law*, vol. 36 no. 1 pp. 59–67, 2008

Notes

Chapter 1

1 Gambroon is a twilled cloth of worsted and cotton, or linen and cotton, used for summer trousers.
2 A postillion is a rider who steers a team of horses where there is no coachman.
3 A bridewell is a prison for petty offenders.
4 A contusion is a bruise, but presumably John Oxford suffered from something more serious.
5 A beadle is a parish officer who deals with petty offenders.
6 A halberd is a sort of pike, although in this case, presumably not a real one.
7 Coiners are makers of counterfeit coins.
8 Crêpe is a type of silk that is used in mourning clothes.
9 The Board of Green Cloth was only formally abolished in 2004.
10 This plot to assassinate the First Consul of France, Napoleon Bonaparte, happened on 24 December 1800.
11 Much of the Treason Act is still in force today.
12 Insanity was believed to be largely hereditary.
13 Dr Thomas Hodgkin discovered Hodgkin's Disease.
14 The bitter evergreen leaves of rue had long been used as an antidote to 'prison fever', the endemic contagious disease often present in Newgate Gaol.
15 The origin of the word 'bedlam'. Now known as Bethlem Royal Hospital, it can trace its origins back to 1247, and is the world's oldest institution for the mentally ill, admitting its first patients in 1357.
16 Part of the Bethlem hospital building today houses the Imperial War Museum.
17 The steward was the general manager.
18 An oedema is a swelling.
19 Emerald Hill is known as South Melbourne today.
20 A levee is a social event, tracing its origins back to Louis XIV and his ceremonial rising from his bedchamber.

Chapter 2

1 This represented a significant percentage of the total population, which was about sixteen million in England & Wales in 1841; with another eleven million living in Scotland and Ireland.
2 A barouche is a four-wheeled carriage with a collapsible hood over the rear half.
3 Limelight is a very bright light produced by heating a block of quicklime with a hydrogen and oxygen flame.
4 The poor performance and slow communication between Metropolitan districts in catching Daniel Good led to the setting up of the Detective Force later that year.
5 A stock is a cravat.
6 A hurdle is a wooden frame.

7 This sentence was enacted in the 1814 Treason Act, which replaced the medieval punishment where the offender was disembowelled and emasculated when only half-dead from hanging, before being beheaded.

8 Nine Elms was the original terminus, situated between Vauxhall and Battersea.

9 Spithead is an area of the Solent, off Portsmouth.

10 Caulking is a waterproof mixture of hemp and tar rammed into the seams between the ship's wooden planks.

11 Not today's biscuit, but compressed bread, which often became home to small grubs once damp.

12 In dry-holystoning, dry sand was sprinkled on the deck and then scoured with a piece of freestone (typically sandstone or limestone).

13 'Picking oakum' refers to the process of pulling hemp fibres from old ropes to be used for caulking.

14 Pease were dried garden peas or a type of chickpea.

15 Catechu was an astringent extract from a species of acacia tree.

16 Although the use of lemon or lime juice had been standard in the Royal Navy for fifty years, nobody knew why it worked, and an understanding of vitamin C only emerged in the twentieth century.

17 Hemeralopia is the inability to see clearly in bright light.

18 Potassium nitrate or saltpetre is a constituent of gunpowder and was alleged by some in the 1830s to combat scurvy.

19 'Unnatural crime' meant homosexuality and bestiality.

20 In fact, Paterson changed his surname to Launceston, so the town was actually named after its founder.

21 The 'American wheel' was probably a device like a carousel.

22 The house where John is believed to have lived still stands, now a licensed brothel called 'Cherry Blossoms'.

23 An aneurism is a swelling in the wall of the artery.

Chapter 3

1 A landau is a convertible carriage with facing seats over a dropped footwell.

2 A surtout coat was a man's frock coat, of the kind worn by cavalry officers.

3 A colourman was a retailer who, in addition to colours and the oils to make paints, also usually sold a range of household and other goods.

4 'Toby' was a slang word for buttocks, and to 'tickle someone's toby' meant to spank or beat them.

5 Millbank Prison stood where Tate Britain stands today.

6 A lighterman transferred goods between ships and quays in the Port of London, using a flat-bottomed barge called a lighter.

7 A monthly nurse attended a mother during the four weeks or so of the lying-in period.

Chapter 4

1 Drawing-rooms were events where many people were presented to the sovereign.

2 The royal closet in St James's Palace was a small reception room.

3 Between 1840 and 1930, when the population of Europe doubled, the population of Ireland halved, from around eight down to about four million.

4 Blucher boots were high shoes or half boots.

5 A Grand Jury considers whether there is a *prima facie* case against the accused, a practice abandoned in England in 1933.

6 A true bill constituted a charge and indicates that there was a case to answer.

7 Pensioner guards were men who would act as guards one last time and then settle in Australia.

8 A gill was a quarter of a pint; five fluid ounces, so half a gill was just over half a British standard small glass of wine.

Chapter 5

1 A corn factor was a middleman in corn sales, corn being the generic term for wheat and other cereal grains.

2 Fen ague was a type of malaria carried by a breed of mosquito now extinct.

3 Lucubrations are pieces of writing which are typically pedantic and over-elaborate.

4 An omnibus was a horse-drawn bus with seating inside and above.

5 Today we might possibly have diagnosed that 'diseased brain' rather more accurately. He clearly had obsessive compulsive disorder, a chemical imbalance that causes obsessive repetitive behaviour, and may have suffered from paranoid schizophrenia.

6 A fellmonger was a dealer in sheep's hides.

7 The watch house was a local lock-up.

8 A phaeton is an open carriage usually drawn by a single horse.

9 Pig-sticking was hunting for wild boar on horseback using a spear and encouraged by the army as good training.

10 Prince George of Wales was the son of the Prince of Wales, crowned in 1910 as George V.

Chapter 6

1 The gene that transmits haemophilia could not genetically have come from Albert, and as there are no known haemophiliacs in the Queen's maternal ancestors, it has been suggested that the Duke of Kent was not Victoria's father (and therefore she was not entitled to the throne). The other possibility is that it was a spontaneous mutation. See *Queen Victoria's Gene: Haemophilia and the Royal Family* by D. M. Potts and W. T. W. Potts, as detailed in the 'Sources' appendix.

2 Stomach cancer, rather than typhoid fever, now seems a more likely diagnosis.

3 Schleswig and Holstein were two duchies situated between Denmark and Prussia, which were connected to the Danish throne, but had large populations of German descent. The 'question' was whether Schleswig, in particular, should become part of Denmark, or both should be independent states in the German Federation.

4 A ghillie or gillie was an attendant on a hunting or fishing expedition.

5 This is the same Feargus O'Connor described in Chapter 4 as the Chartist leader.

6 The cause of Feargus O'Connor's insanity was probably syphilis.

7 A scrofulous condition is a disease causing glandular swellings, especially tuberculosis.

8 An oil and colour warehouseman was a wholesaler of oils, pigments, and dyes for painters and the textile trade.

9 Coldbath Fields House of Correction was sited where the Mount Pleasant sorting office of the Royal Mail stands today.

10 Imbecility meant at this time a weakness of the mind and some sort of brain malfunction as in, for example, dementia. The word 'idiot' was used to describe the mentally retarded.

11 This letter survives to this day in his case notes.

12 On Christmas Day later that year, the *Helenslea* was in collision with a Cunard liner off the Irish Coast and sank with the loss of nine lives.

13 Muffs were a humane method of hand restraint.

Chapter 7

1 'Sweeping a crossing' meant clearing the dung from the path of popular road crossings in fashionable areas in return for tips.
2 Although Bradlaugh later said he would swear allegiance, a select committee said he could not, as he was an atheist. He was re-elected twice more as the member for Nottingham and was finally instrumental in establishing the Oaths Act of 1888, which allowed members to affirm their allegiance instead.
3 George Chesney Wilson was seventeen at the time. He later married Sarah Spencer-Churchill, an aunt of Winston Churchill.
4 Charles's surname and that of his family was variously written McLean, MacLean, or Maclean.
5 Nothing to do with Maclean's toothpaste, which is a twentieth-century product.
6 *Fun* magazine continued right through the nineteenth century until 1901.
7 The failure of the Overend, Gurney & Company bank was the last run on a British bank until the events at Northern Rock in 2007.
8 Sweet nitre is ethyl nitrite and was used to reduce fever, aid urination, and for other common ailments.
9 A fly was a single-horse carriage.
10 In 1964, Parliament changed the law again so that the verdict became 'not guilty by reason of insanity'.
11 The poor law parish of Kensington also accepted a settlement by residence and agreed to pay 14s a week to the governor for Roderick Maclean's maintenance.
12 Apoplexy is a cerebral haemorrhage or stroke.

Chapter 8

1 This was the old Metropolitan Police headquarters in Whitehall Place, which backed onto Great Scotland Yard.
2 Erysipelas is a type of skin infection caused by streptococcus bacteria, manifested as a crimson swollen sore.
3 Gladstone Street is, coincidentally, less than a hundred yards from where Edward Oxford had lived nearly fifty years earlier.
4 As revealed in *Fenian Fire* by Christy Campbell (see Sources).

Epilogue

1 Hafiz is a title meaning somebody who has learnt the Qur'an by heart.
2 Munshi means 'teacher' or 'clerk' in Urdu.
3 Aphasia is an inability to talk caused by some kind of brain damage.